Blessing of a New Dawn

## PRAISE FOR *BLESSING OF A NEW DAWN*

"A book of towering stature, an immense contribution to one of the greatest religious and moral revolutions of all time: Christianity's repentance and revision of its relationship to Judaism. Mary Boys's respectful reading of sacred Scriptures and foundational texts and her analysis of modern Jewish and Christian scholarship model a way forward for Christians to foster a loving, dialogical relationship with Jews." — **Rabbi Irving (Yitz) Greenberg, President, J.J. Greenberg Institute for the Advancement of Jewish Life**

"A vitally persuasive book! Drawing on a wealth of knowledge and deep personal experience, by turns it cajoles, pushes, and invites the church to let the sun rise on a new day. The beautiful flow of its argument rearranges the furniture of your mind. Read it and be inspired to act." — **Elizabeth Johnson, Distinguished Professor Emerita, Fordham University**

"With clear sight and keen expression, Mary Boys offers guidance on the fractious past of Christian-Jewish relations and hope for harmony as we walk God's path together into the future." — **Rabbi Burton Visotzky, Director, Milstein Center for Interreligious Dialogue, Jewish Theological Seminary**

"Speaking both from within and to the Church, Mary Boys gently and persuasively helps readers to recognize how reorienting their relationship to Judaism not only corrects distortions of the Gospel but also encourages a deeper understanding of Jesus. Pastoral and personal, lucid and challenging, Boys's work is more important than ever." — **Amy-Jill Levine, Rabbi Stanley M. Kessler Distinguished Professor of New Testament and Jewish Studies, Hartford International University for Religion and Peace**

"*Blessing of a New Dawn* is nothing less than a theological tour-de-force, accessible but also authoritative. Readers will come away from reading this volume not only more educated but also enthused and edified by her vision of Christianity's relationship to Judaism based on hope and partnership." — **Dr. Ed Kessler MBE, Founder President, Woolf Institute**

"Mary Boys narrates the diverse ways in which the first Christians inhabited Judaism, but how 'the Jews' became an abstraction through the hands of early Christian writers. Inviting readers into a complex view of Christian origins and offering a robust reconstruction of the histories of Jewish-Christian relations, Boys illuminates long-standing patterns of thought, the damage they have wrought, and ways forward for change." — Jeannine Hill Fletcher, author, **Grace of the Ghosts: A Theology of Institutional Reparation**

"A compelling, fresh, and honest meditation on Christianity's relationship with Judaism from one of the field's leading scholars. Boys draws readers through the historical and theological arc of this relationship, though not from a scholar's distance. Instead, she invites readers into her own journey as she has navigated the tension of being a faithful Catholic while acknowledging Christianity's often troubled history with Judaism." —**Mahri Leonard-Fleckman, Associate Professor of Old Testament, Princeton Theological Seminary**

"Mary Boys deftly presents the major advances in Christian understandings of Judaism that have developed since the Holocaust. With clarity and nuance, she offers to Christian readers clear ideas on how to put into practice these ideas. This book will be an essential resource for all those looking to teach and learn about Christian solidarity with Jews today." — **Daniel Joslyn-Siemiatkoski, Center for Christian-Jewish Learning, Boston College**

"Mary Boys takes her readers on the path she has herself walked for decades, dismantling anti-Jewish traditions one by one. True Christian faith does not require a negation of Judaism, nor asserting supremacy over other religions. But it does require rethinking distorted ideas of an alleged Christian superiority over Jews. Mary Boys develops a language of Christian self-understanding that affirms Judaism as Judaism. This eschewing of false superiority is truly a new dawn for Christianity." — **Barbara U. Meyer, Tel Aviv University**

# Blessing of a New Dawn

## Reorienting Christianity's Relation with Judaism

Mary C. Boys

Maryknoll, New York 10545

Founded in 1970, Orbis Books endeavors to publish works that enlighten the mind, nourish the spirit, and challenge the conscience. The publishing arm of the Maryknoll Fathers and Brothers, Orbis seeks to explore the global dimensions of the Christian faith and mission, to invite dialogue with diverse cultures and religious traditions, and to serve the cause of reconciliation and peace. The books published reflect the views of their authors and do not represent the official position of the Maryknoll Society. To learn more about Maryknoll and Orbis Books, please visit our website at www.orbisbooks.com.

Copyright © 2025 by Mary C. Boys

Published by Orbis Books, Box 302, Maryknoll, NY 10545-0302.

Scripture texts used in this work, unless otherwise noted, are taken from the New Revised Standard Version Updated Edition. Copyright © 2021 National Council of Churches of Christ in the United States of America. Used by permission. All rights reserved worldwide.

All rights reserved.

No part of this publication may be reproduced or transmitted in any form or by any means, electronic or mechanical, including photocopying, recording, or any information storage or retrieval system, without prior permission in writing from the publisher.

Queries regarding rights and permissions should be addressed to: Orbis Books, P.O. Box 302, Maryknoll, NY 10545-0302.

Manufactured in the United States of America

**Library of Congress Cataloging-in-Publication Data**

Names: Boys, Mary C. author
Title: Blessing of a new dawn : reorienting Christianity's relation to Judaism / Mary C. Boys.
Description: Maryknoll, NY : Orbis Books, [2025] | Includes bibliographical references and index. | Summary: "A review of the ancient divide between Judaism and Christanity and how it can be bridged"— Provided by publisher.
Identifiers: LCCN 2025017471 (print) | LCCN 2025017472 (ebook) | ISBN 9781626986213 trade paperback | ISBN 9798888660768 epub
Subjects: LCSH: Christianity and other religions—Judaism | Judaism—Relations—Christianity
Classification: LCC BM535 .B647 2025 (print) | LCC BM535 (ebook) | DDC 261.2—dc23/eng/20250530
LC record available at https://lccn.loc.gov/2025017471
LC ebook record available at https://lccn.loc.gov/2025017472

To Sara S. Lee, Carol K. Ingall, and Shuly Rubin Schwartz

and

Members of the Christian Scholars Group on Jews and Judaism

# Contents

*Acknowledgments* . . . . . . . . . . . . . . . . . . . . . . . ix
*Prologue* . . . . . . . . . . . . . . . . . . . . . . . . . . . . . . xiii

1. Memory and Imagination . . . . . . . . . . . . . . . 1
2. In Pursuit of the Pharisees . . . . . . . . . . . . . 25
3. The Early Church and
   Its "Construction" of Judaism . . . . . . . . . . . 65
4. Early Judaism: Resilience, Reorientation,
   and Reinvention . . . . . . . . . . . . . . . . . . . . . 124
5. Recovering the Jewish Jesus and
   Rediscovering Judaism . . . . . . . . . . . . . . . . 156
6. The Past Is a Foreign Country:
   A Guide for Traversing Its Terrain . . . . . . . 193

*Epilogue* . . . . . . . . . . . . . . . . . . . . . . . . . . . . . 223
*Resources on Judaism* . . . . . . . . . . . . . . . . . . 231
*Bibliography* . . . . . . . . . . . . . . . . . . . . . . . . . 233
*Index* . . . . . . . . . . . . . . . . . . . . . . . . . . . . . . 253

# Acknowledgments

Although writing is a solitary craft, many voices and relationships become partners in the process. Here I thank those whose insights and support enliven my thinking. The Dedication reflects my gratitude to a trio of Jewish women and to a collegial group of scholars. Over the years I have had the privilege of teaching in various settings with Sara S. Lee of Hebrew Union College–Jewish Institute of Religion and with Carol K. Ingall and Shuly Rubin Schwartz of the Jewish Theological Seminary of America. Our collaborations were never merely professional but occasions that engendered deep and lasting ties of friendship. I learned new insights into Judaism as we prepared lectures and classes together—and I have sought to absorb the wisdom of their Torah-inspired lives.

For close to forty years, I've belonged to the Christian Scholars Group on Jewish–Christian Relations. Originating in 1969 as a gathering of scholars who met together regularly to study theological issues regarding Christian relations with Jews, its stimulating discussions have consistently provided impetus for deeper exploration while exemplifying the best of scholarly collaboration. Current members include Victoria Barnett, Robert Cathey, Philip Cunningham, Daniel Joslyn-Siemiatkoski, Heather Miller-Rubens, Katharina von Kellenbach, John Pawlikowski, Peter Pettit, Elena Procario-Foley, Jesper Svartvik; and Jewish consultants Adam Gregerman and Ruth Langer. I express my gratitude as well to former members I've known over the years. Family responsibilities, new positions, retirement, or health reasons have necessitated their withdrawal from active membership, but their presence is not forgotten. Neither are those who have gone before us in death. Their memory is indeed a blessing.

I extend special thanks to Philip A. Cunningham for his stellar leadership in interreligious institutions and collaborative projects and, most of all, for our many years of friendship.

I am grateful for Union alumna and professional editor Jerri Hurlbutt's generous offer to review my manuscript-in-the-making and for the many conversations we had online and in person about ways to enhance its readability. I thank Amy-Jill Levine and Joseph Sievers for providing early access to their edited book *The Pharisees*, which proved so helpful in the process of my writing. Thanks also to my wonderful colleagues at Union Theological Seminary, especially those in the Interreligious Field from whom I learn so much: John Thatamanil, Jerusha Rhodes, Greg Snyder and, most recently, Simran Jeet Singh. My thanks also to Jeremy Hultin, whose astute observations provided help. I am grateful for the support of Union's President, Serene Jones, and its Dean and Academic Vice-President Su Yon Pak.

I have (mostly) enjoyed the intellectual challenge of writing this book—and even more the pedagogical process of thinking how best to formulate a concept or develop my ideas. For that I am especially appreciative of the privilege of working with students who bring their own convictions, experiences, and aspirations; their concerns and questions complicate and energize my thinking, including my current doctoral students Tony Amoury Alkhoury and Thelma Ranjitsingh. Thanks also to those whose invitations to lecture have prompted me to find ways to express complicated ideas in an accessible manner. I seldom return home without pondering the questions and concerns of audience members.

*Acknowledgments* xi

I extend thanks to Robert Ellsberg for his patience as my editor and for his leadership as publisher of Orbis Books. I am grateful for the resources of the Columbia University Library, which have significantly enabled my research, including the staff at Union's Burke Library. My life has been profoundly shaped by my belonging to the Sisters of the Holy Names—this lively, feisty community of women for whom educating in faith for the flourishing of humanity and the planet animates us. No words suffice to express my gratitude for the rich friendships that sustain and inspire me. I also thank the Sisters of Our Lady of Sion, as it is a privilege to collaborate in their visionary work in deepening relations between Christians and Jews. And to Barbara King Lord, journalist extraordinaire emerita and friend of many years, my gratitude.

Mary C. Boys, SNJM
New York City
March 24, 2025

# Prologue

"I'll never know enough to write this book."

I wrote this observation in my notes in September 2024 while participating in a seminar with scholars from a range of theological specializations pertinent to relations between Judaism and Christianity. Listening to my learned colleagues, I was overwhelmed by the breadth and depth of the theological questions involved in this complicated relationship that spans the course of two millennia.

Strangely, the recognition of the limits of my own knowledge gave me new energy to complete this book. Precisely because the topics involved in reorienting Christianity's relation with Judaism have such deep roots in history, concern important claims of Christian theologies, encompass new ways of understanding Scripture, and impact what Christians teach and preach, I see a need for an overview. That is precisely what I have aspired to in writing this book.

It's a work of synthesis, an attempt to offer a "big picture" of how contemporary biblical and theological studies provide a horizon within which Christians today might reimagine our intertwined origins and complicated history with Jews. It's a work of advocacy, summoning Christians to learn why and how we should assume a new posture vis-à-vis Jews. In short, *Blessing of a New Dawn* is a call to reorient our relationship with Judaism and with Jews.

It's a work indebted to the scholarship of many as refracted through the lens of my own knowledge and experience. Yet it's not a book primarily for scholars. I write for thoughtful Christians desirous of living out their faith through just relationships. It's also a book I hope church leaders, including clergy and teachers, will take seriously so as to incorporate its claims in church life.

And I welcome Jewish readers, many of whom have a keen awareness of Christianity's troubled history with their tradition. It is my hope that they will find reasons for hope that the Christian tradition will live more fully into the Apostle Paul's affirmation that Jews are God's "beloved" because "the gifts and the calling of God are irrevocable" (Romans 11:28–29). When the Second Vatican Council cited this avowal in its historic decree *Nostra Aetate* in 1965, it opened new possibilities that the past sixty years have only begun to explore.

So read this book to trace contemporary Christianity's circuitous journey into honoring that affirmation. And to explore new possibilities for living into it.

# 1

# Memory and Reimagination

It all began in 1982 with an essay "Questions 'Which Touch on the Heart of Our Faith'" (Boys 1982, 636–56). I have long since forgotten what prompted writing it, although I do remember the sentence that inspired my title: "These signs"—the vitality of Jewish faithfulness to God, dedication to studying the Scriptures, and commitment to recreate its peoplehood over the course of centuries—"pose questions to us Christians, which touch on the heart of our faith" ("Statement by the French Bishops Commission for Relations with Jews" 1987, 61). The notion that Judaism posed questions touching on the heart of the faith life of Christians rang true to my experience, not only intellectually but personally. There was *something* in this relation with Jews and Judaism that drew me more forcefully than did other interesting and noteworthy theological questions. It transcended knowledge of the New Testament and factual knowledge of Judaism, though both were intricately connected.

Although the process of writing that essay had sparked something within me, the implications were unclear. In the meantime, I was busy with work in my early years as an assistant professor at Boston College. Teaching absorbed much of my energy, as did research for a book that would appear in 1989, *Educating in Faith: Maps and Visions*.

And then a wholly unexpected phone call in early 1985 from a stranger, Rabbi Michael Signer of Hebrew Union College–Jewish Institute of Religion in Los Angeles. He and a colleague, Professor Sara S. Lee, the Director of the Rhea Hirsch School of Education, were involved in planning an interreligious event for the seminary faculties of the metropolitan area. They had read my essay and wondered if I'd be willing to come to L.A. to speak at the gathering. And, were I willing to consider their invitation, Professor Lee would be pleased to share more about the conference, as she would be in Boston in a couple of weeks in the early spring.

At the time I had published nothing else specifically on the topic of Christian–Jewish relations, so the invitation seemed a bit unreal. And intimidating! But Rabbi Signer was such an affable, encouraging caller that I couldn't refuse. And I was intrigued to meet his colleague. So, yes, I would seriously consider their generous invitation. Little did I know.

It turned out that Professor Lee was herself a Boston native and had come to help her daughter Aviva, then a medical student at Tufts University, prepare for hosting a Passover seder. Aviva dropped her off at my office. From the moment Sara and I met, our conversation flowed, much to Aviva's frustration because we talked far longer than either of us had anticipated. The connection we experienced came from an unspoken recognition that we shared in common both a deep involvement in the life of our own tradition and a passion for educating religiously. Our friendship continues some forty years later.

I accepted the invitation and went to Los Angeles—the first of many times I would enjoy Sara's hospitality at her then-home in the San Fernando Valley. When she came to Boston, she spent time with my colleagues at Boston College and with my community. I came to know Sara's family and friends, both informally and at seders; she met my parents and deepened her place in their hearts through her kindness by sending packages of chocolate orange sticks from Trader Joe's to my mother. Professionally, we went to one another's classes or lectured together. We even spent a wonderful week at the Hong Kong International School as Charles Dull Visiting Scholars (the "Dull Scholars"!). For several years we led the Catholic–Jewish Colloquium, a program for Catholic and Jewish educators supported by the Lilly Foundation. This called for extensive collaboration, and we prepared assiduously. The Colloquium met over six sessions in three years, and we continued to reflect on what we learned by editing a special issue of the journal *Religious Education* (Boys and Lee 1996). Through the intense sessions Sara and I spent in preparing for both the Colloquium sessions and our joint editorial work, I began to understand Jewish life. And our preparations often included intense conversations about how each of us understood the other's tradition, including Sara's question to me, "So what about the Trinity?"

My connection with Rabbi Signer also had a profound effect. A learned medievalist with a delightful sense of humor, his doctoral mentor at the University of Toronto was a Catholic priest who ultimately became the Vatican librarian. Consequently, Michael knew a great deal about Catholicism, not only in the Middle Ages but in the present; he reveled in having a certain insider knowledge of the ways of the Vatican. Ultimately, he accepted a position at the University of Notre Dame as its inaugural Abrams Professor of Jewish Studies, where he flourished—even though, despite my encouragement, he lacked a passion for Notre Dame football.

And it is at Notre Dame that I will always remember him. In August of 2008, he hosted a meeting of a collaborative project of Jewish and Christian scholars in which I participated. Arriving on campus, I looked forward, as we all did, to meeting up with the ebullient Michael, only to encounter him under sobering circumstances. Days beforehand, he and his wife Betty had learned of his diagnosis of pancreatic cancer. They were, understandably, shaken to the core. His diagnosis pervaded our conference. Feeling helpless in the face of such a deadly cancer, we decided that we could at least gather to bless him and Betty. And so, on our final day in South Bend, we set aside our papers and assembled in one of the small chapels in the building where our group met for a simple service led by one of the group, Rabbi Professor Ruth Langer. We read a few texts; there was some music and a great deal of silence. However vague my recall of specifics, I will never forget the ending of the service. Each of us approached Michael and Betty to bless them and, in turn, to receive their blessing. I don't remember the words, but I do the many tears, which flow even now as I recall that sacred moment. Above all, there was the realization that illness and death transcended our differences as Jews and Christians. And that it is for the flourishing of our shared humanity—and in our inarticulateness in the face of mortality—that we stood together before the One Beyond All Understanding.

Michael died January 10, 2009. He was 63.

All this is by way of saying that my study of relations between Jews and Christians has never been merely academic. My desire to delve deeply into the world of Christian origins involves questions that *touch on the heart of my faith* in large part because of rich friendships with Jews whose own intense questioning touching on the heart of their tradition expands and energizes my own. In our mutual probing, we meet both in the history of our encounters and in the present of our shared lives on a fragile planet in a divisive era. The opportunities to team-teach with Professors Carol K. Ingall and Shuly Rubin Schwartz in courses jointly offered by my home institution, Union Theological Seminary and theirs, the Jewish Theological Seminary of America, have added immeasurably to my knowledge of Jewish life—both academically and through our many conversations. I have learned a great deal about Jewish life through its festivals, in studying about them (Greenberg 1988) and more through informal conversation with friends as they prepared and lived the events in the Jewish life cycle. Participating in a seder is a privileged experience, different in every home—and sometimes different on the second night from the first. Each Shabbat table I've been privileged to join has proven especially formative; the rich conversation with hosts and other guests are always the highlight of the week. What I have learned at their tables gives depth and breadth to what I've learned in the library. Hospitality, as I've experienced through such experiences, is a key virtue of interreligious learning.

To be gifted with Jewish friends also entails a deepened sensitivity to the grief and anxiety that antisemitism generates, especially in this time of its global resurgence. Antisemitism has a long and complex history, appearing in multiple guises: political, racial, economic, and religious. In our time, it exists at the crossroads of Christian anti-Jewish teachings and conspiracy theories, nationalism, racism, White supremacy, and xenophobia. In its various manifestations, antisemitism has caused tremendous harm to Jews—and the wounds continue into the present. The contribution of Christian theology to antisemitism is painful to confront, yet it is absolutely necessary that Christians do so if we are to live by the gospel we proclaim.

To study the history of the many vicious ways in which Christians have expressed their contempt for Jews and for Judaism in word and deed gives rise to great shame. In particular, characterizing Jews as a perfidious and treacherous people because of their alleged culpability for the crucifixion of Christ fundamentally distorted Christian theology. The promulgation of Vatican II's decree *Nostra Aetate* in October

1965 contributed significantly to the slow awakening of the churches to their responsibility to interpret the New Testament texts about the death of Jesus in their historical and sociocultural contexts, and to educate its adherents more adequately about Judaism. Perhaps because of its ubiquity and shape-shifting manifestations, antisemitism resists simplistic definition. The complexity is compounded by the question of the extent to which Christianity's anti-Jewish teachings over the centuries are related to antisemitism. While there is no consensus on this question, I have found Susannah Heschel's argument insightful. She builds upon Helen Fein's comprehensive and complex definition of antisemitism as a

> persisting latent structure of hostile beliefs toward Jews as a collectivity manifested in individuals as attitudes, and in culture as myth, ideology, folklore, and imagery, and in actions—social or legal discrimination, political mobilization against Jews, and collective state violence—which results in and/or is designed to distance, displace, or destroy Jews as Jews. (Fein 1987, 67)

Susannah Heschel notes that scholars from various disciplines have used the term antisemitism as "hostility toward Judaism and Jews" that is expressed in a variety of ways, including through economics, politics, nationalism, religious discourse, or race. Given the breadth of that perspective, Heschel categorizes anti-Judaism *as term for a discourse that expresses antisemitism in theological language* (emphasis added). In the view of many scholars today, "antisemitism cannot be confined in its descriptive applicability to the modern era, despite the term having been coined in the nineteenth century" (Heschel 2011, 259–60). She draws on her extensive scholarship on Christianity and the Third Reich in her 2008 book, *The Aryan Jesus: Christian Theologians and the Bible in Nazi Germany,* to show that pro-Nazi German Protestants drew on classic racial theories and mythology in their efforts to eradicate Judaism from Christian life. Yet the manner in which these theologians drew upon Nazi concepts and their susceptibility to Nazi propaganda does not mean that theologians and religious thinkers of earlier ages were unaffected by the contextual realities of their own times. Heschel cites New Testament scholar Adele Reinhartz's judgment that "even in the patristic and medieval eras, long before the coinage of the term antisemitism as such, it is almost impossible to distinguish between the racist and religious/ethnic elements." In a personal note to Heschel, Reinhartz says that many of the authors she researched for her 2011 book, *Caiaphas the High Priest,* assumed that "Jews were by their nature evil, and their rejection/killing of Christ is evidence of that evil nature."

My book addresses the issue of theological antisemitism from two varying angles. On the one hand, I trace the way in which over the course of the third and fourth centuries early Christianity's "construction" of Judaism as its rival and adversary metamorphosed into a vilification, even demonization, of Jews, thereby setting the stage for Christianity's heightened hostility toward Jews in the Middle Ages—and beyond. On the other, I argue that despite its very real and lethal theological antisemitism, Christianity's theology is *not intrinsically* antisemitic. Rather, its antisemitism developed out of a period when significant early leaders argued against Judaism from the position of an insecure minority in the Roman Empire, passionate in their dedication to the Way of Christ, skilled in rhetoric but ill-informed about the other. Nevertheless, their theological judgments—that Judaism was mired in the law, had failed to recognize the messianic character of Jesus, and wrongly interpreted its own Scriptures—unwittingly laid the theological foundation for centuries of teaching and preaching in opposition to Judaism and to Jews themselves. Yet distinctions must be made. The early interpreters, such as Ignatius of Antioch and Justin Martyr in the second century, considered Jews wrong but not evil. In the rhetoric of John Chrysostom and the teaching songs of Ephrem of Syria in the fourth century, however, Jews were both erroneous *and* iniquitous.

In our time the Hamas–Israel war has revealed antisemitism in its political and social guises. I witnessed the vitriol directed against Israel in the course of protests about its treatment of the Palestinians and its bombardment of Gaza in the wake of the unspeakable cruelty of the pogrom by Hamas on October 7, 2023. Living in an area where the protests were particularly ferocious, I found the singular focus on "genocidal Israel" and, too often, the evocation of classic antisemitic stereotypes, deeply offensive. I have my own critical perspectives about Israel's incursions into Gaza: its horror—the terrible toll of death, destruction, and famine—inflicted upon the Gazans, as I have discussed in a recent essay (Boys 2025). The continuing violence done to Palestinians in the West Bank by right-wing Israeli Jews remains a deep concern.

Yet, many of the protests around the country and world often involved a shallow, one-sided understanding of the history and complexities of the Middle East as well as of Zionism. I think of protestors who flooded campuses with pamphlets defining Zionism as an "ideology of racist and religious supremacy that aims to create a Jewish ethnostate on indigenous Palestinian land through settler-colonialism, ethnic cleansing, and the genocide of the Palestinian people." Was there no awareness of the ways such a simplistic description distorted the origins and complexity of Zionism, including the varied perspectives that live under Zionism's big tent?

Zionism is certainly not beyond critique, nor should it be. Some who identify as Zionist hold reprehensible beliefs about Palestinians or even about non-Jews in general. But no movement should be judged on the basis of its most notorious adherents, nor should the movement as a whole be so carelessly and misleadingly characterized in the name of protest. The critique of Zionism, Jonathan Karp argues, might better be understood as "anti-Israelism": an "irrational feeling of repulsion" against Israelis, a blanket disapproval of all things Israeli, attributing "inherent negative characteristics to an entire national group." Israel is, he writes, "a tiny country whose all-too-real flaws have been blown into cosmic significance in the global imagination. Anti-Israelism, then, is not a mere policy stance with which one might agree or disagree.... It is a prejudice, a sweeping judgment of an entire people, country, state, and culture that we would not tolerate if it were directed at anyone else" (Karp 2024). Anti-Zionism and anti-Israelism can serve as code words expressing hostility to Jews—and often do. It is too easy to forget that real people live behind those abstractions.

Of even greater concern is the current increase in nationalism in democracies of the West, including in the United States where some powerful officials in the newly elected Trump administration express support for right-wing political parties and movements. Social media sites reveal an alarming surge in antisemitic views, exacerbated by the world's richest man who owns and controls "X," formerly Twitter.

These developments are not innately tied to the church's theological antisemitism. They can, however, readily build upon the negative images of Jews that have long been a part of ecclesial tradition. For example, Simon D. Mayers ably traces the process by which English Catholics moved from stereotypical images of the Pharisee to the "Zionist Menace" in the period from 1917 to 1922 (Mayers 2012, 140–51). His work demonstrates how once a stereotype takes hold (e.g., of Pharisees), its hostility to a particular group gives rise to disparagement of another in a later age.

Stereotypes of Jews are rife in our time. Christians have an obligation to counter them, particularly within our own theologies. Analysis of theological antisemitism is woven throughout the book, but my focus is principally directed to advocating for a fuller, more adequate understanding of Judaism among Christians. My principal aims are interrelated:

- To describe and show the significance of the complex, often conflictual, process by which Christianity emerged in tandem with Judaism in the early centuries of the Common Era.
- To analyze texts of selected early church writers whose works significantly shaped the church's oppositional stance to Judaism. That these writers are generally little known today tends to obscure recognition of their effect on theology and liturgy.
- To depict Judaism as a resilient tradition that reinvented and reoriented itself in the wake of crushing military defeat, exile, and the Christianization of the Roman Empire, and that continues as a dynamic, robust tradition.
- To emphasize the importance of situating Jesus, his early generations of disciples, and the texts of the New Testament within their Jewish matrix, and to show the significance of the Jewish Jesus for the life of the church today.
- To offer recommendations for teaching and preaching that build upon a more profound understanding of the relation of Judaism and Christianity.
- To suggest the value of interreligious dialogue and scholarship for enhancing Christian commitment.

We are now privileged to live in a time when Christians and Jews are no longer enemies on the theological battlefield, even if substantial remnants of past antagonism remain.

Our ancestors in faith would find this development astonishing. We need no longer live by an oppositional imagination that requires disparaging the other in order to uphold one's own tradition. We can now more fully envision ourselves as brothers and sisters, partners in working and waiting for the full redemption of the world. If only we could appreciate the wonder of this time in history when so much else divides humans from one another.

In sum, in this book I am arguing for a vision of Christianity's relation to Judaism that relinquishes its oppositional imagination and replaces it with a hopeful imagination that envisions our two traditions as partners in hope and commitment to God's Reign.

### The Book in Closer Focus

It's difficult to grasp the significance of this new era between Jews and Christians because the story of this long and troubled relationship is little known, particularly among Christians. This story, I am convinced, needs to be told—but in ways that enable people to understand when and why the relationship went awry, the consequences of that misdirection, and the dynamics that unfolded. It is a story with a complicated beginning.

Some endeavors get off to a clear start and unfold systematically. Others may have a rocky inception and flounder; a midcourse adjustment may rectify the problem. But some beginnings, which once seemed straightforward, are far more complex than has been typically understood. Further knowledge necessitates reconsideration.

In the case of Christianity's origins, the problem is not simply that its point of departure is typically dated too early (e.g., the thirties of the first century, the time of the ministry of Jesus) but that the entire process by which Christianity emerged as a tradition distinct from Judaism has been oversimplified. And this distorted depiction took hold for nearly two millennia, forming the ground on which other problematic claims and categories were planted.

There was nothing nefarious about the misconstrued genesis of Christianity, though its many problems contributed significantly to a detrimental relationship with Judaism that deteriorated even further over the ages—and with tragic consequences. An abundant literature documents and explains the long and painful history of this fractious relationship. In this book, however, my interest lies primarily with showing how new perspectives on the first several centuries of the Common Era (CE; what was previously called *anno Domini*, "in the year of the Lord," or AD) bears relevance for significant new perspectives on Christianity and on its relationship with Judaism for our time.

These new perspectives are possible because today we have resources previous ages did not have. The work of archaeologists, biblical scholars, historians, and theologians enables us to expand and reimagine our understanding of the emergence of Christianity in the first centuries of the Common Era and of the study of religion more generally. It is a privilege to have access to such learned works, even if only to a modest sampling of a vast literature. In addition, we live in an era when the church is widening the horizon of its self-understanding vis-à-vis other religious traditions—a crucial enlargement if the diverse peoples of this world are to live together in peace on earth, our common home.

The expansion of knowledge and greater openness to the other can be unsettling, especially insofar as it upends the conventional story about how Christianity arose out of and then separated from Judaism. It disturbs the traditional account in which Judaism and Christianity became fundamentally incompatible at an early stage and were regarded as inherently conflictual. Further, it complicates the Jewish world of antiquity that most Christians have regarded as monolithic, exposing a diverse range of perspectives. It differentiates groups of Jesus's followers, revealing variations in belief and practice between his Jewish disciples, Paul's communities of "God-fearing" Gentiles, and the later generations of Gentile followers without connection to Jewish life. It resituates the polemic of New Testament texts and traces the development and consequences of later arguments about which community was more faithful to God's covenantal love. In short, scholars take us into a time when communal identities were being formed in relation to one another over a period of several centuries in various regions and cultures, allowing us to glimpse a much messier reality than we had previously seen.

So, if this new knowledge has unsettling effects, of what benefit is it? First, by allowing ourselves to learn a more complicated portrait of antiquity, we gain a truer view—one corresponding to facts and carefully calibrated arguments—of our origins. Second, we gain valuable insights into the New Testament world, including new perspectives on texts that have been used to disparage others, especially Jews. Third, we acquire a better grasp of how and why an argument with Judaism began—and why the terms of that argument have proven so deadly over the centuries. That is *not* to claim that Judaism and Christianity should now be viewed as indistinguishable traditions. Clearly, they became and remain deeply different traditions. Yet their dissimilarities should no longer be a source of antagonism. Fourth, how we frame the development of Judaism and Christianity in relation to one another establishes a framework for how we might understand our relation today—and what that relationship might imply for Christianity in a religiously pluralistic world. Fifth, encountering the resources of contemporary scholarship contributes to the development of a self-critical faith.

A further word about self-critical faith. Religions can and do inspire and sustain persons to live generously, committing themselves to the care of others, fostering a more just society, and seeking an integral ecology. But a shallow grasp of religious teaching and ignorance have too often resulted in intolerance and demonization of the other. Throughout the ages, religious ideas have fueled division, harsh judgment of others, and violence; history bears witness to the disastrous consequences of religious fanaticism. Many denounce religion precisely because of the evil done in God's name.

Just as coming to personal maturity requires us to know our shadow side, so also healthy religious traditions recognize how the ideals they teach have been (and continue to be) hijacked by ignorance and used for power and domination. In the case of Christians, it behooves us to understand our initial friction with (other) Jews and what happened over history to turn arguments into animosity and hostility into persecution: In too many centuries, Christianity fostered perspectives that demeaned Judaism and maltreated Jews. This is a stubborn fact, however discomfiting.

When a Vatican commission writes, "The history of relations between Jews and Christians is a tormented one" (Commission on Religious Relations with the Jews 1998), it has made a historically verifiable claim. What is missing, however, is confession of who did the tormenting, for what (ostensible) reasons, and with what effects on the tormented. Jews were by no means the sole victims of the church's intolerance, but they were its most frequent objects.

This book will not recount the long "tormented" history of relations between Jewish and Christian history, although it will draw on particular events and controversies as appropriate. Nonetheless, what I have learned from this history impels the present project (Boys 2013). In narrating the complex emergence of Christianity over the course of several centuries, I aim to show that *Christian hostility to Jews and Judaism is not an essential trait of Christianity, but rather resulted from historical contingencies*—that is, occurrences due to certain circumstances. The following are the principal factors in shaping the tormented history:

- The apparent hostility to Judaism expressed in certain New Testament texts, particularly in the Gospels of Matthew and John as well as the Book of Revelation;
- The loss of connection to the cultural–ethnic dimensions of Judaism—in a word, to its peoplehood—beginning in the second century of the Common Era;
- The rhetoric of early church writers, the prominence of their literature in subsequent centuries, and their influence in shaping Christian identity;
- The enactment of imperial legislation resulting in Christianity becoming the religion of the state.

Scholarship today enables us to interpret New Testament and early church writings in historical, literary, and sociocultural contexts as well to understand the dynamics by which the Catholic Christianity came to be upheld by imperial authorities. Thus, the question that generates the way I have structured the book: *How might the scholarly resources of our age reorient and revivify how we Christians understand our tradition and inspire us to be truer to our calling vis-à-vis the religious other and for the life of the church?* Behind this question is my commitment to make those resources accessible to those who lack the time and/or the specialized knowledge to follow all the contours of scholarly discussion. So, I am foregoing my attachment to extensive footnotes and lengthy analyses in order to compose as lucid and lean a synthesis as possible on a complicated topic. I write particularly for those desirous of absorbing new insights into what the experiences of our ancestors in faith say to us in this era when just relations with the "other" are imperative.

In searching out insights we might discern from our ancestors in faith, I explore several key questions, probing for implications that provide direction for reorienting understanding:

- What are key dimensions of Jewish life that illumine the world of Jesus and his disciples? What is most salient to our understanding of Jewish practices and beliefs that provide the critical context for the emergence of Christianity?
- What continuities and discontinuities from the time of Jesus might we perceive in the life of Paul, a Jewish, second-generation follower of Christ? With the gospel writers, who were third or fourth generation followers of Christ in late first century?
- What continuities and discontinuities characterized the followers of Christ in the second through the fourth centuries? What legacy did they leave and with what consequences?
- So what? What difference does it make to rethink the early centuries in the twenty-first century? How might our reorientation revitalize Christian self-understanding and relations with Jews? In what ways might this reorientation serve to counter anti-semitism? What might that reorientation suggest for Christian relations with other religious traditions?

I will in part address these questions by tracing the role the Pharisees played—and continue to play—in Christian self-understanding. Drawing upon the Pharisees also provides something of a familiar point of departure for many people, enabling me to put more flesh on the historical skeleton, and adding a bit of color, as their varied depictions are memorable, if also a deeply disturbing testimony to the endurance of a stereotype. Moreover, the Pharisees have become a major focus of recent scholarship, offering more resources than one could read and absorb in a lifetime. To be clear, this is not in the first instance a book about the Pharisees. Rather, it is a book in which the varying lenses on the Pharisaic movement, as well as the various streams of Judaism, offer a narrative device for an initial foray into new insights on Christianity's origin story that hold meaning for the present.

The Pharisees must take their place, however, in the historical period after Alexander the Great in 324 BCE and extending to the devastation of Judea in 135 CE.

### Viewing Antiquity from the Present

Before introducing the Pharisees, however, I offer a few comments about the complications of viewing antiquity from one's present vantage point. It is important from the outset to recognize three impediments to understanding: *anachronisms, binaries,* and *flawed metaphors*. A word on each.

Anachronism, the imposition of meanings and categories from the present on the past, presents a major hindrance to allowing the past to speak on its own terms. For example, in a speech celebrating the Fourth of July 2019, President Donald J. Trump, in his first term, said, "[During the War of Independence] Our [Continental Army] manned the air, it rammed the ramparts, it took over the airports, it did everything it had to do, and at Fort McHenry, under the 'rockets' red glare,' it had nothing but victory." The forty-fifth president—and now the forty-seventh—seems to have been on a flight of fancy in asserting the Army's takeover of airports in the 1770s when the first airplane flight by brothers Wilber and Orville Wright happened only in December 1903.

And when it comes to antiquity, anachronism is all the more a temptation; the past is truly foreign territory. Much damage is done by those who impose their contemporary experiences and understandings on antiquity. For example, the term "religion," which naturally springs to mind when studying the New Testament, is a modern category and thus distorts the complex of rituals, ethnic customs, practices, and beliefs that characterizes antiquity. We who are accustomed to listing our religion—or lack thereof—on forms only need to consider that Jews of the time of Jesus, for example, would be mystified by such a request (had there been such forms in their times) and would not have entered "Judaism" as their religion because it was a category unknown to them (Lieu 2016, 206).

Other anachronisms that hinder our understanding include speaking of "Christianity" before the late second century, translating the New Testament's Greek term *ekklēsia* as "church" rather than as "assembly," and classifying Paul as a "convert" from "Judaism" to "Christianity." How these anachronisms hinder accurate understandings will become clearer in subsequent chapters. In general, here it is sufficient to say that they obscure the complex processes by which the institutional dimensions of both Judaism and the church developed over time and through mutual connection and antagonism. Willingness to recognize and to discard anachronisms is central to the study of antiquity and thus to absorbing and appreciating the process by which what we know today as Judaism and Christianity emerged in relation to the other over the course of several centuries. And we must recognize that because anachronism seeps in with ease, it is challenging for us moderns to truly enter into the world of antiquity.

Abandoning anachronisms, however, can also be disconcerting. Most of us have fixed understandings of Judaism and Christianity—and learning the ambiguities, messiness, and entanglements of their historical evolution can be destabilizing. Contributing to the disequilibrium is the temptation to homogeneity with regard to the other, often by way of binaries. Binaries simplify things, offering some general categories to make sense of our worlds. Good and evil. Natural and unnatural. Oppressor and oppressed. Women and men. Religious and secular. True and false. Heaven and earth. Jews and Christians.

So, binaries are useful. Yet they are deceptive, often constraining our imagination by providing deceptively clear distinctions. Reality, as we all know, is messy and muddled. And binaries can be dangerous insofar as they lead us to categorize groups of people in ways that erase particularities and oversimplify complex attributes. Conspiracy theories such as QAnon, for example, work on the premise that traditional sources of knowledge—government, academia, "mainstream" media—are corrupt; thus, conventional versions of reality are not trustworthy and thus must be rejected. Because only "we" (QAnon adherents) who buy into this theory really know what's happening, we reject *in toto* what "they" claim. Biblical texts can and often are misinterpreted as proof texts, used, for example to attest to the division of humankind into two camps. Revelation 13 about those marked with the sign of the beast and those who resist it is a text particularly susceptible to such misinterpretation.

Binaries constrict our understanding of religion, as if religious identity were a stable identity when in fact our religious traditions are "porous, permeable, and perpetually fluid" (Thatamanil 2020, 15). The complex realities we term "religion" develop in diverse ways, shape and are shaped by distinctive cultures and historical events, assume varied organizational structures, and serve as a very "big tent" for peoples with widely different views.

Christians necessarily speak about Judaism in seeking to understand their own identity, but too often binaries impede an accurate comprehension. For example, it is not uncommon for Christian homilists to assert that "Jews believed (or believe) a particular principle or idea"—but, I mutter to myself, "Which Jews? When? Where? With what evidence?" All too often, teachers and homilists employ binaries to contrast Jewish "belief" with that of Christians. Moreover, they assume that Jewish belief is the same now as it was in antiquity, just as they assume that Jesus founded the church (another anachronism) and that his disciples became Christians despite the fact that Jesus and his first disciples were an entirely Jewish movement. Moreover, Judaism is often talked about as if it existed only in the past; too few who teach and preach have any sense of contemporary Jewish life. It may well be that a fundamental problem for Christians is that they regard Judaism as old—outmoded and antiquated. As a consequence, most Christians don't think of Jews as flesh-and-blood people living in the present. That failure of the imagination stifles Christian self-understanding.

But the principal binary is the zero-sum problem: Because Christianity is the true religion, Judaism is not true; it doesn't lead to salvation. This binary has many variants regarding which religion is false in relation to one's own. It's an easy binary to fall into if one lacks reliable knowledge and sustained contact with practitioners of the other tradition. It is far too simple to generalize about the other when that other is only a figment of one's imagination. In the face of real people, generalizations often fall apart. Sadly, history provides numerous examples of one tradition or group assuming they alone are the true believers. So, too, does each day's news chronicle arrogant dismissal of the traditions of others outside the realm of the true believer. This is particularly evident in Christian nationalist circles, most (in)famously in the current ReAwaken America movement led by Lieutenant General (ret.) Michael Flynn and political operative Roger Stone. They and others have been touring the United States in recent years, encouraging their followers to save America through spiritual warfare against those who are not Christian (or not sufficiently Christian in their eyes). Flynn illustrates the zero-sum problem in his assertion: "If we are going to have one nation under God, which we must, we have to have one religion. One nation under God, and one religion under God, right?" Wrong! Similarly problematic is the metaphor so often used in Christian circles about the Jewish "roots" of Christianity. It is not entirely wrong, but it is misleading insofar as it restricts Judaism to the role of preparation for Christianity. The roots metaphor further suggests that Judaism remains as it always has been, while that to which it gave rise continues to grow and flower. In many cases, it rests on the assumption that Judaism is the religion of the Old Testament, an erroneous depiction that obscures the ethnic and cultural dimensions of Judaism—its peoplehood—and neglects the rich and continuous textual commentary that characterizes the rabbinic interpretation so formative for Jewish life.

To abandon anachronism, avoid binaries, and apply fresh metaphors requires engaging the imagination. In this case, it necessitates envisioning a considerable period of Jewish belief and practice before there was "Judaism" as such and the Jewish Jesus Movement before institutional Christianity. Rather than presenting a picture of Christianity arising from a fully formed Judaism, historical reconstruction reveals how both traditions emerged in relation to each other through *contact, contestation, conversation, conflict,* and *cooperation* (Runesson 2000, 244–64). In other words, historical reconstruction requires a willingness to set aside conventional understandings that can no longer be considered as reliable and to search for more truthful accounts. Thus, it entails forgoing the "need to be right and [committing to] the pain of learning" (Hull 1991, 89–146).

Exploring the implications of historical reconstruction is a theological and a spiritual journey involving wandering in the wilderness of ambiguity, traversing some difficult terrain, and discovering expansive new vistas. This exploration will not only invite new perspectives on antiquity but will also provide a glimpse of new pathways by which to walk Christian commitment in a religiously pluralistic world. My interest in a historical reconstruction of the emergence of Christianity is not simply an intellectual undertaking. Rather, it flows from a passionate conviction that Christians immeasurably enrich their understanding of faith by engaging in relation with Jews and Judaism. Even as engaging with Jews and Judaism enhances our understanding and practice of Christianity, it also confronts us with disturbing realities. A consequence of deepening is being unsettled by discovery of the long history of Christian antagonism toward Jews undergirded by theological antisemitism. A response to that history is learning to tell the story of our origins in a way that does justice to what Judaism was then as a way of deepening who we are as a church community today in relation to Jews.

**A Synopsis**

Here's the big picture of this book:

The early chapters focus on establishing the fundamentals of the oppositional stance that so shaped the formation of Christian identity in opposition to Jewish identity, In Chapter Two, I argue that a fundamental element in Christian identity development came in large measure from the New Testament's depiction of the Pharisees as hypocrites and legalists who represent the religious perspective Jesus came to remedy. As popular religiosity has developed over the years, the Pharisees have come to symbolize what was wrong with Judaism. In Chapter Three, I analyze the work of early church writers committed to articulating what it meant to be a Christian. It is clear that leading thinkers did so by drawing firm lines of opposition between the followers of Christ and Jews. Certain emphases evident in their works bequeathed a legacy still apparent today, especially in the claim that Jesus Christ, as revealed in the New Testament, fulfills the Old Testament and that, consequently, Judaism was rendered theologically obsolete. The old law had value primarily as the promise fulfilled in Jesus's law of love. What becomes clear in retrospect is that writers in the early church "constructed" what Judaism was; their depictions lacked Jewish self-understanding at the time. Crucially, by the fourth century, in certain circles, their writings reveal not merely opposition to "Judaism," but hatred of Jews.

In Chapters Four and Five, I take up the work of "reconstruction." Or, to put it another way, I am building the fundamentals of a "replacement theology" to the conventional replacement theology that holds that Christianity replaced or superseded Judaism. My goal is to replace the fundamentally flawed construct that portrayed Judaism as a homogenous relic with a portrait of a living, postbiblical Judaism. I offer a portrait of Judaism as a resilient reorientation and reinvention of Jewish life in the wake of immense destruction. In the fourth chapter, I am asking what we might learn from historians, theologians, and rabbinic scholars about what Judaism was in the first five centuries or so of the Common Era. This involves brief forays into the nature of the Diaspora and role of the synagogue, the capacious concept of "Torah," and into the Jewish literary world of the Mishnah and of the Talmud. I also examine the consequences of the "Christianization" of the empire on Jewish communities—a reality that resulted in long-lasting effects on both Jews and Christians, albeit in starkly different ways.

The fifth chapter continues my reconstructive project by probing for what it might mean for us Christians to reimagine Jesus as a Jew. How did the fact of his Jewishness become obscure in much of Christianity, and what might it mean to recalibrate our image of Jesus in light of a "rediscovery" of the

Judaism of the first century CE? Having worked primarily in Matthew's Gospel in Chapter Two, in Chapter Five, I take up the challenges of "the Jews" as depicted in the Gospel of John. Given the enormous literature on this topic, I have limited my own analysis, taking up the implications of reading John "within Judaism." In a final section, I sketch some images of a Jewish Jesus as "other," as "the living Torah of God" and as "wisdom."

The sixth and final chapter considers specific ways of implementing the insights provided in the copious literature that has proven so important to this book. I have long realized that it is one thing to comprehend what can be learned through study, but there is another challenge altogether to succinctly and meaningfully articulate that learning in situations where people have little background and/or there is limited time to engage in a careful exposition of a concept or argument. I am under no illusion that my suggestions will prove entirely adequate, but my hope is that they might at least inspire some creative thought for those responsible for teaching and preaching. But, convinced that Jews and Judaism offer questions that "touch on the heart of our faith," I feel obliged to suggest ways we might address those questions in the everyday life of the church.

And now, on to the Pharisees....

## 2

# In Pursuit of the Pharisees

Among the dramatis personae of the New Testament, the Pharisees stand out, assuming the role of Jesus's primary antagonists. Depicted in the gospels as a "brood of vipers," "blind guides," "blind fools," and, most memorably, as "hypocrites," the Pharisees are nefarious characters. So, it is not surprising that most Christian writers over the ages render the Pharisees as archetypes of malevolence. The most familiar portrayal of Pharisees describes them as exemplars of extreme religiosity, captive to legalism. They are hypocrites because they don't practice what they teach. They misuse their authority by imposing heavy burdens on others yet are unwilling to shoulder such burdens themselves. They lack humility, craving acknowledgment of their piety, asceticism, and charitable giving. They are self-important, seeking places of honor and titles of respect. They are obsessed with meticulous details of religious practice, flouting the deeper meaning of religious commitment. The Pharisees, in short, seem to represent everything a Christian disciple should *not* be—in fact, *everything a person should not be.*

When it comes, however, to deriving implications of the gospels' criticism of the Pharisees, it appears that the interpreter's own ideological stance prevails. For example, in *Social Justice Pharisees: Woke Church Tactics and How to Engage Them,* author AD Robles represents Pharisees as the "woke church," that is, those preoccupied with social justice. These social justice advocates, says Robles, use the Bible as does Satan, drawing upon it as if it were a book of slogans about righteousness and justice. Pharisees are those who use the "satanic methods of the woke church" (Robles 2021; Kindle edition, no page numbers). In contrast, James Butcher, a Southern Baptist preacher, tells of his dawning conviction that contemporary conservative Christians look shockingly similar to Pharisees. In his book *Christian Pharisees,* Butcher charges his conservative colleagues with being self-appointed experts in religion "well known for their abrasiveness in their moral judgments, but not for their humility.... Renowned for being confident in the truth of their opinions, but not for their compassion" (Butcher 2017, 43). Along an analogous line, a letter to the editor in the July 3, 2021, issue of *The Tablet,* a Catholic periodical published in the United Kingdom, accuses the majority of the US Conference of Bishops of being in a "giddy rush to swap mitres for MAGA hats" by threatening to refuse Communion to President Joe Biden because of his stance on abortion, and thus they "have embraced Pharisaical transactional politics and squandered the residual trust of their flock."

Then there is *The Pharisees: The Party Game.* As its website describes it,

> **PHARISEES: The Party Game** is a new twist on Mafia, the classic party game we all know and love. Except, this time, it's got a little less organized crime ... and a lot more Bible verses.
>
> Picture this: you live in a distant land, many centuries ago. You've recently begun following a controversial new prophet named Jesus ... and the religious leaders of the day, the Pharisees, aren't very happy about it.

Each night, the Pharisees sneak into your community in search of one of Jesus' disciples to stone.

## Can the disciples find and excommunicate the Pharisees before they stone them all?

Pharisees is the perfect party game for anywhere from **5 to 48 players**. Each player has a mission. As a disciple, find and excommunicate the Pharisees. As a Pharisee, convince the disciples you're innocent while secretly trying to stone them each night, one by one.

To my knowledge, in the long history of Christian disparagement of the Pharisees, this is the first depiction that compares the Pharisees to mafia thugs desirous of stoning the disciples of Jesus (to show how one "offs" enemies in the first century CE?). Or that suggest the disciples of Jesus should excommunicate them. Perhaps this game gave some of the players a sense they were engaging in an entertaining form of Bible study. Having taught high school many years ago, I appreciate playful approaches to biblical texts that open new possibilities of understanding. But not when the players are mindlessly misrepresenting a group. Were there Pharisees today, they would be well advised to sue for libel.

While liberal or conservative convictions help to shape how the Pharisees are interpreted for the twenty-first century, the examples above share two notions in common. First, they accept the New Testament's typically negative portrayal of the Pharisees as historically reliable and thus as an accurate judgment about the Pharisaic movement. Second, while not explicit, their interpretations virtually always rest on the assumption that the Pharisees' preoccupation with the law symbolizes the legalism of Judaism. Indeed, for many Christians, the Pharisees epitomize Judaism as a religion of law, not love.

And yet a dramatically different characterization of the Pharisaic movement has developed among biblical scholars in the past fifty years or so. To summarize briefly, many scholars situate the Pharisees among the various Jewish voluntary associations that developed in late Second Temple Judaism (516 BCE–70 CE). Similar groupings included Essenes and Sadducees; presumably other groups existed for which evidence is scanty. In distinction from other Jewish associations, the Pharisaic teachings were broadly similar to those of Jesus. In the years after the destruction of Jerusalem's (second) Temple in 70 CE in the war with Rome in 66–70, the Pharisees assumed a more prominent role in Jewish life. It is likely that the Christ followers in the postwar period when the gospels were written perceived the Pharisees as their principal rivals and thus sought to delegitimize them by way of polemic. The diatribe in the gospels, most vociferous in Matthew, was not unusual in the Greco–Roman literature of the day. Its relentless negativity, however, has had lasting effects, with the result that "Pharisee" and "hypocrite" became synonyms.

The perspective presented in the previous paragraph is not new and has been widely available for several decades. Yet, it hasn't become widespread. Several reasons may account for its limited dissemination. The scholarship about the Pharisees requires approaching the New Testament through the lens of historical criticism, that is, interpreting texts in the fuller context of their historical, literary, and sociocultural contexts. In general, stereotypes tend to enjoy a long shelf life, particularly when there is a group one can portray as dishonorable and hypocritical. And the texts disparaging the Pharisees are both numerous and memorable. In short, they preach! So, the hold the conventional understanding of Pharisees has had on the church is not surprising.

Precisely because they are both familiar and easily (mis)characterized, the Pharisees deserve a closer study. Yet, thinking anew about the Pharisees can be disorienting.

They've so long been cast as Jesus's shady antagonists that repairing their reputation requires several stages of reconsideration. So, playing my own role as a sort of "reputation defender," I will proceed by first noting examples of ways Pharisees have been depicted in Catholic sources. Second, I will situate them in their historical context, drawing on current exegesis. My intention is less to restore their reputation than to reveal the complex world of Jesus's Judaism by comparing elements of Pharisees' characterization in the gospel accounts with that of the first-century Jewish historian Josephus. And, because the Gospel of Matthew devotes so much attention to the Pharisees and does so with such a jaundiced eye, I explore a plausible hypothesis that accounts for Matthew's negative portrait.

## The Pharisees in Catholic Religious Education and Pastoral Settings: Some Examples

Erroneous depiction of the Pharisees has given rise to binary formulations Christians often use to distinguish themselves from Judaism. Here the oppositional imagination pictures Jews as mired in legalities rather than living in the freedom of Christ's love. Christianity's (mis)representation of the Pharisees has had deleterious effects on relations with Jews because the hypocritical and legalistic Pharisees came to represent the Jewish rejection of Jesus and his new commandment of love.

A few examples make the point. In his analysis of how Catholic education textbooks portray the Pharisees, Philip Cunningham notes entries such as the following (Cunningham 2021, 388–93):

> Wherever Jesus, the new king of Israel went, he was followed about by angry men who argued with him because they did not like what he was saying or doing. Some of these men were Pharisees. Some of the Phari-

sees were so concerned with the special laws that God had given them through Moses that they often forgot about loving God and others. Instead, they thought only of themselves. They thought they were perfect, and they wanted to look perfect by following every law without making one little mistake. But their hearts were cold, proud, and unloving. (A fourth-grade text.) Jesus faced difficulties throughout his public life. Sometimes people did not understand or accept him. From the beginning, the religious leaders watched his every move with suspicion. They did not like his popularity and his criticism or their rigid view of the law. Instead of being open and changing their narrow-minded attitudes, they gradually built a wall of opposition. (A high school text.)

[Jesus strongly reproached the] scribes, the Pharisees, and the priests ... because, wanting to fulfill the 613 precepts and prohibitions of the Torah in an exceedingly scrupulous manner, they ended up losing sight of the deeper meaning, that which gives it soul, namely love. Scribes, Pharisees, and priests, instead of loving, have become teachers of obedience, instead of children loved by the Father, they have become slaves. Thus, the Law ended up stifling love. (From an Italian Catholic textbook, as identified by Maria Brutti.)

Although the first two examples Cunningham cites are from his 1992 dissertation, the thinking they represent enjoys a very long shelf life. For example, as I was working on this chapter, I happened to pick up the week's parish bulletin dated February 12, 2023, from a Catholic Church in the metro New York area where I sometimes participated in the Eucharist. The pastor wrote:

The scribes and Pharisees were masters of the Old Law. Now that the Messiah had arrived, they were unwilling to go deeper and move beyond the Old Testament teachings that they often misrepresented. They preferred a black-and-white approach to morality that had been with them for centuries and did not want to change when presented with Jesus' new and higher calling.

His column continued:

> Today's Gospel [Matthew 5:17–37] continues the Sermon on the Mount, which began with the Beatitudes. In today's portion of Jesus' sermon, we are taught about anger, adultery, and oaths. In every case Jesus refers to the Law as it was taught in the Old Testament but then elevates it to an entirely new level. The quote above makes it clear that to accept these new teachings of Jesus, one had to surpass the "righteousness" of the scribes and Pharisees. And the dire consequences of not surpassing their righteousness would be the loss of the Kingdom of Heaven.
> ... It is helpful to understand these new teachings in the context of the approach that the scribes and Pharisees took in regard to the Old Testament. About that, Jesus says, "Do not think that I have come to abolish the law or the prophets. I have come not to abolish but to fulfill." Thus, the primary problem with the scribes and Pharisees is not that they failed to teach the Old Testament properly. The primary problem is that now that the Messiah has arrived and has ushered in a new time of fulfillment and righteousness, they would not go deeper and would not

embrace the fulfillment of the Law of God. They are not willing to grow in holiness and embrace the fulfillment of all that had been taught before.

The pastor ended with a summons to "live in His New Law of grace," and to become "truly radical in your faith." He exhorts parishioners to "commit to surpassing the old and limited righteousness of the scribes and Pharisees, and God will do glorious things in your life."

With respect to pastors who struggle each week to say something meaningful to their congregants in their homilies and weekly bulletins, commenting on the Scriptures requires study. And in this case, it is doubtful this pastor's words roused any defense of the scribes and Pharisees because at the level of popular religiosity, how he characterized them is all too common.

Consider that an attentive reader might reasonably infer from the pastor's commentary that the Sermon on the Mount, or at least that Sunday's portion of it, advances an understanding of God contrasting with what had been previously taught in the "Old" Testament. This reader might further infer that the scribes and Pharisees, given their commitment to the "Old" Law and its "black-and-white approach to morality" exemplify Judaism. Unable to move beyond the teachings of the "Old" Testament and unwilling "to grow in holiness and embrace the fulfillment of all that they had been taught before," his column might easily be understood as claiming that the scribes and Pharisees epitomized the (Jewish) failure to "go deeper" and acknowledge the Messiah as fulfilling God's Law. At the root of the pastor's criticism lies a stereotyped, implicit caricature of Judaism.

His column underscores a tendency among Christians to expound on the teaching of Jesus by contrasting it with Jewish teachings—as if Jesus were not a Jew and the first generation of his followers all Jews. *In my experience, one rarely hears a* positive word about the Jews of Jesus's day. Rather, the reiteration of Judaism's alleged deficiencies serves to accentuate the superiority of Christ's teaching and thus of Christianity. Moreover, it is rare that I hear reference to Judaism beyond the biblical period. In June 2022, for example, the first day of the Jewish festival of *Shavuot* (see Exodus 23:14–17) overlapped with Pentecost Sunday. Closely connected with the festival of Passover (*Pesach*) that had been celebrated fifty days prior, *Shavuot* today is a resonant occasion that celebrates the giving of the Torah at Mount Sinai. It also marks the beginning of the wheat harvest and the bringing of the first fruits to the Temple. Among many Jews, it is a custom to study the Torah all night—or at least for a considerable amount of time. On that occasion in June 2022, I happened to be in a parish where the pastor was generally quite knowledgeable about Scripture. He rightly mentioned that the origins of Pentecost, celebrated fifty days after Easter, developed out of *Shavuot*. Yet he missed a teachable moment by connecting the timing of the two feasts in the present. No wonder congregants associate Judaism with the past.

These two experiences in local parishes illustrate well two of the familiar problems. The first is a well-worn claim that Jews of Jesus's day were mired in the Law, in contrast to the "New Law of Grace." The second is that even the occasional mention that Christian feasts are related to Jewish festivals is presented in such a way that it often implies those festivals form the "root" of Christian liturgical life whereas contemporary Jewish life goes unmentioned. One of the missed "teachable moments" in both cases is that the parishes are in an area where Jews constitute a significant part of the populations; presumably congregants in both parishes would know Jews. What they heard from the pastor's column and from the pulpit did little to enhance their knowledge—and, in the case of the scurrilous condemnation of the Pharisees, contributed to a negative, stereotypical view of Judaism.

Another, more fundamental reason for the lack of an accurate understanding of the Pharisees may be discerned. To comprehend the Pharisaic movement in its historical setting involves a panoramic knowledge of the New Testament in its Jewish matrix, of methods of contemporary biblical scholarship, and of Christianity's moral responsibilities after the *Shoah*, particularly in view of the resurgence of antisemitism in recent years. Seeing the Pharisees as other than Jesus's hypocritical major antagonists rests on a web of knowledge in at least seven interrelated areas, including

- Interpreting biblical texts in their sociocultural, literary, and historical contexts.
- Recognizing Jewish diversity in the Second Temple period (516 BCE–70 CE) and beyond.
- Honoring the Jewish character of the early Jesus movement.
- Grappling with the distinctiveness of each gospel account.
- Explaining the emergence of Judaism and Christianity in relation to each other over the course of centuries.
- Critiquing the nature, function, consequences, and critique of polemics in Scripture, particularly the New Testament's slanderous portrayal of Jews, including the Pharisees.
- Taking seriously the imperative in church teaching to engage in knowledgeable relations with other religious traditions. For Catholics in particular, "knowledgeable relations" entails understanding the legacy of *Nostra Aetate* and the imperative to counter theological antisemitism.

Entering the world of contemporary scholarship on each of these topics is like walking a labyrinth in which the center is not merely reliable knowledge of the Pharisees and a surer grasp of the New Testament but also an opening to a new appreciation for the relation of Judaism and Christianity in our time. How we frame the development of these two traditions over the centuries in relation to one another establishes the foundation for how we approach that relationship today—a relationship of enormous importance for our world.

## Two Perspectives on the Pharisees:
## The Historian Josephus and the New Testament

The Pharisees appear with such frequency and play such memorable roles in the New Testament that it is natural to assume that their lineage would be widely known. In fact, however, there is a paucity of reliable information about their origins, organizational structures, way of life, and degree of influence. The Pharisees seem to have left no document that articulates their perspectives, no text that we can assuredly claim has Pharisaic authorship other than Paul's self-identification as a Pharisee in Philippians 3:5–6. "Data on the Pharisees is so sparse and difficult to evaluate that any historical reconstruction must remain incomplete and uncomfortably hypothetical" (Saldarini 1988, 277).

Although probing their history reveals only a modest return in terms of reliable information about the Pharisaic movement, it yields two important results. First, it illumines aspects of Jewish practices and beliefs in the late centuries BCE and early CE. Second, it offers a caution to those who make assertions about the Pharisees—and the world of antiquity more generally—with more self-assurance than knowledge, as it will become clear that conventional understandings of the Pharisees are oversimplified and, in many cases, simply erroneous.

### Josephus on the Pharisees

So, we begin with what others said *about* them, beginning with Flavius Josephus (37–ca.100 CE). The eminent historian of the ancient eastern Mediterranean world, Steve Mason (2021), considers Josephus "the most consequential ancient writer in the West." Jerusalem-born to an aristocratic, priestly family as Yosef ben Mattiyahu, he became a well-educated priest, served as a regional commander in Galilee for his people in the Jewish War against Rome of 66–70, surrendered in the onslaught by Roman legionnaires and was taken captive. He then was fortunate enough to come under the protection of Vespasian and his son Titus, Roman generals who became emperors, so he went to Rome in 71 and began his extensive historical accounts. Besides his knack for impressing persons in prominent positions, Josephus had a keen interest in politics and the philosophy of government, wrote in Greek, and was knowledgeable about Greek philosophy as well as his own Jewish culture.

The Pharisees, whom Josephus regarded with both respect and disdain, are marginal figures relative to his production of thirty volumes. The Pharisees appear on only about twenty occasions in the massive corpus of his work. Pharisees, he observed, were known for their careful exposition of the Torah. But in his judgment, they were *too lenient* in their interpretation of the laws of Moses. Moreover, they were critics of rulers whom Josephus deemed virtuous and devout, particularly his favorite, John Hyrcanus (135–104 BCE), and too often turned the populace against their leaders. Although Josephus gave no indication of precisely when the Pharisees originated, we can infer that at least some were active and relatively prominent in the second century BCE, that is, during late Second Temple Judaism. This was the period when Jews had reconstituted their life in the land of Israel only to see the Second Temple and Jerusalem destroyed by the Romans in 70 CE.

In his seven-volume *Judean Wars* (ca. 74–81 CE), a tragic testimony to Judean "fortitude of spirit" despite the impossibility of defeating the Romans, Josephus classified the Pharisees, Sadducees, and Essenes as three Judean philosophical schools. The term he uses is *hairesis*, which might also be translated as "schools of thought" or "lines of thought" (not as "sects"). Although the Pharisees come first in the list of the three philosophies, likely an indication of their influence in society, it is clear that Josephus was more fascinated by the Essenes, whom he portrays at greater length because of their adherence to the Torah, disciplined conduct, self-restraint, and frugality. It may well be that a group of Essenes lived at Qumran and were among those responsible for the Dead Sea Scrolls. These scrolls, discovered by accident in 1947, have become the source of vast information about a dissenting faction of Jews in the Second Temple period. This faction was notable for vehement opposition to the Temple and priesthood, withdrawal into the Judean desert, and the conviction that they were the "sons of light" in opposition to the "sons of darkness."

Nevertheless, Josephus compared the Pharisees favorably to the Sadducees. Unlike the boorish Sadducees, the Pharisees related well to one another and promoted harmony among the people. The Sadducees denied fate—that is, things are brought about by certain powers or divine providence—believing that humans controlled their own destiny. In contrast, the Pharisees ascribed everything to fate and to God, leaving room for an individual's own decision-making. They believed in the imperishability of the soul and the punishment of the wicked as well as the reward of the good; the Sadducees thought that the soul perished after death.

A similar comparison and contrast with the Sadducees occur in Book 18 of his twenty-one volume *Jewish Antiquities* (ca. 94 CE, including two appended volumes of his autobiography, *Life*). Here Josephus added that the Pharisees have a simple standard of living and demonstrate respect and deference to their elders. In contrast, the Sadducees pay little heed to their ancestral teachers. In Book 13 of *Antiquities*, the historian expounded on the distinctive Pharisaic interpretational method: "the Pharisees passed on to the people certain ordinances from a succession of fathers, which are not written down in the laws of Moses. For this reason, the party of the Sadducees dismisses them, averring that one need recognize only the written ordinances, whereas those from the tradition of the fathers need not be observed. Conflicts and major differences developed between the two groups over these matters" (13:297–98). Josephus repeats the judgment about Pharisaic accuracy in interpretation in *Antiquities* 17:41: "There was also a certain bloc of Judean people that prided itself greatly on great precision in relation to the ancestral heritage and laws."

Although Josephus was clearly no fan of the Sadducees, he also rejected what he regarded as the Pharisaic leniency with the law. This is evident in the two-volume *Against Apion* (ca. 97 CE), both a defense of Judean historiography and culture vis-à-vis Greek historiography and culture, and a refutation of slurs against Judeans. In this relatively brief work, Josephus decried those who, like the Pharisees, sought to mitigate harsh punishments (e.g., by death) for transgressing the Law of Moses such as Deuteronomy 21:18–21:

> If someone has a stubborn and rebellious son who will not obey his father and mother, who does not heed them when they discipline him, then his father and his mother shall take hold of him and bring him out to the elders of his town at the gate of that place. They shall say to the elders of his town, "This son of ours is stubborn and rebellious. He will not obey us. He is a glutton and a drunkard." Then all the men of the town shall stone him to death. So you shall purge the evil from your midst; and all Israel will hear, and be afraid.

Ultimately, Josephus considered his own interpretation of the "constitution" Moses had bequeathed his people to be the proper one, honoring the Judeans' rigorously righteous traditions. Josephus also adds a fourth member to his "schools of thought": the "Fourth Philosophy" cofounded by Judah the Galilean with the Pharisee Zakok who led an armed revolt against Roman rule in 6 CE (*Antiquities* 18:23–25). The soldier–statesman Josephus blamed their early resistance movement as contributing to the turbulence that eventually led to the outbreak of Jewish War in 66 and resulted in the destruction of the Temple and the city of Jerusalem in 70.

Several observations about this brief excursus into Flavius Josephus:

- Josephus was not primarily interested in the Pharisees as a religious group in the narrow sense of that term. He didn't comment on their ritual practice or take issue with their beliefs about the soul's imperishability or about fate. Consistent with his focus on political life and government, the Jewish historian emphasized their effect on Judean society, such as influencing the people against certain rulers or the consequences of their interpretational methods for Judea's reputation in relation to Greek societies.
- Roman rule had begun in 63 BCE under the Roman general Pompey, resulting in Judea coming under direct Roman rule after eighty years of independence. Rome's cult of the emperor and the high taxation of the people led to resistance groups, such as that of Judah the Galilean, and continued until Rome's devastating victory over Jewish rebels in 70 CE.
- The Pharisees were relatively unimportant in the corpus of Josephus's works. The negligible attention

Josephus gave to them contrasts dramatically with the outsize role they play in the New Testament.

- In the New Testament, particularly the Gospel of Matthew, the Pharisees are depicted as exacting and severe in their interpretation of the Torah. In contrast, Josephus, while respecting the precision of their interpretations, found them too lenient.
- In the New Testament, both in Matthew and Luke, the Pharisees are accused of being "full of greed." Yet Josephus notes they had a simple standard of living.

In brief, Josephus's depiction of the Pharisees is in tension with that of the New Testament. At minimum, the differences raise questions about the historical reliability of the evangelists' more negative portrayal. This suggests that the gospels may not have been intended as a dispassionate report on the nature of the Pharisaic movement. It may well be that what the gospels portrayed were the sorts of conflicts that arose in the latter part of the first century CE when the gospels were composed, suggesting the evangelists were offering a religious narrative about Jesus and his significance rather than providing a historically reliable documentation of his life. That being said, it is time for a closer look at the Pharisees as the New Testament writers characterize them.

## The New Testament's Pharisees

### Paul

The time frame of the composition of the various books constituting the New Testament roughly corresponds to that of Josephus, with the exception of the letters of Paul, typically dated to the 50s CE. Paul doesn't reveal much about the Pharisees but he makes one important declaration in the Letter to the Philippians that is too often overlooked:

Beware of the dogs, beware of the evil workers, beware of those who mutilate the flesh! For it is we who are the circumcision, who worship in the Spirit of God and boast in Christ Jesus and have no confidence in the flesh—even though I, too, have reason for confidence in the flesh. If anyone else has reason to be confident in the flesh, I have more: circumcised on the eighth day, a member of the people of Israel, of the tribe of Benjamin, a Hebrew born of Hebrews; *as to the law, a Pharisee;* as to zeal, a persecutor of the church; as to righteousness under the law, blameless. (Emphasis added)

Yet whatever gains I had, these I have come to regard as loss because of Christ. More than that, I regard everything as loss because of the surpassing value of knowing Christ Jesus my Lord. For his sake I have suffered the loss of all things, and I regard them as rubbish, in order that I may gain Christ and be found in him, not having a righteousness of my own that comes from the law, but one that comes through faith in Christ, the righteousness from God based on faith. I want to know Christ and the power of his resurrection and the sharing of his sufferings by becoming like him in his death, if somehow I may attain the resurrection from the dead. (Philippians 3:2–10)

Paul is an immensely complicated figure whose writings defy facile explanation. Paul wrote letters, not systematic theological treatises. We don't know precisely what questions and concerns the recipients of his letters had brought to him, nor do we have evidence of their responses to what he wrote them. Moreover, most scholars distinguish between his genuine letters, that is, those directly from him, and those written in his name. So, we have Paul and the "Pauline school," as it were. Nor were Paul's letters easily comprehensible, even to his contemporaries, as the writer of another New Testament epistle, 2 Peter, observes of the letters of his "beloved brother Paul": "There are some things in them hard to understand, which the ignorant and unstable twist to their own destruction, as they do the other scriptures" (3:16). Hard to understand, indeed! Those of us today who sometimes find Paul perplexing and inconsistent may be relieved to know that even those far closer in time to him were at times mystified.

Just to add further complications, in the Acts of the Apostles, Luke's second volume, Paul figures prominently. Yet the apostle's own letters differ markedly from the "Lukan Paul." Parsing those differences has given rise to a massive literature, with many today dubious about the historical accuracy of Paul's depiction in Acts. Ultimately, Luke's theological commitments shaped his presentation of events and personages of the early communities of Christ followers, and his portrayal of Paul provided a memorable narrative device, including Luke's attribution of this claim by Paul: "I have belonged to the strictest sect of our religion and lived as a Pharisee" (Acts 26:5). Earlier in Acts, taking note of Sadducees and Pharisees in the crowd when he is called before the Jewish council (Sanhedrin), Paul exclaims, "Brothers, I am a Pharisee, a son of Pharisees" (23:6).

And then there is the long history of Paul's many interpreters from Augustine of Hippo to the present as well as Paul in the life of the church today. In my own tradition, he is "Saint Paul," the Jew who converted to Christianity and became a missionary. In Paul's day, however, there was as yet no "Christianity" to which he could convert.

So, what to do with Paul's own curriculum vitae? Never one to be reticent about his own qualifications, he touts his Jewish credentials, as it were: "circumcised on the eighth day, a member of the people of Israel, of the tribe of Benjamin, a Hebrew born of Hebrews; as to the law, a Pharisee; as to zeal, a persecutor of the church; as to righteousness under the law, blameless" (Philippians 3:5–6).

Note also in the citation above from Philippians, likely written in the early 50s CE, that Paul sets tact aside, mocking false teachers as "dogs," a derogatory term in antiquity (with apologies to modern readers with different sensibilities about canines). Paul believed those teachers were misleading Gentiles attracted to Christ by claiming that circumcision was requisite for them as well. Paul's vision was radically different: Jews became righteous by following the law, that is, by faithfully living the Torah. That included circumcision, that is, the way in which male Jews entered into the covenant community. But non-Jews who aspired to follow Christ had a different communal call for which following Jewish ritual practices was not appropriate. Not everyone in the early communities of Christ followers saw eye-to-eye with Paul on this matter, especially Peter and James.

In Philippians, however, Paul doesn't develop this argument. Rather, he takes a more personal turn. There's nothing inherently wrong with circumcision, he clarifies. He himself was circumcised on the eighth day after birth, becoming a member of the people Israel. He was of Hebrew heritage from the tribe of Benjamin, living the Torah through the tradition of the Pharisees.

But Paul doesn't tell us precisely what that way of interpreting the Torah meant, only that he was righteous, that is, living justly. Yet despite Paul's impressive credentials, he has learned another way of living righteously, through trust in Christ and a desire to know the power of the resurrection—spoken as one formed as a Pharisee, for whom the soul was imperishable. For Paul being a Pharisaic Jew and following Christ were consistent ways of being.

Apropos of Paul's complexity, he will reappear in further chapters. For now, I suggest we muse on this phrase: *The Apostle Paul, a Christ-following Pharisee.* And Paul was not alone. Being a "Christ-following Pharisee" was not an oxymoron in the first century. For example, in the Acts of the Apostles, Luke refers to "some believers who belonged to the sect of the Pharisees" (15:5). Earlier in Acts, Luke writes about the Pharisee Gamaliel, a respected sage and scholar, who warned his fellow members of the Sanhedrin to refrain from persecuting Peter and other Christ followers whose preaching and healing in Jerusalem were drawing large crowds in Jerusalem. Gamaliel instructed them that "if this plan or this undertaking is of human origin, it will fail; but if it is of God, you will not be able to overthrow them—in that case, you may even be found fighting against God" (5:38–39). Acts 23:9 recounts a similar intervention on behalf of Paul when he is brought before the Sanhedrin when "certain scribes of the Pharisees' group stood up and contended, 'We find nothing wrong with this man. What if a spirit or an angel has spoken to him?'"

### Pharisees in the Gospels and Acts

In the relative brevity of the New Testament, the Pharisees are mentioned nearly one hundred times, primarily but not exclusively as foils for the central figure, Jesus of Nazareth. For the most part, they are on the losing side of every controversy, except for Luke–Acts, which has a somewhat more sympathetic portrayal. In fact, each of the four canonical gospels and Acts has its own depiction of Pharisees, the subject of a detailed study by British scholar Mary Marshall (2015).

In the interests of brevity, I have chosen to sketch only a few of the most salient characteristics by which Mark, Luke–Acts, and John depict the Pharisees. I will then turn to examine Matthew's Pharisees in somewhat more detail because they play a colorful and dominant role in his gospel. Most famously, the Matthean Jesus—that is, Jesus as Matthew characterizes him—engages in a sustained and intense diatribe against the "hypocrites." I will also explore one scholar's hypothesis about this denunciation and suggest implications for grappling with Matthew's antagonism toward this school of thought.

A number of the tensions between the Pharisees and Jesus surface around eating—or in one case, not eating, since the Pharisees question Jesus about why his disciples don't fast when the disciples of John the Baptist do so. Mark and Luke portray Pharisees as being scandalized by Jesus's table companions: tax collectors and sinners. Such a scurrilous company for this teacher from Nazareth! Jesus, on the other hand, has his own objections. The Pharisees, Jesus says, are preoccupied by washing before meals, both their customs about rinsing their hands and cleaning "cups, pots, and bronze kettles." In his perspective, their obsession with exterior cleanness entirely misses the point of inner cleanliness. Citing Isaiah (29:13), Jesus accuses the Pharisees of honoring God with their lips while focusing their hearts elsewhere. In Luke's version, Jesus accuses them of fixating on cleaning the outside of the cup while themselves being "full of greed and wickedness" inside.

Interestingly, Luke includes three details about Jesus dining with Pharisees. The encounters lead to an extended teaching. Simon, a Pharisee who had invited Jesus to his home for dinner, becomes a recipient of teaching about the meaning of hospitality and abundant love after a "sinful woman" enters the scene, bathing Jesus's feet with her tears and anointing him with an expensive ointment (7:36–50). Later in his gospel (14:1), Jesus is on his way to eat a Sabbath meal with a leader of the Pharisees when he encounters a man with dropsy, or edema, perhaps symbolizing greed. Apparently, a crowd of scribes and Pharisees was nearby, watching whether Jesus would heal on the Sabbath. Jesus queries them: "If one of you has a child or an ox who has fallen into a well, will you not immediately pull it out on a Sabbath day?" (14:5). Luke notes they had no reply to this. And when Jesus arrived at the Pharisee's house for the

Sabbath meal, he saw how the guests vied for seats of honor and instructs them to seek the lowest seat (14:12–14). This teaching echoes Jesus's admonition to the Pharisees for seeking seats of honor in the synagogue (11:43). And, he instructs, when you are issuing your invitations to a meal, make sure the needy are included.

In addition to stories of Jesus's healing of persons and animals on the Sabbath, all three of the synoptic gospels describe an incident when the disciples plucked grain while walking through a grainfield on the Sabbath; Matthew adds that this was to assuage their hunger (Mark 2:23–28; Matthew 12:1–8; Luke 6:1–5). At issue here is obedience to the command, "Keep holy the Sabbath." Essential to keeping the Sabbath holy was cessation from work. And for these particular Pharisaic interpreters of the Torah, that law meant refraining from the work of healing and picking grain.

While a great more detail about the synoptic writers' depictions of the Pharisees could be said, it is important to pay attention to what the passages cited here suggest. They represent Jesus and the Pharisees as interpreting Jewish practices around eating and Sabbath observance differently. The evangelists portray Jesus as having the more compassionate interpretation and suggest that the Pharisees are more intent to preserve their customs than to be faithful to the Torah. For the most part, they portray the Pharisees' focus on externals as obscuring the deeper meaning of Jewish practices around Sabbath and food.

John, as usual, presents a somewhat variant view. He reports that Nicodemus, a leader among the Jews and a Pharisee who came to Jesus in the night, addresses Jesus as a "teacher who has come from God; for no one can do these signs that you do apart from the presence of God" (3:1–2). So, in this case, it is Nicodemus the Pharisee who discerns Jesus's closeness to God. In chapter 9, however, the Fourth Gospel offers another perspective on the Pharisees in a well-told tale about

## In Pursuit of the Pharisees

a blind man in which the Pharisees reveal themselves to be the truly obtuse ones. It's a lengthy account, composed in the distinctive Johannine mode of fashioning a theological account around a healing. A condensed version of the story is told in John 9: Jesus cures a man born blind. The man's skeptical neighbors quiz the blind man whom they knew as a beggar: "Then how were your eyes opened?" The blind man, no theological genius, sticks to the facts: A man named Jesus smeared mud on his eyes, sent him to wash in the pool of Siloam; when he washed, he received his sight. Then Pharisees appear on the scene, expressing their disapproval that the healing had taken place on the Sabbath. Like the skeptical neighbors, they ask the blind man how he came to see and receive a similarly straightforward response: "Jesus put the mud on my eyes, I washed and now I see." Some of the Pharisees remain offended that such a deed would be enacted on the Sabbath, and others are puzzled how a sinner could perform this healing. So, they further interrogate the blind man, asking what kind of a person he believes the healer to be. More enlightened than in his previous responses, the formerly blind man responds, "He is a prophet."

Yet, the narrator notes, unbelief continues, among "the Jews" and then even among the man's parents, who probe how this healing had happened. As the exchange nears its end, the formerly blind beggar expresses his faith in Jesus. Meanwhile, the Pharisees reappear, asking a rhetorical question: "Surely, we are not blind, are we?" Jesus retorts, "If you were blind, you would not have sin. But now that you say, 'We see,' your sin remains." In John's perspective, the Pharisees are oblivious to their own haughtiness, a view that while expressed in a dramatic interplay of characters, resonates with the dominant perspective of the synoptic writers that the Pharisees lack insight into the Torah's true meaning.

Yet, in the accounts of the Gospels of Mark, Luke, and John, there are also intimations of the Pharisees' hostility to

Jesus. Mark accuses Pharisees of conspiring with the dynasty of Herod the Great, the Herodians (3:6 and 8:14), and of seeking to entrap Jesus with their questions about divorce (10:13). Luke expands upon the accusation of greed and wickedness to lament how the Pharisees neglect justice and God's love, seek honor and respect, interpret the Torah in ways that burden people while failing to offer them wiser counsel, and dishonor the prophetic traditions. Matthew has an even longer list of "woes" against the Pharisees, which will be addressed below.

In the Gospel of John, the indications of hostility become more explicit. He portrays them as colluding with the chief priests and the Temple police in order for Jesus to be arrested. Later the trio summons a meeting of the Sanhedrin about Jesus, and then joins the chief priests in giving an order to the people to let them know where Jesus was so that "they might arrest him" (11:46–57). Ultimately, John says that Judas brought a detachment of soldiers along with the police, chief priests, and Pharisees to the garden to arrest Jesus. Like John, Matthew associates the Pharisees with the death of Jesus, most explicitly after the crucifixion when they accompany the chief priests to ask Pontius Pilate to secure the tomb, since the "impostor" Jesus had said, "After three days I will rise again" (23:62–63).

When we scrutinize major emphases in Mark, Luke–Acts, and John, the Pharisees are alternatively curious about Jesus (e.g., why he and his disciples were not fasting) and scandalized by what they perceive as a disregard for observing Sabbath. They disagree with his interpretations of the Torah (e.g., on divorce) and are threatened by his teaching to the extent that they seek to entrap him. The reader comes to understand Jesus's teaching by virtue of contrast with the teaching and behavior of the Pharisees. Matthew includes nearly all of these encounters in his own fashion, but his portrait of the Pharisees is bleaker. Of all the New Testament writers, Matthew singles out the Pharisees most frequently (twenty-nine times) and most negatively. Thus, it is imperative to explore his distinctive portrait, its repercussions, and a framework for grappling with how we might interpret his characterization in our time. In Matthew the Pharisees function as a brilliant literary device, but his depiction has had deadly consequences because later ages projected Matthew's depiction upon Jews as a whole.

## Matthew on Jesus and the Pharisees

In a word, Matthew's Pharisees are hypocrites, a charge the Matthean Jesus directs at them eight times and implicitly four times. In chapter 23, Jesus adds a few more colorful terms to complement the charge of hypocrisy: brood of vipers, snakes, whitewashed tombs, blind guides, blind fools. In their interpretation of the Torah, Pharisees decree burdensome norms yet fail themselves to live by them. They wear their religious garb ostentatiously so that others will be impressed by their religiosity. They expect to be greeted with respect in the marketplace, to enjoy the seats of honor at banquets and at synagogues, and to be called by titles such as "rabbi." When it comes to tithing, their offerings are mere herbs; just as they fail to tithe more nourishing foods, they neglect the weightier values of the law: faith, justice, and mercy. Obsessed with cleaning their vessels, interiorly Pharisees are filled with greed and self-indulgence. They have crucified or flogged prophets, sages, and scribes.

One might say that Matthew has provided a prelude to this diatribe in Jesus's instruction: "Beware of practicing your piety before others to be seen by them" (6:1). So, he charges his disciples not to boast about their almsgiving, nor to flaunt their godliness in synagogues and in public. Further, Jesus instructs them not to pray in elaborate and empty word salads, piling up words as do the Gentiles! When fasting, they should avoid the appearance of long-suffering; they should wash their face and comb their hair (6:2–18). Those churches that use the lectionary often proclaim these instructions on piety in Ash Wednesday services. I am always struck by the irony of walking around the streets and workplaces of New York City with ashes on my forehead. Do those of us so marked realize that we contradict the instruction in Matthew's Gospel to wash our faces when fasting and to avoid showing off our piety? Irony aside, however, it is no wonder Jesus's invective against the Pharisees has proven so memorable. The "cultured despisers of religion" of our time rightly rant against the hypocrisy religion seems to breed, although often oblivious to the fact that hypocrisy is not limited to the religious sphere. And who among religious practitioners doesn't occasionally rage against hypocrites? And, in moments of stillness, when we come face to face with our own hypocrisies, do we not feel shame?

Nor was Jesus alone among Jews in deprecating hypocrisy. Israel's prophets had plenty to say on this score. Isaiah is particularly outspoken:

> What to me is the multitude of your sacrifices?
>   says the Lord;
> I have had enough of burnt-offerings of rams
>   and the fat of fed beasts;
> I do not delight in the blood of bulls,
>   or of lambs, or of goats.
> When you come to appear before me,
>   who asked this from your hand?
> Trample my courts no more;
>   bringing offerings is futile;
>   incense is an abomination to me.
> New moon and Sabbath and calling of convocation—
>   I cannot endure solemn assemblies with iniquity.
> Your new moons and your appointed festivals
>   my soul hates;
> they have become a burden to me,
>   I am weary of bearing them.

> When you stretch out your hands,
> > I will hide my eyes from you;
> > even though you make many prayers,
> > I will not listen;
> > your hands are full of blood.
> > Wash yourselves; make yourselves clean;
> > > remove the evil of your doings
> > > from before my eyes;
> > cease to do evil,
> > learn to do good;
> > seek justice,
> > > rescue the oppressed,
> > defend the orphan,
> > > plead for the widow. (Isaiah 1:11–17)

Thus, the issue is not about whether the denunciation of hypocrisy in the gospel accounts accords with Jewish tradition, but rather *whether the Pharisees themselves can be accurately understood as the principal exemplars of hypocrisy?* Should we judge the Pharisaic movement as fundamentally hypocritical? Or might hypocrisy in religious matters be a temptation common to all who profess a faith? Moreover, why does the Matthean Jesus criticize the Pharisees so vociferously? After all, the evangelists portray Jesus more typically as showing mercy and compassion toward his interlocutors. Jesus's heightened condemnation of Pharisees in Matthew seems uncharacteristic, even jarring—and a striking contrast with Josephus's opinion that the Pharisees were too moderate.

- Pondering what may have prompted the particularities of Matthew's harsh portrait of Pharisees necessitates a brief review of some important details not commonly understood by readers of the New Testament. By way of summary thus far: Pharisees were

not homogeneous. At least some were open to Christ's teaching; others were themselves among the believers (e.g., Nicodemus). There was no evidence that Pharisees were beholden to a single rule. What they had in common was commitment to interpreting the Torah in a way that considered development in tradition—what came, at least in part, to be the Oral Law.
- Nor did contemporaries of the evangelists agree with their overall portrait. Josephus, although not developing his views on the Pharisees at length, thought that their interpretation of the Torah was too lenient.
- By his own account, Paul belonged to the Pharisees. There is no evidence that his devotion to the Way of Christ precluded belonging to the Pharisaic movement. This biographical fact stands in tension with the common assumption that already by the time of Paul in mid-first-century that "Christianity" had developed a distinctive identity from Judaism.
- In Acts, Luke identifies Paul's teacher Gamaliel as among those Pharisees who called for further discernment about following Christ.
- Some scribes identified as Pharisees.
- Overall, the gospel writers present the Pharisees as foils to Jesus. From a literary standpoint, the Pharisees' skepticism about (at best) or disagreement with Jesus illumine the teaching of Jesus by way of contrast.

Grappling with the invective of Matthew's depiction of the Pharisees will be helped by some background information and hypotheses that suggest important context. This involves some basic information about Judaism in the Second Temple Period: the development of synagogues, and some general notions about the meaning of the Torah in the first century CE. A brief word on each, to be developed further in Chapter Four.

## Synagogues

Whenever we meet a word from antiquity that is still in use today, anachronism is always a temptation. Although there is continuity between ancient and modern synagogues, over the centuries they have evolved in varying ways. The common thread is that synagogues in antiquity were/are sites where Jews gathered. The word synagogue is Greek (*synagogē*), means an assembly, a coming together, a gathering. Yet, synonyms abound; some seventeen terms were used in Hebrew and Latin as well as Greek for synagogue. Two of the more frequently used were "prayer house" *(proseuchē)* and "holy place" *(hieron)*. Another is *ekklesia,* a term that occurs often in the New Testament and is typically translated as "church." In the first instance, however, it means an assembly. More on this later.

Precisely when and where synagogues began is difficult to date with assurance. Among the earliest dates proffered thus far—study of the past is always developing—is a third-century BCE *proseuchē* in Middle Egypt. The Egyptian Mediterranean city of Alexandria, famous for its ancient library, had a number of synagogues. Synagogues extended across the Mediterranean world and even to the Black Sea and India—and of course, to Israel. In 2009, archaeologists discovered one of the oldest synagogues in Israel dating from the first century BCE in the Galilean fishing village of Migdal (Magda), the hometown of the disciple Mary of Magdala, "Apostle to the Apostles."

Synagogues were multifunctional, with specific activities varying according to time and place. Among them were

- Study, instruction, and discussion of the Scriptures, laws, traditions, moral norms;
- Prayers, ritual, and worship;
- Communal dining, celebration of festivals, and remembrance of central events in Jewish history;

- Adjudication of disputes, meetings, formulations of local norms, keeping of community archives—something of a village hall for civic matters;
- Votive offerings and dedicatory offerings (Gruen 2012, 100).

Although synagogues originated within Jewish communal life, they were not exclusive to Jews. Even when synagogues became increasingly recognized as sacred spaces in the late first and second centuries CE, non-Jews were welcome. Alexandrian Gentiles, for example, joined Jews in annual celebrations of the completion of the Greek translation of Israel's Scriptures, the Septuagint. For the most part, Gentiles (non-Jews) drawn to aspects of Judaism, often known as "God-fearers," took on aspects of Jewish practice, such as Sabbath observance, yet retained their worship of native gods. Jews worshiped the one God of Israel, but were accepting of those with different cultural traditions, particularly in urban centers where interaction with non-Jews was part of daily life.

Two types of synagogues have been identified in Israel (Runesson, 2008). One refers to a town assembly, a sort of municipal or civic institution. Among its various functions were the political and juridical decisions a functioning community needs to make but also the Sabbath gatherings in which the Torah was read and discussed. They were open to all Jews, and leadership was local; there was no normative ritual or ruling group. It was in this type of synagogue that a teacher from Nazareth, Jesus, occasionally worshiped, preached, and healed.

The other type of synagogue paralleled the Greco–Roman institution of the *collegia,* or association. Association synagogues were communal institutions in which specific groups of Jews developed and deepened their particular approach to Jewish life. Each was independent from the other and specified their own rules and leaders. According to Philo, the

Essenes had their own synagogues, as did the Therapeutae. Luke reports in Acts 6:9 about a "synagogue of the Freedmen" in Jerusalem consisting of formerly enslaved Jews who had received manumission. Voluntary associations like the Pharisees had their own synagogues. It is likely that Matthew is referring to the distinction between public and association synagogues when he distinguishes between "their" or "your" synagogue and synagogues more generally. Matthew uses "their" on five occasions: 4:23, 9:35, 10:17, 12:9–10, 13:54; "your" synagogue is used in 23:34. In contrast, he uses "synagogues" without pronouns three times: 6:2, 5, and 23:6.

### Interpretation of the Torah

Torah is a capacious term—far more layered than the usual Christian reductionistic rendering of it as Law—designating not only the first five books of the Bible (Gk., Pentateuch) but also encompassing the Jewish Bible—*Tanakh*—and ultimately, the Oral Torah, the compendium of Jewish teaching over the ages.

The threefold division of the Jewish Bible came to be known in the Middle Ages by the acronym *TaNaKh*, that is *Torah, Nevi'im* (Prophets), and *Ketuvim* (Writings). Of these, the Torah holds primacy, enfolding the key narratives by which the Jewish people originated and were chosen to live in such a way as to bear witness to a just and merciful God—a call in which they failed time and again, only to experience God's redeeming power. Genesis (*Bereshit*) tells the story of creation, recounts the divine call to form a people through Abram (Abraham) and his wife Sarai (Sarah), and their progeny. Exodus (*Shemot*) picks up the narrative with the people enslaved in Egypt and God's call to Moses to challenge Pharaoh, "Let my people go." Their ensuing liberation—their exodus—from Egypt finds them in the wilderness of Sinai, called to live in covenant with God so as to be "a kingdom of priests and a holy nation." Leviticus (*Vayikra*) narrates some of the dimensions of living a holy life: sacrificial worship, abiding by norms of purity, and commemorating God's redeeming actions. Numbers (*Bemidbar*) revisits the years in the wilderness, including the people's rebellion. Deuteronomy (*Devarim*) gathers all this together, retelling Israel's story and reminding the people of their obligation to live faithfully. Above all, Israel is called to listen to the Divine Voice: "Hear, O Israel! The LORD is our God, the LORD alone. You shall love your God with all your heart and with all your soul and with all your might" (6:4).

The Torah certainly includes law—how Jews were to live out the covenant—but more generally might be understood as teaching or instruction, from its Hebrew stem *yrh*, "to shoot an arrow" or "hit the mark." In the first century CE, the Torah was at the center of Jewish identity. Flavius Josephus noted that education in the Torah constituted the mark that distinguished Jewish children from their Gentile counterparts (*Against Apion* 1.60).

The Christian equation of the Torah with law and legalism developed primarily in the second through fifth centuries, a story that the next chapter tells in part.

## The Heightened Intensity of Matthew's Depiction of the Pharisees

Matthew's Gospel was likely composed at least fifty years after the death of Jesus and in the wake of a traumatic event. Considerable social unrest by Jews disillusioned with Roman rule had led to a revolt that eventuated in the Jewish War of 66–70 CE. Given the disparity in power, the war ended, predictably, with Rome victorious. The consequences were dire: the (Second) Temple was left in ruins and many Jews were taken captive. One can only imagine the postwar instability and upheaval, including crises in leadership, since those groups associated with the Temple, such as the high priests and Sadducees, no longer had a functioning institution. The groups like the Essenes, who had settled in the wilderness to establish what they viewed as a Jewish life of greater holiness, hid their writings deep into caves in the Judean wilderness; many perished or fled elsewhere. The dry desert heat preserved those documents, discovered only in 1947, the Dead Sea Scrolls, which contain, among their other documents, the oldest biblical manuscripts.

By the time the gospels were composed (ca. 70–110 CE, with Matthew dated ca. 80–90 CE), the Pharisees had become the more prominent group. At the same time, Jesus's movement had grown, spreading beyond Judea and Galilee. While some Gentiles had been drawn into the following of Christ—some likely through the preaching of Paul—it seems to have remained a predominantly Jewish group until the advent of the late first and early second century. Many scholars have suggested that Matthew's negative depictions of the Pharisees emerged in this postwar period, when both Christ followers and Pharisees became rivals in advocating for their respective positions on what it meant to observe the Torah.

Why did the Torah require interpretation? Simply put, it was already a document of antiquity with perspectives and laws that needed clarifying in a different age. And since there was as yet no norming body with the authority to adjudicate between authentic and inauthentic interpretations, Jews debated matters among themselves, often vociferously. Arguing the Torah was regarded as an act of fidelity to the tradition—and remains so.

*It is important to recognize that Matthew's Gospel does not criticize Judaism as such.* In fact, his community manifests many connections with Jewish practices: observing Sabbath, tithing, almsgiving, fasting, prayer, paying the yearly Temple tax, and a public reading and discussion of the Torah in synagogue settings.

Matthew's anger is directed primarily and passionately toward a specific group: Pharisees. It wasn't that they failed to honor the Torah with their teaching, but rather that they failed to "walk their talk." The Matthean Jesus advises, "The scribes and the Pharisees sit on Moses' seat; therefore, do whatever they teach you and follow it"—"*but do not do as they do because they don't practice what they preach*" (23:2–3, emphasis added). The critique is personal and meant to sting.

## Matthew's Pharisees:
## One Scholar's Perspective

So, what might have made Matthew's particular argument so strident? The prolific Swedish New Testament scholar Anders Runesson offers an intriguing hypothesis that illumines a possible explanation regarding Matthew's representation of the Pharisees and suggests the kind of dynamics that may well have lain behind late first-century Torah debate in one particular community (Runesson, 2008).

In brief, Runesson posits that the conflicts Matthew portrays so intensely came out of a Pharisaic association in which Matthew's community had been a minority subgroup—after all, we know that at least some Pharisees were Christ followers. The tensions between the two seem to have come to a boiling point, resulting in a split that left the Matthean community irate. Social psychologists note that groups that hold many ideas in common may experience more intense friction than between groups who have less in common. Anyone active in religious groups, for example, is aware of conflicts in which greater hostility—often unedifying—is expressed against members of their own group than against outsiders. This may well have been the case between the Mattheans and other members of this Pharisaic association to which they had once belonged and with whom they still shared many similar beliefs (Saldarini 1992, 659–80).

What, then, might have led to this bitter break, likely sometime in the 80s CE? In terms of belief, it may be that Matthew's messianic community interpreted the Temple's destruction and the increasing number of Gentiles becoming followers of Christ as signs that the End Times were approaching. In terms of group dynamics in the postwar climate in which leadership among Jewish groups was at issue, it may well have been that the Mattheans were vying with the Pharisees to assume leadership. This would explain, at least in part, why their hostility was expressed in such a personal vein, even suggesting in chapter 23 (vv. 13,15, 33, 35–36) that the Pharisees had no place in God's Kingdom. Matthew is engaging in de-legitimizing Pharisaic leadership (Saldarini 1992, 659–80).

Two final points. Nothing in Matthew's Gospel suggests that it is other than a document from a Jewish community—albeit in vigorous disagreement with another Jewish group, namely, the Pharisees. To regard Matthew as emerging from within Jewish life challenges Christians to turn their imagination, acknowledging that (1) when Matthew wrote his gospel there was not yet Christianity; (2) there were diverse ways of understanding and living Jewishly; (3) there were "Christ-following Pharisees," such as Paul; and (4) even sacred texts have polemics reflective of tensions of their times.

### Reflection

If the gospel writers depicted Pharisees as Jesus's unscrupulous sparring partners, why should we today have scruples about accepting their portrayal?

The question is significant for three reasons. First, as I noted earlier, arriving at the true identity of the Pharisees is an elusive quest because we do not have sources that allow definitive answers. We do, however, know enough in our time to argue that their representation in the gospels does not do justice to the diversity among Pharisees, exaggerates the differences between the principal lines of their teaching and that of Jesus, and obscures later first-century conflicts over leadership that influenced the writing of the gospels in the latter third of that century.

Second, exploring the context in which Christ followers in the latter part of the first century condemned Pharisaic behavior contributes to a more nuanced and accurate understanding of the New Testament. If, according to Runesson's argument, key members of Matthew's community had left a Pharisaic association because they bitterly disagreed with how they lived their interpretation of the Torah, then it should not be difficult to hear aspects of their disillusionment in our own experience of religion. Which of us hasn't criticized the way certain of our co-religionists understand and practice their faith? Which of us hasn't regarded a group with whom we passionately disagree as hypocrites?

Accordingly, the critique of the Pharisees in Matthew directed at those with whom they disagreed may and should be turned on *us* as interpreters: In what ways might the depictions of the Pharisees serve as a mirror for our own hypocrisy? How might a deeper understanding of the New Testament's depiction of the Pharisaic movement allow us to see more vividly how religious sensibilities can be misdirected by our need to flaunt our own righteousness and to disparage others who differ from us?

A third reason the question about the Pharisaic identity is important is that the numerous incantations of "hypocrites" have given rise not simply to relegating the Pharisees to the lowliest of the low but also to disparaging Judaism: Pharisees are seen as exemplifying the scrupulosity and superficiality of its religious system. The equation of Pharisaism with hypocrisy is well attested in a range of sources: dictionary definitions of "hypocrite," biblical commentaries, theological literature (academic and popular), art, film, and homiletics.

This equivalence even gave rise to a cocktail, the *Pharisäer*. Originating in late nineteenth-century Germany, this concoction of coffee, rum, and whipped cream allowed one to sit in cafés ostensibly sipping coffee while enjoying alcohol unbeknownst to the onlooker—truly a hypocrite's drink!

Historians Susannah Heschel and Deborah Forger, from whom I learned of this drink, summarize German Protestant perspectives of that era on Pharisaic religion as "rigid, petrified, degraded, cankered, disfigured, wrathful, violent." They considered Judaism a religion of "materialism, deception, hypocrisy, abomination and shackles; it murders the conscience, gentleness and the true religious spirit and, in the end, persecutes Jesus with frenzy." They cite nineteenth-century German theologians, such as the biblical scholar Julius Wellhausen, who described Pharisees as "Jews in superlative, the true Israel," characterized by "blind, absolute obedience to the law." Theologian Karl Theodor Keim wrote, "All these heavy burdens, an infinity of legal ordinances which not only occupied and diverted from higher moral pursuits every moment of life, but also filled life with a continual fear of omissions, were imposed by the Pharisees upon themselves and upon the nation." Biblical scholar Franz Delitzsch differentiated between Hillel, a leading sage of the first century and Jesus: "The tendencies of these two diverged as widely as heaven from earth. The teaching of Hillel is juristic, casuistic, and narrow-minded nationalism, while that of Jesus is universally religious, moral and humane" (Heschel and Forger 2021, 365–66).

These judgments about the Pharisees attributed to nineteenth-century German Protestant theologians were neither restricted to Germany of that epoch nor to Protestants. They suffused Christian thinking and have yet to disappear, as the examples cited earlier in this chapter attest.

It may well be that the stereotypical view of the Pharisees has proven difficult to dispel because it has typically been embedded in a complex network of assumptions about Judaism. Three assumptions in particular are rooted in invidious contrasts between Judaism and Christianity. One of the most harmful is the notion that Judaism's God, as revealed in the Old Testament, was violent and capricious in comparison to the loving God revealed in Jesus Christ. Similarly troubling is the assertion that the oppressive and constricting norms of the (Jewish) Law contrasted with the freedom of the followers of Christ. Third, one of the most detrimental contrasts is that of old and new: Once Jesus Christ "founded" Christianity, Judaism, the religion of the Old Testament, became obsolete; the "new" covenant superseded the "old" covenant.

Thus, amending the typical negative assessment of the Pharisees involves reassessing Christian assumptions about Judaism. It involves recalibrating how we imagine Judaism itself, including the Jewish world of the first century CE, the sociocultural, historical, and religious context of Jesus and his earliest disciples. Above all, it involves attention to ways that we make meaning of the Scriptures by becoming "religious-critical" interpreters—an undertaking that enables us to reread ancient texts in ways that further the work of justice in our time.

In the literature of the early Christian writers in the second through fourth centuries, the Pharisees received less attention. But what becomes painfully obvious is that the disparagement of Judaism implicit in the New Testament's depiction of the Pharisees becomes explicit. To their literature we will turn to in Chapter Three so as to understand how Christian self-understanding was developed in opposition to "Judaism."

I conclude with two further notes:

1. Attentive readers may notice that I have used the term "oppositional imagination" without further clarification. I first heard the term from my friend Philip Cunningham during discussions in various projects in which we've been colleagues. His phrase struck me

immediately as a concise summary of the way many Christians envision their relationship with Judaism. Conventional preaching and teaching about the Pharisees may be the most typical instances of the oppositional imagination at work. Since I could not find the term in Phil's published work, I asked him directly. Following a conversation on Zoom, he sent me the following explanation, which, when it appears in a forthcoming book, *Disruptive Readings*, will be his first full elaboration in print. Cunningham writes (with minor edits on my part):

> The oppositional imagination ... is an operative paradigm that over centuries became conditioned in Christian culture, prompting people to consciously or unconsciously presume that Judaism and Christianity—and so Jews and Christians—conflict with each other at a fundamental, existential level. Readers possessed of the oppositional imagination will see episodes of Jesus debating with Jewish contemporaries as supporting this basic presupposition and so overlook any biblical counterindications. They will tend to imagine that Jesus himself stood outside the Judaism of his day in opposition to it, and that the Judaism of his day must have rejected him, leading to his execution.
>
> Reading the Bible through this lens inclines readers to actualize the Scriptures accordingly when it comes to Jews in their own times. "Jews" are the eternal "other." This binary outlook also tends to essentialize Jews and Christians alike. Both groups are conceived to be monolithic and uniform in their dissimilarity and antipathy to each other.

2. Given the frequency with which the Pharisees appear in the lectionary, I urge those who preach and teach to take seriously their responsibility to offer sound commentary on the many passages in which the Pharisees appear. They have a "teachable moment" to challenge the oppositional imagination by offering a word of context about the Pharisees and suggesting that we Christians might take stock of our own hypocrisies.

And now to Chapter Three, where the oppositional imagination developed in significant ways.

# 3

# The Early Church and Its "Construction" of Judaism

It's likely most Christians give little thought to details of the church's origins. Some assume that Jesus "founded" Christianity and that the event of Pentecost marked the church's birth. Others attribute its beginnings to the Apostle Paul, whose letters in mid-first century CE recounted his formative experiences with diverse communities of Christ followers throughout a large swath of the Mediterranean.

So, I was startled one day in the early 1980s when my mother, a lifelong practicing Catholic who had no interest in theology, announced, "I'm going to start a church." Her declaration roused my attention, particularly her subsequent claim: "We'll announce that Elvis has been raised from the dead."

Now my mother was known for her zany sense of humor, and we all had a good laugh. But her madcap announcement made sense when juxtaposed with some of the extravagant claims of the televangelists, such as Tammy Faye and Jim Bakker whose *PTL Club* ["Praise the Lord"] aired from 1974 to 1987. A church that promoted a risen Elvis Presley, my mother cynically reasoned, would become a colossal fund-raising enterprise—not unlike the Bakkers' PTL Club that raked in millions of dollars from its fervent fans. Not all donors were fooled: Jim Bakker, charged in 1989 with twenty-four counts of fraud and conspiracy, later served time in prison. And in 2020 the state of Missouri sued Bakker and his production company for selling a fake cure for the coronavirus.

So how *did* the Christian church begin? Its origins defy straightforward narratives and precise chronologies. There was no strategic plan, no orderly accomplishment of priorities, no immediate construction of buildings, no clear lines of authority: Christianity did not so much *start* as *emerge* over the course of several centuries. It developed out of the life and teaching of Jesus, a Jew from Nazareth whom his followers saw as the "Christ"—God's anointed one—the *messiah* (Hebrew, *mashiach*; Greek, *christos*). Amazed by the encounter of some of their number with the crucified Jesus now experienced as alive—"raised" by God—these Christ followers told of what they had seen and heard. They formed small communities, striving to live in the spirit of Jesus Christ and to share widely what they were experiencing.

A fact seldom given sufficient acknowledgment, these early generations of Christ followers were Jews. As they sought to understand the life and teaching of Jesus, they drew on their sacred writings, the Septuagint, the third-century BCE Greek translation of Jewish holy texts, which Christ followers would have known as early as Paul's time (the mid-fifties CE).

Yet, many of their Jewish contemporaries did not construe the holy texts as did the Christ followers. That he might have been a prophet, a charismatic teacher—yes. But the messiah? Not when the messianic world of divine peace and justice had yet to dawn. In their view, Israel's Scriptures were yet to be fulfilled. Thus, they disputed with the Christ-following Jews over how the sacred writings they held in common were to be understood.

In working out the meaning of their way of life—their identity—the followers of Christ necessarily had to situate themselves in relation to the other. How should they understand themselves vis-à-vis other Jews? Vis-à-vis non-Jewish Christ followers, who came in larger numbers late in the first century and then increased in the next several centuries? Vis-à-vis followers of Greco–Roman traditions ("pagans"), many mystified by this new movement? Vis-à-vis civic and imperial authorities who viewed them as beyond the scope of Rome's definition of a licit religious tradition.

In grappling with these questions, Christ followers fashioned varying responses. Practical matters demanded decisions, especially about their relation to Judaism. Did non-Jewish (Gentile) Christ followers need to keep the dietary laws? And if they did not, then what did that mean for Jesus's Jewish followers? Need Gentile men who became disciples be circumcised? Should the rituals of Christ followers involve both Jewish festivals and meals in memory of Jesus?

The most pressing question of all, *In what ways did discipleship in the name of Christ reorient understanding of the holy texts of the Jews that Christ followers accepted as their own after some debate?*

And then there was the matter of articulating belief. Jesus taught in poetry, parables, and enigmatic sayings. He spoke about his father and the advocate to come, about God's Kingdom, about losing one's life as did a grain of wheat fallen to the ground. But how to convey this in more systematic ways that accorded with the ways of philosophers? How to express profound poetry in a philosophers' prose?

It is through this complicated, often-contentious and messy project that the Christian church emerged. It's an important story to know because what happened in the second through fifth centuries shaped Christianity in decisive ways. Yet this narrative is largely unknown; few Christians, particularly in the West, have even heard of the writers featured in this chapter. Thus, the complexity of Christianity's origins is unknown to most Christians, thereby often giving rise to simplistic and mistaken notions of its tradition's beginnings.

In retrospect, it is painfully clear that the way early church writers envisioned Judaism—how they "constructed" Judaism—did not do justice to that tradition. Their distorted perspective, however, became embedded in the church's theology, liturgy, and popular religiosity. Only with key developments in the twentieth and twenty-first centuries did a more accurate understanding of Judaism develop and with that a keener recognition of the complexity of Christian origins. The significance of these recent insights becomes clearer when contrasted with the distorted vision of Judaism that endured for so long.

What we think of today as Judaism and Christianity emerged over the course of several centuries. Contestation was a principal dynamic of the relationship, but recent literature suggests there was more exchange than had been previously thought. Each tradition in formation developed fundamental elements of its institutional identity in relation to the other, often by way of difference though also at times in similar ways. Just to complicate the picture, contestation between and among early Christian thinkers themselves was intense—and even more so with their opposition to what they thought of as "Judaism" as well as "paganism." It was this former disputation that proved to be the most enduring, as it became thoroughly interwoven with Christian theology.

It is precisely the myriad ways in which formative Christianity's disparagement of Judaism became part of the warp and woof of its doctrinal system and liturgical life that overshadows relations between Jews and Christians in our time. Yet the new theological understandings that have been maturing over the course of the past seventy-five years, as well as a dialogical engagement with Jewish belief and practice, necessitate a critical assessment of the past centuries of contestation and the articulation of perspectives grounded in contemporary scholarship.

Thus, in this chapter we move to the wider realm of early Christian perspectives on Judaism that establish the larger context in which negative views of the Pharisees should be understood, as should be John's judgment that "the Jews" bore responsibility for the death of Jesus. What this chapter reveals is a problem that has long plagued Christianity—and not only Christianity—the *inability to differentiate without denigrating the other.*

### Christ Followers and the Construction of Judaism

As Christianity developed in the second and third centuries, leaders among the followers of Jesus, whom a later age designated as the "church fathers," were committed to articulating Christian belief in clear categories. As Gentiles lacking little connection to lived Judaism, they were generally unacquainted with those Jewish practices and beliefs embedded in cultural and ethnic customs such as language, the meaning of *Torah* and *halakah*, and land. Unfamiliar with Jewish life in its diversity, "Judaism" became an abstraction against which Christian identity was articulated, a sort of a "reversed 'religious' mirror image against which 'Christianity' would make sense as the only salvifically viable option" (Runesson 2017, 247). The oppositional imagination began to take shape.

That the Christ followers of the second and third centuries would seek to differentiate their movement from others is understandable because the process of identity formation necessarily includes distinguishing one's group from others. Identity formation is a complex process, involving concepts of boundaries, sameness and difference, continuity and discontinuity; it often includes regarding the other as homogeneous (Lieu 2004, 12). Christ followers, moreover, would have been aware of how others articulated their identities over against other peoples. They weren't the only people who formulated their identity in ways that set themselves apart from—and superior to—others.

The ancient Greeks, for example, regarded others as "barbarians" (*barbaroi*), which originally meant "non-Greeks."

In the wake of Greece's wars with Persia in the fifth century BCE, barbarian acquired a pejorative sense, connoting a foreigner's inferiority culturally, morally, and religiously. With Rome's ascendancy in the Mediterranean world, its status changed among the Greeks who no longer saw them as barbarians but as Hellenes. Greco–Roman culture then established the standard whereas other peoples, such as those without Roman citizenship and nations beyond the empire's border, were the barbarians. Over the course of the centuries and varying sociopolitical developments, "barbarian" acquired a broad sense of meaning. It could simply denote foreign languages and ethnicity, but it often encompassed a wide range of deleterious behaviors or marginal status, such as sexual immorality, cannibalism, inferior education and intellectual ability, and physical deformity. *Barbarian* functioned as an all-purpose stereotype. Stereotypes, however, are malleable and often inconsistent, as history reveals.

The literary works of distinguished Roman figures offer examples of how stereotypes of the other functioned. Cicero (ca. 106–43 BCE), lawyer–statesman, orator, and eminent stylist of Latin, characterized Judaism as anti-Roman superstition (*barbara superstitio*) contrasting with Roman gravitas and ancestral custom (*mos maiorum*). This depiction occurs in his defense of Lucius Valerius Flavius (d. 95 BCE), governor of the Roman province of Asia accused of financial impropriety. Among the issues was Flavius's edict in 62 BCE forbidding the Jews under his rule to send their annual tribute to the Temple in Jerusalem; instead, the funds came under Flavius's control. In his oration *Pro Flacco*, Cicero impugned the reliability of witnesses from Rome's Jewish community, using the standard rhetorical technique of caricaturing a people. The historian Tacitus (ca. 56–120 CE) portrayed Jews as utterly other, fearing that those attracted by Judaism might come to "revile the gods, repudiate their native land, and despise parents, children and brothers" by assuming its "alien rites" and thereby relinquishing their Roman identity (*Histories* V:4–5).

In the Hebrew Bible, the primary distinction is between Israel and "the nations" (*goyim*/Gentiles). They may be named—"the Hittites and the Amorites, the Canaanites and the Perizzites, the Hivites and the Jebusites" (Deuteronomy 20:17)—but more typically were regarded as without ethnic particularity. Much of what the Greeks and Romans considered "barbarian" was also characteristic of "the nations." And, similarly, the "other" changes according to new cultural and sociopolitical realities. As Judith Lieu notes, in Deuteronomy, Edom is kin to the Israelites but by the time of the Second Temple literature, Edom exemplifies a people opposed to Jews. She observes, "The people behind that mask of otherness will change, from Idumaea to the Roman Empire in rabbinic writings, to its Christian successors, but the mask remains, with all its sibling ambiguity" (Lieu 2004, 280). Yet, as is often the case, what is asserted about the other in texts is far more equivocal in the social world. Moreover, even within the literature certain non-Jews—for example, Ruth, the Ninevites transformed by Jonah's preaching, and the Persian King Cyrus who freed the Israelites from their Babylonian captivity—reflect a different appraisal of the nations.

So, it hardly surprising that those proto-Christian and Christian writers who articulated Christian belief did so in ways that assumed its superiority over the other, namely, Judaism. And they had many challenges. Once Christ followers made the decision to retain Israel's scriptures, they had to distinguish their interpretation from that of the Jewish world. So, too, did they need to consider to what extent they would adopt or adapt or abandon Jewish rituals and festivals, as will be evident particularly in the ways in which the early church appropriated symbols of Passover. Furthermore, their teachings needed to be articulated in a coherent way, lest the following of Christ be seen as intellectually inferior, as the pagan philosopher Celsus had claimed. Then, too, there had been a linguistic shift from the Aramaic-speaking Jesus and his disciples to the Greek East and the Latin West—and with the change of language came cultural shifts.

The urgency to articulate clear and compelling teachings is understandable. In a polytheistic world, it became imperative to articulate what was distinctive about the claims of Christ followers, particularly as Gentiles began to outnumber Jews in the community. The texts that would come to constitute the New Testament—canonized only in the late fourth century—present a diverse witness more suggestive than systematic, thereby raising many questions. How should Christ followers articulate his relationship with his "Father" and "Spirit" referred to in these texts? What norms for the moral life might be discerned from the gospels and from Paul? What practices would sustain Christ followers in a new age? What, in short, did it mean to assert, "We are Christians"?

There were, of course, numerous attempts to articulate an answer to this fundamental question—and disagreements, some vehement, among the various church writers. Hence, certain arguments within their communities were condemned as "heresy." But this charge was a slippery slope. Those who accused others of heresy could (and did) later have that same allegation hurled at them.

Moreover, for the most part, early church writers were skilled rhetoricians, schooled in Greco–Roman modes of argumentation in which making one's case did not rest on an accurate appraisal of one's opponent, but rather on cogent and convincing arguments in opposition. And while compelling arguments are important in the process of identity formation, the clarity and elegance of an argument often cloaks messy complications. The texts that the early church writers bequeathed to subsequent generations reflected the thinking of their authors, not necessarily the facts on the ground. Often, for example, their letters or sermons asserted that the other's practices or beliefs were incompatible with the Christian way of life. The boundaries they drew definitively, however, were far more fluid in reality. So early church writings need to be read with a critical lens: What was stated clearly about the other in a text was likely considerably more ambiguous in the daily round of life.

In short, giving voice to what Christians should believe and practice was a complicated process. Christianity gradually and through considerable contestation took shape over several centuries, developing structures of leadership and authority, distinctive rituals, and theological formulations.

It is clear in retrospect that efforts to offer a coherent understanding of Christian beliefs defamed Judaism. The tragedy is that this distorted depiction of Judaism set the theological stage for centuries to come. The patristic writers' "construction" of Judaism—*that is, how church writers depicted Judaism, not how Jews themselves understood it*—became embedded in Christian teaching and preaching until the twentieth century and lingers well into the twenty-first. The church's defamatory depiction of Judaism remains both in contemporary theological formulations and in key aspects of its liturgical life. Consequently, many Christians receive a false notion of Judaism, in conflict with the imperative "You shall not bear false witness against your neighbor" (Exodus 20:16).

The literature of this period is extensive, varied, and significant. In keeping with the aims of this book, I approach it selectively, pointing to patterns that have a ring of familiarity because they reappear in liturgy and theology today, sometimes in more nuanced fashion. As will become evident, hostility to Judaism became more pronounced in the fourth century. This animosity was taken up into the medieval period and beyond. Ultimately, such theologies persisted throughout modernity and remain in the church today. In my experience, it is all too seldom that accurate depictions of Judaism are offered in the pulpit; even less is Judaism portrayed positively. Too often the teachings of Jesus are presented in contrast to Judaism, a religion that is viewed as old and obsolete. Or, even if Judaism is not depicted as inferior, few preachers and teachers have a grasp of its core teachings and diversity, both past and present. And yet, Christianity cannot be understood without reference to Judaism.

Critically, over time many writers of the early church directed their animosity not simply against the perceived other religious and cultural system *but against its adherents*. *That is, their rhetoric inveighed not simply against Judaism itself but against Jews themselves. It is in this process we see the origins of theological antisemitism.*

### The Shaping of Christianity vis-à-vis Judaism: Key Influencers in Context

To explore the role selected writers played in shaping Christian identity in relation to Judaism, I first focus on two second-century figures, Ignatius, bishop of Antioch, and the philosopher Justin Martyr. Then I describe the evolving theological landscape, particularly the "Christianization" of the Roman Empire and the Council of Nicaea (325) before turning to two immensely influential fourth-century figures: Jerome and John Chrysostom. I then explore the early church's appropriation of the symbolism of Passover, the context for analysis of two other influential writers of the fourth-century, Athanasius, bishop of Alexandria, and the Syriac poet Ephrem of Syria. A personal reflection concludes the chapter.

### Ignatius of Antioch

The city of Antioch in Asia Minor, founded on the Orontes River circa 300 BCE, became the capital of the Roman province of Syria in 64 CE. As the third largest city in the Roman Empire (after Rome and Alexandria), Antioch had a prominent Jewish community. It also became a key site for Christ followers working out their identity vis-à-vis Jews. Early indications of this process surface in Paul's debate with Peter as described in his Letter to the Galatians (2:11–14). Antioch is the likely setting of the Gospel of Matthew; Luke identifies it as the city where the disciples were first called "Christians" (Acts 11:26). Over the centuries, it remained an important city. Tragically Antioch—now the Turkish city of Antakya—was largely destroyed in the February 2023 Turkey–Syria earthquakes. Among the many buildings reduced to rubble was its Antakya Synagogue, built in 1890 and the sole institutional remnant of the nearly 2,300 years of Jewish presence in Antioch.

Early in the second century CE, Ignatius, bishop of Antioch, addressed letters to various church communities in Asia Minor as he journeyed under guard to Rome, where he was to suffer martyrdom under the aegis of the Roman Emperor Trajan. His seven letters, written in Greek, are relatively brief; a larger trove of letters attributed to Ignatius is now regarded as fourth-century additions. While some of his phrasings seem odd to modern ears, Ignatius's conviction about the imperative of unity and concord among Christ followers is abundantly clear—as is his belief in the importance of a bishop's authority. Apparently, not all in Antioch shared that belief.

His letters provide a glimpse into early church life in the late first and early second centuries CE, among the earliest literature that would ultimately constitute the patristic writings that have proved so influential in the development of Christianity. He was, in fact, the first to use the noun "Christianity" (or "Christianism"), seemingly as constituting a "life system" (Lieu 1996, 31). So it is to Ignatius that we owe the term "Christianity." In Greek it is *christianismos*, analogous to the term *ioudaismos* ("Judaism"), the latter term found only in the literature of the Maccabees (2 Maccabees 2:21, 8:1,

14:38; 4 Maccabees 4:26); the books of the Maccabees are not included in the canon of the Jewish Scriptures. Ignatius perceives the relation between *christianismos* and *ioudaismos* as one of stark contrast. In his letter to the church of Magnesia, Ignatius instructs the Magnesians neither to be deceived by "erroneous opinions" nor by "old fables," that is, Jewish teachings. If the church were to "continue to live ... according to 'Judaism,'" Ignatius asserts, "we confess that we have not received grace" (8:1; translations from Schoedel 1985). Those who "lived in old ways" have now come "to newness of hope," thus no longer keeping Sabbath, but "living in accordance with the Lord's Day on which also our life arose through him and his death (which some deny), through which mystery we received faith, and therefore we endure that we may be found disciples of Jesus Christ, our only teacher" (9:1). He follows this by exhorting:

> Therefore, let us become his disciples and learn to live according to Christianity.... Set aside, then, the evil leaven, old and sour, and turn to the new leaven, which is Jesus Christ.... It is ridiculous to profess Jesus Christ and to Judaize; for Christianity did not believe in Judaism, but Judaism in Christianity, into which every tongue that has believed in God has been gathered together. (10:1c–3l)

Related themes arise in his letter to the church of Philadelphia in which Ignatius states his love for the prophets "because they also made their proclamation with the gospel in view and set their hope on him and waited for him, in whom by believing they were also saved." Seemingly, Ignatius has high regard for the prophetic writings because for him they were not really a part of the Jewish Scriptures—for which he has little regard—but rather pointed the way to the Christ and the gospel. By implication, Ignatius excludes the prophets from Judaism. Further, he exhorts:

> If anyone expounds Judaism to you, do not listen to him; for it is better to hear Christianity from a man who is circumcised than Judaism from a man who uncircumcised; both of them, if they do not speak of Jesus Christ, are to me tombstones and graves of the dead on which nothing but the names of men is written. (6:1)

This echoes his claim in Magnesians that "Christianity did not believe in Judaism but Judaism in Christianity" (10:3). Ignatius rejects anyone proposing to explain Judaism; one should pay no heed to such a person. Getting involved with Judaism is problematic. Nevertheless, it's far better to hear about it from one who has moved from circumcision to Christ, as had the apostles in his view, rather than from a Gentile (and thus uncircumcised) person. Anyone drawn to Judaism rather than solely focused on the Christ has become an outsider to the church.

As is often the case with the early church writers, what they argued intensely did not necessarily reflect the situation on the ground. The boundaries between Jew and Christian were far more porous than their arguments suggested, and thus a concern to church authorities, if not to the people themselves.

Yet these early second-century letters reveal claims that would resurface consistently. Moreover, remnants of Ignatius's polemic linger in many contemporary Christian communities: Judaism is old—and sour, in need of being replaced by the new leaven, Jesus Christ. Its teachings are "fables" and thus incompatible with Christianity; they do not grace its believers. Sunday—the day that celebrates the Lord's resurrection has replaced Sabbath. Ignatius was the first to devalue the Sabbath—and not the last (Lanfranchi 2008, 257). Notably, Ignatius makes his arguments *against* Judaism: "There is no awareness of 'the Jews' nor of *their* Judaism" (Lieu 1996, 35). This, too, became—and remains—typical of much Christian rhetoric, as is also evident in the writings of Justin Martyr. Judaism has become something of an abstraction—a tradition against which Christian identity is formulated by comparison-contrast.

## Justin Martyr

Born around the turn of the first century in Flavia Neapolis in Samaria (modern Nablus), Justin Martyr hailed from a pagan family and received a philosophical education. At some point, he became an ardent follower of Christ who wrote well-crafted defenses of "Christianity"—still very much in the developmental stage—including his *First Apology* and *Second Apology*. Although a prolific author, only one other work survives: *The Dialogue with Trypho*. It is this latter document, dated circa 150–160 CE, that reveals Justin's advocacy of a well-defined border between Jewish and Christian belief and practice.

*Dialogue with Trypho* is less dialogue and more disputation. It reveals a philosopher's conviction of the utter truth of the Way of Christ as he engages in debate with a learned Jew, Trypho. Christ's way is for him "the only sure and useful philosophy" (8.1). As the author, Justin's standpoint dominates. Trypho, however, reveals himself the better listener, showing openness to his new friend Justin's logic yet convinced of the necessity of fulfilling the "whole written law" (8.3). In the end of this lengthy work (142 chapters), no clear resolution appears: Trypho remains faithful to his Jewish way of life despite Justin's attempts to persuade him otherwise. Yet though he had failed to convince Trypho, Justin nonetheless established grounds for argumentation that has had a lasting effect on the church. Traces of the borderline he drew remain in many Christian theologies today, particularly his assertion that "your Scriptures" [the Jewish Bible], are no longer "yours, but ours. For we believe and obey them, whereas you, though you read them, do not grasp their spirit" (29.2).

Justin's primary argument with Trypho is that Jews do not regard Jesus as the Messiah of Israel. Trypho's teachers, "ignorant of the meaning of the Scriptures" (9.1), are responsible for having led him astray. They—and therefore Trypho—simply do not grasp the meaning of Scripture, failing to see how the prophets speak of Christ: "The Lawgiver has come, and you do not see him; the poor have the gospel preached to them, the blind see, yet you do not understand" (12.2). To that end, Justin, showing extensive familiarity with a Greek text of the Jewish scriptures, cites numerous prophetic texts at length as proof of Jesus's messianic nature. But he does not convince his interlocutor. Rather, Trypho tactfully responds with "All the words of the prophets which you just quoted are ambiguous, sir, and they certainly do not prove what you want them to prove" (51.1).

Justin heaps scorn on two key dimensions of Jewish practice: circumcision and Sabbath. His diatribe against circumcision is unrelenting. "What you really need is another circumcision, though you prize that of the flesh" (12.3). Circumcision, the philosopher opines, was given as a "distinguishing mark, to set you off from other nations and from us Christians." Its purpose was that "you and only you might suffer the afflictions that are now justly yours, that only your land be desolate, and your cities ruined by fire" (16.2). Circumcision, moreover, was merely a "type" (or foreshadowing) of the "true circumcision by which we are circumcised from error and wickedness through our Lord Jesus Christ" (41.4). The followers of Christ, in contrast, "have the salutary circumcision, namely, that of the heart." Further, Justin writes,

"We, indeed, who have come to God through Jesus Christ, have received, not a physical, but a spiritual circumcision" ... by means of baptism" (43.2). Regarding Sabbath, Justin accuses Jews of failing to understand its real meaning: "The New Law [of Christ] demands that you observe a perpetual Sabbath, whereas you consider yourselves religious when you refrain from work on one day a week, and in doing so you don't understand the real meaning of that precept" (12:3). God commanded circumcision, Sabbath, sacrifices, oblations, and festivals because of "their [Jews'] hardness of heart" (41.3). God "issued his ordinances about the Sabbaths and oblations" so that they might not worship idols and forget God, becoming "impious and godless, as indeed, you always seem to have been" (92.4). In effect, the cultic dimension of the Torah is irrelevant. It is in Christ that its ethical demands are fulfilled.

As a result, "The law promulgated at Horeb is already obsolete" and was only intended for Jews. In contrast, Christ is the "everlasting and final law," and it is Christ's law that is in "opposition to an older law" and "abrogates" it, just as the "trustworthy covenant" offered in Christ voids the earlier covenant (11.2). So, Justin concludes, "we are the true spiritual Israel, and the descendants of Judah, Jacob, Isaac, and Abraham" (11.5). Followers of Christ are "both called and in reality, are, Jacob and Israel and Judah and Joseph and David and true children of God" (123.9). For Justin "we, hewn out of the side of Christ, are the true people of Israel" (140.3). Jews, in contrast, are unable to drink from the living fountain of God but only from the broken cisterns that can hold no water" (140.3). Not only have Christians become a "holy people" (119.3), but Christ "founded a new race which is regenerated by him through water and faith and wood, which held the mystery of the cross" (138.2; on race, see Lieu 2004, 239–69).

While it is apparent that Justin was a knowledgeable student of the texts Jews held holy, his sweeping judgments about Judaism indicate far less familiarity with how

Jewish communities interpreted those texts and strove to live by them. His characterization of Sabbath, for example, as instituted because of Jews' "hardness of heart," distorts its meaning, particularly the radicality of instituting a day of rest for all, including animals. *In effect, Justin erases Jews as a people: Only those who follow Christ have become Israel's true people.* As the first to deem Christians "Israel," he establishes the theological move from "We are Israel, also" to "We are Israel instead"—a dangerous religious idea, as history would verify (Mikva 2020, 95).

Reading Justin's often callous (mis)representation of Judaism in our time raises many concerns. In essence, his disputation with Trypho was a lengthy argument that Christianity had displaced Judaism. In effect, his rhetoric constituted a theological takeover (Lieu 1996, 136–40). He "constructed" what he thought Judaism was and then deconstructed it by contrasting it with what he believed to be the "only sure and useful philosophy," the Way of Christ.

What escapes Justin is that Jesus the Christ was a Jew from Nazareth in Galilee, as were all the earliest generation of Christ followers. It would be centuries before Jesus's Jewishness would come to bear significance for Christian theologians. In fulfilling the Torah, Justin's Christ made it largely irrelevant except as a promise.

From the perspective of the twenty-first century, it is tempting to denounce Justin for his harsh polemical stance vis-à-vis Judaism in his "dialogue" with Trypho—what Tessa Rajak accurately renames as "Talking at Trypho" (Rajak 1999, 59–80). He was indeed the first to write at considerable length to contrast Judaism with Christianity with such definitiveness. Yet we must situate Justin in his cultural and religious contexts rather than impose the assumptions of our time. To read him in context is to recognize how certain church leaders interpreted what they interpreted as the "signs of the times" regarding the demise of Judaism. In the perspective of many early church writers, Jewish losses in the wars of the first and second centuries meant that Judaism had been defeated. The First Revolt of 66–70 CE, ended in destruction of the Temple, a central symbol of Judaism, followed by the defeat of Jewish uprisings in Egypt in 115–117 that resulted in the destruction of the city of Alexandria, a major site of Jewish life. Then followed the devastation in Judea following the resounding defeat by the Roman army in the Bar Kokhba Revolt 132–135. (Trypho identifies himself as a "refugee (phŭgón) from the recent war" [1.3]). It seemed logical to Justin and his contemporaries to interpret Judaism's defeats as signs of divine displeasure with a sinful people and thus as a prelude to fulfillment in a new community of believers.

Justin's *Dialogue* reveals the (unintended) consequences of the rhetorical style of early church writers as influenced by their Greco–Roman education. To read the *Dialogue* is to be struck by the cerebral character of Justin's depiction of Judaism. He is a philosopher convinced of the "only sure and useful philosophy" (8:1) and shaped by the rhetorical practices of formulating a well-defined argument against one's philosophical opponent. Attempting to understand his opponent's beliefs and practices as part of a diverse people received no consideration: Justin has a construction of what Judaism is in his mind, and nothing Trypho says affects his construct. In Justin's mind, this seems to be a dispute over how to read texts in light of his premise that the coming of Christ fulfilled all that Judaism promised.

Both he and Trypho cite texts to justify their arguments, but there is no possibility of coming to a mutual understanding because in this rhetorical world, vanquishing one's opponent is the goal. To read Justin in the present requires recognition that dispositions such as toleration and pluralism, which emerged only in modernity, were unknown in antiquity. In fairness to Justin, he was following the cultural norm in a world where religious toleration would have been foreign; in the ancient world tolerance was not a virtue. There was, however, a sense in which toleration existed in antiquity as the ability to endure insult or abuse—to engage in what our age terms "anger management" or to shrug off an insult from a person of lower status. In that sense it was a "quasi-virtue" because learning "how to endure insult and abuse could be an excuse for someone working toward the near unattainable idea of the impassible wise man"—presumably, a "wise woman" would have been an oxymoron (Streeter 2021, 365). A further question arose as to the proper response when the insult was directed to someone in authority or on whom one was dependent.

How early Christians responded to this question suggests an important perspective on Justin's harshness toward Judaism—and on that of many early church writers. In relation to God, Christians were indeed dependent, regarding themselves as servants of God or as God's children. As their logic played out, insofar as the Christians saw themselves in a relationship of dependence on God, "any attack on them as Christians would be an insult against God ... [leaving] no space for religious tolerance, since most Christian ideologues were agreed that heretics, Jews, and pagans by their very existence insult God" (Streeter 2021, 372). Thus, for Christians in antiquity, "almost any mistaken theological claim could be interpreted as an insult against God, and therefore as something the individual Christian, as a slave of God bound to defend his master's honor, was required not to tolerate" (Streeter 2021, 375).

Justin Martyr wrote as one Christian who held no church office and thus as a philosopher whose arguments had no intrinsic authority. Nevertheless, *Dialogue* marked the earliest, most extensive refutation of Judaism;

its influence can be detected in many of the works of early church writers that a later age classified as *adversus Judaeos*, "against Jews." Justin established a template for interpreting the Jewish scriptures and depicting Christ as fulfilling God's promises to the Jewish people.

In the immediate centuries after Justin Martyr, church and empire began to develop closer ties. By the fourth and fifth centuries, this came to mean that the Roman Empire became "Christianized." This process is described below and further discussed in Chapter Four.

### Roman Emperors and Christian Orthodoxy: Nicaea's Teaching Upheld

Constantine, emperor of a unified Roman Empire by 324 CE and mindful that the success of his rule depended in part on a Christianity less riven by bitter theological disputes, summoned bishops to Nicaea in 325 for what would become the church's First Ecumenical Council. A prime issue involved identifying the correct understanding of who Jesus was in relation to the One whom he addressed as Father, especially the claim of the priest Arius that Jesus was similar and subordinate to the Father. It was from this Council and a subsequent one in Constantinople in 381 that the formulation of the Nicene Creed emerged. So now the church had delineated a creed to which adherents—believers—were to assent. This conciliar decision, however, did not prove acceptable to the followers of Arius; controversy continued with various church leaders championing the orthodoxy of Nicaea and others, especially the Arians, dissenting from it. After Nicaea, however, authorities had a formulation they could—and did—enforce.

Constantine's three sons, who succeeded him after his death in 337, upheld the orthodox position of Nicaea. Following in the tradition of their father, they extended patronage to the church. But after the death of his third son Constantius

II in 340, a radical change occurred when Constantine's great nephew Julian became emperor. A devotee of Greco–Roman religious traditions and hostile to Christianity, he undermined its status. Julian extended support to Judaism, encouraging Jews to rebuild their Temple in Jerusalem. Christian authorities found Julian's opposition to Christianity and encouragement of Judaism a threat. Thus, they became more attuned to the benefits of the support from imperial leadership, as Christianity's growing prominence could no longer be taken for granted.

Nicaea had made another decisive ruling with serious implications for relations with Judaism by establishing the date of Easter. The earliest known Easter rituals come from Syria and Asia Minor, where Christ followers observed Passover on the fourteenth of Nisan by fasting in memory of the death of Jesus, then at dawn on the fifteenth of Nisan celebrating the Lord's Supper. In the region around the Mediterranean, however, Easter came to be celebrated on the Sunday following Passover. To some leaders, including Emperor Constantine, this discrepancy in date was disturbing. To remedy the chronological difference, Nicaea established uniform practices for calculating the date for Easter by separating its festivities from Passover; eventually the date was standardized as the first Sunday after the first full moon following the vernal equinox for the churches of the West. By separating Easter from Jewish calculations regarding the date of Passover, the bishops at Nicaea thereby indicated a point of separation with Judaism.

According to a letter the historian Eusebius attributed to Emperor Constantine, the motive for separating the date of Easter from Passover concerned more than a desire for a date common to all Christians. Rather, Constantine regarded Nicaea's decree as enacting a clean division between Christians "and the detestable mob of Jews" with whom the followers of Christ should have nothing in common: "We have received from the Savior another way, a course is open to our most holy religion that is both lawful and proper." As to being dependent on Jewish calculations for the date of Passover, "For it is surely quite grotesque for them to be able to boast that we would be incapable of keeping these observances without their instruction. What could those people calculate correctly, when after that murder of the Lord, after that parricide, they have taken leave of their senses, and are moved, not by any rational principle, but by uncontrolled impulse, wherever their internal frenzy may lead them?"

Constantine assures the bishops that the Jews do not see the truth and repeats his assertion that "nothing be held in common with that nation of parricides and Lord-killers." In sum,

> By unanimous verdict it was determined that the most holy feast of Easter should be celebrated on one and the same day, since it is both improper that there should be a division about a matter of such great sanctity, and best to follow that option, in which there is no admixture of alien error and sin. In these circumstances, then, accept gladly the heavenly grace and this truly divine command; for all the business transacted in the holy assemblies of bishops has reference to the divine will." (Eusebius 1999, 3:18–20)

This drawing of boundaries, however, did not mean everyone followed suit immediately. It took a century or so for Nicaea's ruling about the date of Easter to ultimately take hold. In the immediate decades after the council, however, Christianity was divided over the teachings of Arius and others whose perspectives were deemed heretical—unorthodox, like the Jews. In the debate over the proper way of belief regarding Jesus in relation to the One whom he called "Father," the Jews were, in effect, the front line of attack, as will be particularly evident in the fourth century.

If consensus regarding the date for observance of Easter did not come readily, what became increasingly manifest was the linkage between the emperor and ecclesial authorities. A prime example occurred just over a half century later in February 380, when the newly baptized Roman Emperor Theodosius I issued the edict *Cunctos populos* ("All peoples") mandating that all Christians must adhere to Catholic Christianity as defined by the Council of Nicaea in 325. Those who promulgated or held other Christian views, most notably the followers of the teaching of Arius, were to be rejected.

Theodosius strengthened the force of the edict in January 381. All who continued to adhere to other theological perspectives could no longer enjoy the church's privileges and were to be cast out of the towns where their doctrinal views were prominent. Christianity thus became embedded in the law. Five months later Theodosius convened the Council of Constantinople, which promulgated a slightly emended version of the Nicene Creed that is substantially the same as is recited in many church traditions today. In effect, Nicene and Constantinople became the benchmark for doctrinal definition. Now only those orthodox ("right-thinking") Christians had access to public office and were eligible for the full privileges of Roman citizenship. Emperors became enforcers of Christian orthodoxy along with the bishops appointed in key cities throughout the empire—the "monepiscopacy." Christianity gained more status, and the church acquired greater power and wealth. Clarification of religious identity became more central. Christian scholarship flourished.

Increasingly, imperial legislation made life more difficult for Jews, prohibiting them from holding public office in 418 and then forbidding Jews and pagans to practice law in 425. In 438 more legislation prohibited Jews, with their "ill-gotten dignity" to exercise authority over Christians (Linder 1997, 326–39). The process of "Christianizing" the empire was a costly one for Jews—and established patterns in which Christian supremacy became the norm (Teter 2023).

## Jerome and John Chrysostom

Two of the most eminent theological figures of the fourth century, the Latin biblical scholar, writer, and monk Jerome (ca. 340–427 CE) and the Greek orator, priest, and bishop John Chrysostom (ca. 350–407), illustrate the changing dynamics between Christians and Jews that characterized the era. Similar in many respects—erudite, prolific, ascetical, and irascible—each held negative views of Jews and Judaism. They differed, however in their contact with Jews, and in the context and intensity with which their disparaging judgments were articulated.

### Jerome of Stridon

The early Jerome (*Sophronius Eusebius Hieronymous*) was a peripatetic seeker of learning. Born in Stridon on the Dalmatian coast, he received an exceptional classical education in Rome, studying Greek and Latin language and literature under the tutelage of the renowned grammarian and rhetorician Aelius Donatus. Baptized circa 360 or 366 CE, he arrived in Antioch circa 373 to study with Apollinaris of Laodicea after travels through Gaul to Trier and Aquileia. After surviving a serious illness while in Antioch, he left for the nearby desert in Chalcis to study and pray as a hermit. This ascetical sojourn marked his initial foray into learning Hebrew. Returning to Antioch circa 378, he was ordained to the priesthood and moved to Constantinople to study under Gregory Nazianzus. Several years later he returned to Rome to become secretary to Pope Damasus I (r 366–384), where at the pope's request, he began revising the Old Latin Bible, particularly the Psalter and the gospels.

His years in Rome included instructing a number of patrician widows in Scripture. Paula and her daughter Eustochium became his patrons for many years. With local clergy, however, Jerome experienced more fractious relations; after the pope's death, they had him expelled. So, he left Rome to return to Antioch, where Paula and Eustochium joined him for a pilgrimage to the Holy Land and Egypt. While in Alexandria, Jerome studied with the famous teacher Didymus the Blind at its Catechetical School.

After their pilgrimage and interlude in Egypt, they settled in Bethlehem in 388, where he constructed a monastery and lived as a monk until his death in 418/420; a nearby convent was built to house Paula and Eustochium and other women. During his long years in Bethlehem, Jerome drew upon the knowledge he had acquired in his studies by writing extensive biblical commentaries and engaging in voluminous correspondence with many people, including Augustine (354–430) with whom he had a complicated relationship evident in the more than twenty-year correspondence they carried on.

As a biblical scholar, Jerome drew extensively upon the work of his predecessor in the Greek theological tradition, Origen of Alexandria (185–253), principally upon his *Hexapla*. One of the most important resources of the early church, the *Hexapla* was a six-column parallel of the texts of the Hebrew Bible/Old Testament that included Hebrew text, a Greek transliteration of the Hebrew, and four Greek translations, including the Septuagint (abbreviated as LXX). It was this latter translation that shaped early Christianity as the Greek translation of the Hebrew Bible on which the New Testament was formed. Given its importance in shaping the early church, the Septuagint became its authoritative text of the Old Testament and thus the primary source for translation into Latin. By Jerome's time, however, it was evident that its many variants and other textual issues required corrections of the Septuagint. It was in Rome that Jerome began textual analysis of the Septuagint, emending the Latin version of the Psalter accordingly.

In his years in Bethlehem, however, Jerome increasingly realized the imperative of basing his translation not on the LXX but on the Bible's first language, Hebrew. This was an extraordinary realization. Jerome "was the only figure in the early church who regarded the original text of the Old Testament as authoritative over against the Septuagint" (Graves 2014, 104). Yet the Hebrew he had acquired while in the desert in the 370s was inadequate for the scholarship to which he aspired. Thus, Jerome sought out Jewish teachers, a remarkable move for a fourth-century Christian—and for many centuries thereafter. Jerome may have had at least five Jewish instructors; two, he reports, came from centers of Jewish learning in Tiberias and Lydda. In his *Epistle* 84:3, he provides the name of a third teacher, Baranina, who taught him at night, as had Nicodemus (see John 3:2), perhaps lest fellow Jews disapprove of him instructing a Christian monk.

With the guidance of his Jewish mentors, Jerome devoted his energies to a Latin translation from what he called the *Hebraica veritas*, "Hebrew truth," rather than from the Septuagint's Greek. His increased proficiency in Hebrew enabled him to complete a translation based on the Hebrew into Latin. His Jewish teachers, from whom he sometimes sought to borrow books, also exposed him to Jewish traditions of interpretation, thus offering a glimpse into the emerging rabbinic movement.

Jerome worked from about 391 to 405 on his new Latin translation. Nevertheless, for all of its scholarly composition, this Latin translation based on the Hebrew rather than the Septuagint became a source of considerable contention. For several centuries church leaders had regarded the Septuagint as divinely inspired; its authoritative status meant it was the version known and used in the church, even if prior Latin translations admittedly had many defects. In the judgment of the revered Augustine (354–430), Jerome was dismissing a tradition that had become the standard unifying the church. For Augustine, it was the Septuagint that carried apostolic authority. Thus, Augustine's reluctance regarding this new translation from the Hebrew, as he stated toward the end of a very long letter to Jerome, circa 404–405:

> Those who think that I am jealous of your useful labors might now at last understand, if they are able, that the reason I was unwilling for your translation from the Hebrew Bible to be read in the churches was that I wanted to avoid introducing it as something new and as a rival to the authority of the Septuagint, in case it should confuse the Christian congregation when their ears and hearts are used to this translation which even the apostles approved of. (*Epistle* 82)

Even more pointed criticism came from his friend and study partner in Rome and Egypt, Rufinus of Aquileia (345–410), who thought relying on the *Hebraica veritas* was sheer audacity. In his *Apology against Jerome*, he accused his now former friend of betraying Christian tradition by seeking Jewish teachers, such as Baranina, whom he deliberately misnames Barabbas, after the gospel figure whose release from Pilate Jews had sought rather than free Jesus:

> From that other friend of yours, Barabbas, whom you chose out of the synagogue rather than Christ ... you learned ... to love the letter that kills and hate the spirit which gives life.... Now therefore after four hundred years the truth of the law comes forth for us, it has been bought with money from the Synagogue.... What other spirit than that of the Jews would dare to tamper with the records of the church which have been handed down from whom Jews had clamored for release from the Apostles? It is they, my brother, you who were most dear to me before you were taken captive by the Jews. (*Apology Against Jerome* 2:12, 35, 37)

In response, Jerome clarifies that his teacher was Baranina, who was not to be confused with the gospel figure Barabbas. Jerome made clear his Hebrew teachers were not his masters but those who assisted his language learning. And if Jerome devoted so much energy, time, and expense to gain expertise in Hebrew, he informed Rufinus, his major purpose was to enhance his skill in debate "for the refutation of the Jews, even those very copies which they themselves admit are very faithful, so that, if they are ever in an argument with Christians, they may not have an avenue of escape, but may be struck down with their own weapon" (*Apology Against Rufinus* 1.13). In the *Prologue to Isaiah*, Jerome asserts he has exerted himself in learning Hebrew "so the Jews might not jump all day on the errors of the Scriptures in his church."

This shadow side of Jerome's relationship with Judaism and Jews becomes clearer in his correspondence and biblical commentaries. Yes, his Hebrew mentors enhanced his knowledge of the language and, apparently, also of aspects of Jewish interpretation. Yet he had little regard for Jewish traditions and Jews themselves, except, perhaps for his teachers: "If it is expedient to hate any men and loathe any race, I have a strange dislike to those of the circumcision. For up to the present day, they persecute our Lord Jesus Christ in the synagogue of Satan" (*Epistle* 84.3). Jews had "lost their birthright" (*Epistle* 39:4); "the whole cult of Jewish observance was destroyed and they offer all manner of sacrifice not to God but to fleeing angels and unclean spirits" (*Epistle* 121:10). He urges his readers to disregard the "belching and nausea of the Jews" (*Preface, Book on Hebrew Names*); they "conceal the truth with lies" when they interpret passages foretelling Christ (*Commentary on Zechariah* 2:8).

His *Commentary on Matthew* builds upon the familiar theme of Jewish responsibility for the death of Jesus; in his view, the Jews were "continually crucifying Christ." Regarding the evangelist's so-called "blood curse" ("And all the people answered and said: "His blood be upon us and upon our children'" [27:5]), Jerome writes, "This imprecation upon the Jews continues until the present day. The Lord's blood will not be removed from them." He interprets the tearing of the Temple's curtain after Jesus's death (27:51) as a sign of the church's replacement of the synagogue: "The curtain of the Temple was torn, and all the mysteries of the Law that were previously woven together were made known and passed to the Gentile people."

William Krewson observes that Jerome's complexity may be seen in how he differentiates groups of Jews. When the trilingual Jerome refers to his teachers, they are nearly always "Hebrews." In contrast, those he views as carnal and blind to Christian truth are "Jews." Jerome can only be understood, he remarks, as a "complex mixture of an iconoclastic Christian Hebraist, a traditional Christian supersessionist, and the authoritative dispenser of Hebrew truth for the Christian church" (Krewson 2017, 98). In short, a complex figure.

Jerome may have occasionally attended synagogue, as may be inferred from his statement: "The preachers persuade the people that what they invent is true, and when, in theatrical fashion, they have invited applause ... they frown and make weighed and balanced addresses, and usurp the authority of the rulers" (*Commentary on Ezekiel* 34:31). If he had—as unusual as that may have been for both traditions in this era—he likely would have been castigated by his near contemporary in the Greek tradition, John Chrysostom.

*John Chrysostom*

Having begun exploration of patristic literature with Ignatius of Antioch, we return to that prominent city in which John Chrysostom was born (ca. 350) and lived for much of his life, including as a priest between 386 and 397 CE before becoming (ca. 397) bishop of Constantinople, from which he was twice exiled before his death in 407. Chrysostom—"golden mouthed"—received a classical education that included study under the distinguished orator and teacher of rhetoric Libanius. His immersion in Greek language, literature, and rhetoric formed the foundation for his career as a lawyer and teacher of rhetoric—and, ultimately, for the riveting preaching that gave rise to the epithet "golden mouthed." Baptized in 370, he studied theology and Scripture under the tutelage of Diodore of Tarsus, founder of the famous catechetical school of Antioch. Seeking to deepen his faith, Chrysostom left the city to spend four years as a monk and hermit in the desert. The stringent asceticism of the desert life, however, impacted his health and necessitated his return to Antioch, where he served as a lector and deacon before being ordained to the priesthood.

The learned and prolific Chrysostom authored numerous works in three genres: his *opuscala* (minor works, primarily on the ascetical and monastic life), numerous letters, and homilies. His literary legacy is the most extensive of the Greek patristic writers. He wrote on the sacramental life, composed numerous biblical commentaries, and preached extensively; more than eight hundred of his genuine homilies survive. Moreover, he had a prominent platform, as Christians in late antiquity had basilica-style churches enabling them to reach more people, thus offering Christianity mass-market appeal and giving it more visibility in Roman society (Sandwell 2007, 5).

Chrysostom's prolix preaching, on occasion requiring more than two hours to complete (Harkins 1979, 148n.2), revealed his intense desire to form a robust Christian identity among his congregants. He was passionate that they be "correctly Christian," that is orthodox (Shepardson 2019, 94). He left no room for ambiguity in the religious boundaries he established. In part that meant drawing sharp distinctions with Greeks and what he judged to be their superstitious rituals and idolatrous behaviors as sites such as the theater, horse races, public baths, and taverns.

Even as Chrysostom decried the dangers of Greek rituals and behaviors, he assailed Jews and Judaizers in a series of sermons (variously called orations or discourses) likely preached in Antioch's Great Church in August–September 386 and 387. He addressed his congregants, though the ostensible addressees are the "Judaizers," an amorphous grouping of those drawn both to Judaism and Christianity. In his denunciation of Judaizers, however, he engages in a scathing denunciation of the "pitiable and miserable" Jews [*Discourse* I.2.1.) whose festivals "are soon to march upon us one after the other" (I.1.5). "If loyal Christians are the audience of the sermons, the Judaizers are the target of his wrath and the Jews its victims" (Gager 1985, 119).

Unsurprisingly, the religiously fluid Judaizers were a source of agitation for the theologically orthodox Chrysostom, particularly at a season when Jews were celebrating the ritual-rich holidays of *Rosh Hashanah*, *Yom Kippur*, and *Sukkot*. Their liminal status—"half-Christians"–threatened his construal of both Christianity and Judaism. By "mixing what cannot be mixed" (*Discourse* IV.8.6), they had become sick with the disease of Judaism (I.4.8). The Jews are "more dangerous than any wolves," because they are "bent on surrounding my sheep," that is, the Judaizers (IV.1.2). He instructed his congregants to pursue their return to the truth that is Christianity; to rescue a Judaizer surpassed giving alms to the poor:

> When you see the poor, you would not find it easy to pass them by. When any of you see some Christian running to the synagogue, do not look the other way. Find some argument you can use as a halter to bring him back to the Church. This kind of almsgiving is greater than giving to the poor.... The man who gives to the poor takes away the poor man's hunger; the man who sets a Judaizing Christian straight, wins

a victory over godlessness. The first man gave consolation to the poor; the second puts a stop to reckless transgression. The first freed the body from pain, the other snatched a soul from the fires of hell. (*Discourse* VI.7.7–9)

As Chrysostom inveighs against the Judaizers, he makes clear his contempt for Judaism and speaks frequently about his battle with Jews (e.g., *Discourses* IV. 7.1, V.1.3, VIII.1.1). He despises Judaism. More importantly, God hates the Jews. God has turned his back on the Jews and abandoned them by allowing the destruction of Jerusalem and the loss of their homeland. In a rhetorical question addressed to Jews, he asks, "Is it not obvious that he [God] hated you and turned his back on you once and for all?" (VI. 4.4) After all, "You did slay Christ, you did lift violent hands against the Master, you did spill his precious blood. This is why you have no chance for atonement, excuse, or defense" (VI.2.10). Because of the Jews' "mad rage against Christ the Anointed One," there is no room for anyone else's sin to surpass theirs. Jews are thus "in the grip of your present sufferings not because of the sins committed in the rest of your lives but because of that one reckless act [i.e., the crucifixion]. If this were not the case, God would not have turned his back on you in such a way, even if you had already sinned ten thousand times" (VI.3.3). Chrysostom notes he was giving this homily on the feast of martyrs: "For the martyrs had a special hatred for the Jews since the Jews crucified him for whom they have a special love." Evoking Matthew 27:25, he continues, "The Jews said: 'His blood be on us and our children'; the martyrs poured out their blood for him whom the Jews had slain. So the martyrs would be glad to hear this discourse" (VI.1.7).

Chrysostom also hates the Jews because, possessing the Law, they "put it to outrageous use. For it is by means of the Law that they try to entice and catch the more simple-minded sort of man" (VI.6.11). In an earlier homily, Chrysostom notes "there was a time when the Law was useful and necessary but now it has ceased and is fruitless ... Jews are locked in a prison by the curse of the Law" (*Discourse* II.1.7). As for the place where they gather, the synagogue, it is a "stronghold of sin, a lodging for demons, a fortress of the devil, the destruction of the soul, the precipice and pit of all perdition, or whatever other name you give it." Even to call it a brothel would be more of a compliment than it deserved (VI. 7.7). Demons dwell in the synagogues, "not only in the place itself, but in the souls of the Jews" (I.6.6–7). As to the Judaizer who comes to the festivals, "What greater evidence could there be that a man does not love our Lord than when he participates in the festival of those who slew Christ?" (II.3.8). "Does God hate their festivals and do you share in them?" (I.7.2). Going to the synagogue, he thunders, "is a greater crime than going to the theater"; attending the theater may be wicked, but "what goes on in the synagogue is godlessness" (IV.8.3). By directing his hearers to avoid and loathe the synagogue, Chrysostom has instilled what Christine Shepardson terms "*topophobia*," a fear of certain places so as to prevent the members of his church from entering the synagogue (Shepardson 2019, 109).

The unrelenting invective of these homilies is contemptible. But what effect did the homilies actually have? No evidence points to widespread outbreaks of violence against Jewish communities in Antioch, though it is difficult to believe that there were no individual acts of aggression against Jews and Jewish institutions inspired by the sermons.

What if, however, the consequences were more subtle, insidious, and influential, transcending the time and place of their origin? Wendy Mayer, a preeminent scholar of Chrysostom, explores this possibility in a recent essay in *Revisioning John Chrysostom:* "Preaching Hatred? John Chrysostom, Neuroscience, and the Jews" (Mayer 2019). Drawing on moral psychology and cognitive linguistics, she argues that his homilies touch on "modes of thought that are basic to the human brain and thus to at least some degree common across cultures and history" (Mayer 2019, 66). Chrysostom's repeated use of certain metaphors (e.g., Jews as sick and diseased, demons dwelling in synagogues and in Jewish souls)—activates the same circuits in the brain that may stimulate particular kinds of actions: "From a neural perspective, rhetoric triggers neurochemical reactions that produce affective, pre-conscious dispositions that prompt the brain to fit them within the linguistic structures rhetorically constituted through cultural experience" (Mayer 2019, 89).

Violent rhetoric, Mayer observes, "reduces the listener's capacity for conscious critical thought by stimulating the constant activation to the point of habituation of one pattern of thought" (Mayer 2019, 90). It seems that we human beings make rational judgments less often that we assume. Neuroscience reveals that affect more than logic shapes our thinking and action, particularly when constant repetition constrains the critical faculties of the prefrontal regions of the brain. Rhetoric that rouses emotion, such as anger and fear, creates a receptive audience less likely to think critically and more prone to remember what was said.

It is probable that Chrysostom preached six of the homilies (*Discourses* III–VIII) in close sequence in 387. Consider the likely effect on those who heard all six:

> When the audience is told that the Jews are polluted, criminal murderers, who are enemies of God, and the concept that they are impure, polluted, and disgusting is constantly reinforced, the intuitive inference for an individual in whose brain the justice and purity foundations are strongly entrenched is not only that Jews can be killed with impunity, but that they *should* be killed, because they deserve it, the punishment fits

the crime, and the Jew is a dangerous threat to the health/purity of God's Body (the church). The Jew, on the other hand, is external to it and thus her/his killing expiatory, un-polluting, and justifiable. (Mayer 2019, 118)

Nor would the effects be limited only to his hearers in Antioch's Great Church, with a likely maximum capacity of five hundred. Chrysostom's sermons were taken down by stenographers and have had a long afterlife. It is impossible to estimate how many Christians might have heard or read about Jews as dirty and repulsive—as criminals, murderers, and, above all, as God's enemies. In fact, caution is taken even in the present. The Medieval Internet Sourcebook, a website sponsored by Fordham University's Center of Medieval Studies, no longer provides access to Chrysostom's *Against the Jews*. Paul Halsall, the historian who originated this site, as well as the extensive Internet History Source Project, notes that the publisher of Chrysostom's homilies (Catholic University of America Press), requested its removal. When it had been available, Chrysostom's sermons were "more intense than for any other text posted" (Harkins, 1979). Indeed, antisemites have found Chrysostom's homilies a rich resource for stoking hatred.

### Passover and Easter in Early Church Writings

From the early second century, Passover imagery became one of the most important symbols by which early writers expressed the preeminence of Christ and nascent Christianity. The Exodus, the archetypal event of divine deliverance, thus became a tool of rivalry. Early church writers characterized Jewish festivals, most notably Passover, as foreshadowing the great redemptive event: the Passover of Jesus, who became the "true lamb" and "lamb of God" through his sacrificial death. In his Letter to the Magnesians, Ignatius of Antioch (108–140 CE) advised, "Put out, therefore, the evil leaven, which has become old and turned sour and turn toward the new leaven, which is Jesus Christ. Be salted in him.... It is unfitting to say 'Jesus Christ' and live as Jews." Some sixty years later, Melito, bishop of Sardis, depicted Jesus in his "Homily on the Passover" as the "Passover of our salvation.... He is the one who was murdered in the person of Abel, bound in the person of Isaac, sold in the person of Joseph, exposed in the person of David, dishonored in the person of the prophets" ( ca. 160). By the fourth century, John Chrysostom inveighed in his *Discourses Against Judaizing Christians* (ca. 387):

> Why did Christ keep the Pasch at that time [e.g., on the 14th of the Hebrew month of Nisan]? The old Pasch was a type of the Pasch to come, and the reality had to supplant the type. So Christ first showed the foreshadowing and then brought the reality to the banquet table. Once the reality has come, the type which foreshadowed it is henceforth lost in its own shadow and no longer fills the need. (*Discourse* III.4.1)

Later in that same discourse, he suggests another comparison/contrast:

> Do you not see their Passover is the type, while our Pasch is the truth? Look at the tremendous difference between them. The Passover prevented bodily death, whereas the Pasch quelled God's anger against the whole world; the Passover of old freed the Jews from Egypt, while the Pasch has set us free from idolatry; the Passover drowned the Pharaoh, but the Pasch drowned the devil; after the Passover came Palestine, but after the Pasch will come heaven. (III.6.7)

Similarly, Pseudo-Chrysostom, about whom little is known, stated as follows: "The Jews celebrate an earthly Pasch, having refused a heavenly one. [ ... ] The partial and transitory as images and figures of the perfect and eternal, prepared for and foreshadowed the reality that has now emerged. When the reality arrives, the figure is obsolete" (*Homilies on the Holy Pasch, the Excellence of our Pascha*, ca. fifth century).

In portraying Passover as a mere foreshadowing of the salvific death and resurrection of Jesus, these early church writers established a central theological claim of Christianity that also influenced the liturgical life of the church. Yet by framing the relationship as one of comparison and contrast to assert the superiority of the Way of Christ, they distorted the rich layers of meaning Passover had in Jewish life—and of meanings that continued to develop in Jewish communities in subsequent centuries through to the present. Thus, it is important to revisit the fundamental contours of Passover and then the ways in which the New Testament draws upon it, to better understand how early church writers characterized it.

**Passover**

As the biblical writers fashioned their account of Israel's flight from the grasp of Egypt's Pharaoh and his people through the sea into the freedom of the Sinai, the observance of two nomadic, agricultural rituals helped shape their narrative. The festival of the *pesach* (passing over) involved sacrificing a year-old, unblemished lamb and eating it communally; the lamb's blood was then to be smeared on doorposts and lintels to indicate they had performed the ritual. The passing of the old year and arrival of spring was celebrated in the festival of *matzot* (unleavened bread) in which households purged their leavened bread and replaced it with unleavened bread. Both festivals are apparent in the principal biblical account in Exodus 12, with the blood on the doorposts now indicating God's "passing over" the households of the Hebrews in the process of slaying Egypt's firstborn sons. The festival of unleavened bread became a remembrance of "this very day I brought your companies out of the land of Egypt: you shall observe this day throughout your generations as a perpetual ordinance" (Exodus 12:17).

Although details are sparse about precisely how Passover was observed in the Second Temple period, Jerusalem's Temple became the place for the annual slaying of a lamb by the High Priest. Heads of households brought lambs that would be slaughtered as well, with households then sharing in a communal, sacrificial meal. After the Roman destruction of the Temple in 70 CE, however, Passover became a formative remembrance ritualized without sacrifice. This memory became woven into the spring festival of *Shavuot* (seven weeks [since the beginning of the harvest]), celebrating not only the season's first fruits but the giving of the Torah (see Exodus19:1–20, 23). In autumn the festival of Sukkot observed the time when Jews lived in fragile, temporary shelters in remembrance of their perilous existence after leaving Egypt "so that your generations may know that I made the people of Israel live in booths when I brought them out of the land of Egypt: I am the Lord your God" (Leviticus 23:43). The three interrelated festivals became the occasion for pilgrimage to Jerusalem—prime among the "appointed festivals" of Leviticus 2.

That Paul, the Christ-following Pharisee would draw upon Passover imagery in interpreting the death-resurrection of Jesus was absolutely natural: as a Jew who grasped the centrality of Passover, he would have almost instinctively recognized its pertinence to the Christ event. Writing to the community at Corinth in the late 50s of the first century, he admonished them,

> Your boasting is not a good thing. Do you not know that a little yeast leavens the whole batch of dough? Clean out the old yeast so that you may be a new batch, as you really are unleavened. For our paschal lamb, Christ, has been sacrificed. Therefore, let us celebrate the feast, not with the old yeast, the yeast of malice and wickedness, but with the unleavened bread of sincerity and truth. (2 Corinthians 5:6–7)

Passover imagery assumes a key role in the accounts of Jesus's final meal with his disciples, often known as the "Last Supper" or "Lord's Supper." The "synoptic" gospels—Mark, Matthew, and Luke—date the meal to the evening of the "first day of Unleavened Bread" (i.e., the Hebrew month of Nisan 14), when the Passover lamb is to be sacrificed. Jesus instructs the disciples to find a room so that he might "eat the Passover with my disciples" (see Mark 14:12–16; Luke 22:7). In Luke's account, Jesus says, "I have earnestly desired to eat this Passover [in Greek, *touto ta pascha phagein*] with you before I suffer; for I tell you I shall not eat it until it is fulfilled in the kingdom of God" (Luke 22:15–16). In the synoptic narratives, Jesus takes bread, blesses and breaks it, saying: "Take, this is my body" and takes a cup of wine, blesses it and gives it to his disciples: "This is my blood of the covenant poured out for many" (Mark 14:22–24). They conclude the meal with the singing of a hymn and then depart for the Mount of Olives, where Jesus will be apprehended and then put to death the next day by Roman hands.

John's account varies considerably in both chronology ("before the feast of Passover" [i.e., on the fourteenth day of Nisan] and emphasis in which the words of institution ("This is my Body ... Blood") are replaced by the scene of Jesus washing the feet of his disciples: "If I then, your Lord and teacher, have washed your feet, you also ought to wash one another's feet. For I have given you an example, that you also should do as I have done to you" (John 13:14–15). Moreover, the Gospel of John, likely written late in the first century, characterizes Jesus as the "Lamb of God" (John 2:29, 36) and depicts the hour of Jesus's death as the same time that the Passover lambs would have been sacrificed in the Temple. The symbol of "lamb of God" is present in the Acts of the Apostles (8:32) and 1 Peter (1:19), and appears in abundance in some twenty-nine passages of the Book of Revelation.

In the New Testament accounts, the events of the Last Supper offer an overture to the crucifixion. The gospel accounts, however, do not end with the death of Jesus. Rather, each evangelist closes his narrative with vignettes of Jesus's later appearances to various disciples. None of those who bore witness to having seen Jesus alive after his death and burial claimed to have seen him literally "being raised" from the dead. The concept of resurrection that they drew upon developed from a Jewish tradition that God would raise the just at the end of time. The evangelists also had texts such as those from Daniel that spoke of God's deliverance during times of persecution.

> At that time Michael, the great prince, the protector of your people, shall arise. There shall be a time of anguish, such as has never occurred since nations first came into existence. But at that time your people shall be delivered, everyone who is found written in the book. Many of those who sleep in the dust of the earth shall awake, some to everlasting life, and some to shame and everlasting contempt. Those who are wise shall shine like the brightness of the sky, and those who lead many to righteousness, like the stars for ever and ever. (Daniel 12:1–3)

Thus, the disciples' mysterious encounter with the living Christ led to their inference that God had raised Jesus from the dead, a view of at least one stream or "school" of thought in Second Temple Judaism. The evangelists portray Jesus of Nazareth as living in fidelity to the Torah and bearing witness to the arrival of God's Reign of mercy and justice. That is, Jesus lived and taught in such a way that those who ruled in the name of Imperial Rome found him a threat to its exercise of power; thus, they reasoned, Jesus could be permanently sidelined by its preferred mode of execution: crucifixion. But here was the astonishing reality: Jesus, the crucified one, was no longer dead to those who witnessed him alive in enigmatic ways, including Mary of Magdala, Simon Peter, and the disciples. It is their testimony, passed down in varying ways by the evangelists, that lies at the heart of the Christian proclamation of the resurrection.

Beginning with Paul, New Testament writers interpreted the death–resurrection of Jesus through the lens of Passover. In "raising" the paschal lamb Jesus who had been sacrificed, God had performed a new deed: "I am about to do a new thing; now it springs forth, do you not perceive it?" (Isaiah 43:19a). As in the earlier Exodus, God had "made a way in the wilderness and rivers in the desert" (Isaiah 43:19b). God's redeeming ways continued: The God who had made possible the freeing of the Hebrews from slavery in Egypt had freed Jesus from bondage to death. And the redeeming ways continued: Just as Genesis describes God as breathing life into the human, so John portrays Jesus on Easter night as breathing new life into the fearful disciples huddled in the upper room (John 20:22): "Receive the Holy Spirit." Luke varies the chronology; in his Acts of the Apostles, the disciples receive the Spirit on *Shavuot*—Pentecost in Greek (Acts 2:1–4).

Although Passover is the central symbol through which the New Testament writers interpreted the death–resurrection of Jesus, they appended another aspect of his crucifixion: A charge regarding those they saw as culpable for his death. The evangelists vary in how and to whom they attribute responsibility; to some degree, however, they all allege complicity by Jews. The Gospel of John, considered the last of the canonical gospels to be composed, gives the greatest emphasis to this accusation. John embeds Jewish hostility toward Jesus throughout his narrative. It culminates in the charged scene in chapter 19 in an exchange between the Roman-appointed governor of Judea, Pontius Pilate, and "the Jews" (*hoi Ioudaioi*) outside his headquarters:

> When Pilate heard these words, he brought Jesus outside and sat on the judge's bench at a place called The Stone Pavement, or in Hebrew [Aramaic] Gabbatha. Now it was the day of Preparation for the Passover; and it was about noon. He said to the Jews, "Here is your King!" They cried out, "Away with him! Away with him! Crucify him!" Pilate asked them, "Shall I crucify your King?" The chief priests answered, "We have no king but the emperor." Then he [Pilate] handed him over to be crucified. (John 19:13–16)

Today there is a strong consensus among scholars that the passion narratives are primarily theological interpretations rather than historical accounts in the modern sense. From the perspective of history, Judean Jews under Roman rule did not possess the power of capital punishment. Rather, those who ruled in the name of Rome, such as Pilate, were responsible for crucifying Jesus. Given this historical context, we can infer that the crowds Jesus drew, and the beliefs and values he preached about God's Kingdom, threatened Rome's cruel domination of so many peoples. In this sense, Jesus's death by crucifixion was a consequence of his ministry—not of a cruel plot by "the Jews" but the use of state power to demonstrate what happens to those who challenge injustice. It may be that a few Jewish authorities, relatively powerless under Rome's control, cooperated in some manner with Pilate and his henchmen. To blame "the Jews" however, falsifies history and misreads the nature of the genre of the gospels.

This error of attribution of responsibility to "the Jews" is one of the most tragic theological claims in a church that came to regard the Jewish people as "Christ killers." The early church writers, however, had no tools enabling them to interpret the crucifixion as do contemporary scholars. Thus, it may be that they simply assumed that "the Jews" had sought the death of Jesus. What was so catastrophic was that their assumption of Jewish culpability became the principal catalyst in shaping Christian identity over against Judaism and Jews. In a sense, the primacy of Passover imagery became obscured by the vociferousness of allegations of Jewish perfidy. Thus, as we have seen in Ignatius of Antioch, Melito of Sardis, and John Chrysostom, the imagery of Passover itself heightened condemnation of Judaism.

## Athanasius of Alexandria and Ephrem of Syria on Passover and Easter

The juxtaposition of Jewish betrayal and Passover becomes also apparent in two contemporaries: Athanasius, bishop of Alexandria (ca. 296–373 CE) and the poet–deacon Ephrem of Syria (ca. 306–373). In both cases, their ardent support of the orthodoxy of the Council of Nicaea fueled their strident criticism of Jewish Passover observances. Moreover, it could be wielded against other Christians, especially the supporters of Arius and similar dissidents, whose Christology they viewed as deficient as that of Jews. Both Athanasius and Ephrem influenced liturgical practices around Lent/Holy Week and Easter, Athanasius by his energetic attempts to standardize the liturgical calendar and Ephrem by his hymnography.

Shortly after being named in 328 to the see of Alexandria, Athanasius began the practice of issuing an annual *Festal*

*Letter* announcing the date of Easter and offering pastoral exhortation:

> Therefore, my beloved, since we have our souls nourished with divine food, that is, the Word, according to God's will, and we are fasting bodily with respect to eternal things, let us keep this great and saving feast as is fitting for us. Even the ignorant Jews received this divine food, through the pattern, when they ate the lamb in the Passover. But since they do not understand the pattern, they eat the lamb even to this day, going astray since they are without the city and without the truth. (*Festal Letter* 1.7)

Concerned that Christians would properly observe the Pasch, Athanasius instructed them not to "betray the truth through Jewish thoughts and myths like the wretched Judas, who did not keep the Passover properly." As a consequence, Jesus the Lord rebukes "those who keep the Passover in like manner." The Jews' practices were literal and local because their paschal sacrifices were mandated to take place in Jerusalem's Temple, whereas Christians could observe Easter anywhere in the world. Jews partook of the "flesh of irrational animals" while Christians feasted on the "the rational nourishment of the true Lamb, our Lord Jesus Christ" (Brakke 2001, 461). And the Jews had to rely on the temporal instructions specified by Moses; their observance of Passover was thus "unseasonable and parochial," whereas Christians celebrated an Easter feast that was "timely and universal" (462).

Athanasius, a prime advocate of Nicaea's creed, created a view of Judaism that served his agenda of defending the council against his Alexandrian rival Arius; Arianism and similar related theological positions were his chief opponents. His Judaism was static and homogeneous, and his rhetorical construction of Judaism disengaged from actual

Early Church "Construction" of Judaism 109

Jewish communities in Alexandria or elsewhere. Athanasius made plentiful use of binaries to heighten the contrast with Christianity: Material and earthly/spiritual and heavenly, particular/universal, literal interpretation of Scripture/levels of interpretation, and heretical/orthodox. The binaries were applicable as well to Arianism and its variations. But by attacking Judaism and linking it to unorthodox positions within the Christian world, he was able to strengthen the force of his argumentation:

> Not willing to mount a frontal rhetorical assault on his opponents [most notably, Arius], the insecure young bishop turned to a perennial means of uniting divided Christians: he attacked Jews, a practice he would follow numerous times in the remaining 45 years of his life. He could lump together Jews, Arians, Meltians, and all other "heretics" as those who do not "share in the festival." (Brakke 2001, 454)

**Ephrem of Syria**

Moving east, we find an equally ardent and influential proponent of Nicaean orthodoxy, Ephrem, who hailed from the eastern Syrian town of Nisibis. He may have lacked the authority of a bishop of a major see like Alexandria, but as a poet and as a churchman, perhaps as a deacon, he was enormously influential in shaping Christianity in eastern Syria through his prolific composition of hymnody in poetic metered verses (*madrāshē*) as well as homilies in verse and prose compositions, primarily biblical commentaries. Ephrem is best known for the lyric beauty of his hymns in the Syriac language that covered diverse topics, including paradise, the resurrection, virginity, the Virgin Mary, against heresies, and the emperor Julian. In their recent translation of four sets of Ephrem's compositions (*On the Holy Fast, On the Crucifixion,*

*On the Resurrection*, and *On the Unleavened Bread*), the translators render *madrāshē* as "teaching songs," which speaks to their didactic character (Saint Ephrem the Syrian 2022).

According to Syriac tradition, Ephrem founded women's choirs specifically to sing his *madrāshē*; women's choirs played a significant role in Syriac Christianity. As another poet–theologian, Jacob of Sarug (451–521 CE) wrote in his *On Ephrem*:

> Our sisters also were strengthened by you [Ephrem] to give praise;
>
> For women were not allowed to speak in church [cf. 1 Corinthians 14:34].
>
> Your instruction opened the closed mouths of the daughters of Eve;
>
> And behold, the gatherings of the glorious (church) resound with their melodies. (Ashbrook Harvey 2018, 557)

Of the many teaching songs Ephrem composed, those collected in *On the Unleavened Bread* are particularly pertinent to this study. There are twenty-one in this collection, although some are found only in fragments. The teaching that comes most strongly throughout *On the Unleavened Bread* is the stark contrast Ephrem draws between the sacrificial lamb of the Passover and the sacrificial lamb Jesus, and thus the profound disparity between the Exodus and the Passion.

In Teaching Song 19, this differentiation is evident from start:

> The true lamb stood up
> and broke his body
> for the innocent ones
> who had eaten the paschal lamb.

> He slaughtered and ate the Pascha,
> and he broke his body;
> he removed the shadow
> and gave the truth.
>
> The eater was dispersed
> within the unleavened bread;
> his body became for us
> the true unleavened bread.
> (Stanzas 1–3)

Subsequent stanzas play on key events in Israel's history. Then Ephrem heightens the contrast:

> My brothers and sisters, do not take
> that unleavened bread
> from the people whose hands
> are stained with blood,
>
> lest there stick
> to that unleavened bread
> some of filth
> that fills their hands.
>
> Although the meat is pure,
> no one eats
> what has been sacrificed
> because it is defiled.
>
> Thus how impure
> is that unleavened bread,
> since the hands that killed the Son
>     kneaded it?

The hand that is stained
by the blood of animals—
   it is an abomination for us
to take food from it.

Who then shall receive
from that hand,
which is thoroughly stained
with the blood of the prophets?

My brothers and sisters, let us not eat
with the medicine of life
the unleavened bread of the people
as the poison of death.

for the blood of the Messiah
is mixed and dwells in
the unleavened bread of the people
and in our Eucharist.

Whoever received it in the Eucharist
received the medicine of life;
whoever ate it with the people
received the poison of death.

As for the blood for which
they cried out that it be upon them,
it is mixed in their festivals
and their Sabbaths.

And whoever adheres
to their festivals
to him also comes
the splattering of blood.

> The people that does not eat
> from a pig
> is a pig that is
> bathed in much blood.
>
> Flee and keep away from it,
> For look, it is shaking
> lest you be defiled
> by the splattering of blood. (Stanzas 16–28)

Particularly if we consider this hymn a teaching song, it is deeply disturbing to think about what is being conveyed about Jews to those who heard it performed as well as those who sang it. Ephrem views the Jews' Passover as but a shadow, a mere type or anticipation of Christ's true sacrifice—a sacrifice the Jews instigated and carried out—a sacrifice that has forever stained their hands with blood, including the blood of the prophets. Thus, the unleavened bread Jews eat during Passover is toxic, a "poison of death," mixed as it is with the blood of the Messiah—a stark contrast to the "medicine of life." To those Christians who might be tempted to participate in some way in Jewish rituals during Passover season, Ephrem warns they will also be splattered with Christ's blood and thus defiled. Jews may not eat the products of pigs, but they are themselves pigs "bathed in much blood."

The vilification of the Jews this hymn/teaching song conveys would have been intensified by the refrain sung between *each* stanza:

> Praise to the Messiah who, through his body, abolished the unleavened bread of the people in the presence of the people!

Teaching Song 20 continues in a similar vein, with its refrain repeatedly echoing: "Praise to the Messiah into whom, during this feast, the unfaithful people drove nails." Similarly, the refrain for Teaching Song 20: "Praise be to the one who redeems the peoples through his blood *in place of* the symbol that redeemed one people!" (emphasis added). For Ephrem, Jesus is not merely the true paschal lamb. He has superseded the Jews' paschal festival. In these hymns, moreover, Ephrem teaches that Passover has not only become obsolete, but that the Jews have been rejected, as sung in the refrain in Teaching Song 17: "Blessed is he who rejected the people and their unleavened bread because their hands are stained with the precious blood!"

The lyric beauty of Ephrem's hymns is indeed a "terrible beauty," poetry that would have had even more effect because it was sung, likely in a liturgical setting, affecting people at more than a rational level. Yet we are left wondering about Ephrem's hostility to Jews, a question for which historical sources do not provide clear answers. Given Ephrem's commitment to the orthodoxy of the Nicene formulation, it may well be that his antagonism was driven by a perceived need to enforce boundaries between Christians and Jews at a time when those boundaries were not as definitive on the ground as they were in the minds of certain theologians. He "emphasizes the idea of Gentile Christianity without any Judaizing elements, something that appears not yet to have been a clear reality in fourth-century Syria" (Shepardson 2008, 37). Ephrem's rhetoric, embedded in liturgical language, was an attempt at establishing a definitive differentiation with Judaism and, by so doing, upholding the decrees of Nicaea.

While Ephrem was singular in the fourth century for embedding his Nicene orthodoxy in powerful poetry, in other ways he was part of a common trajectory of his time. He exemplifies the way in which polemics served as a tool for forming and deepening group identity during a century characterized by an intensification of anti-Jewish judgments such as those embodied by Chrysostom and Athanasius. If earlier writers, such as Ignatius of Antioch and Justin Martyr, wrote disparagingly about Judaism, by the fourth century the rhetoric was directed as well *at Jews themselves*. Their rhetoric, as Guy Stroumsa analyzes it, "helped transform anti-Jewish theological argument into what can be called antisemitic prejudice" (Stroumsa 2009).

### Reflection

While writing about the six principal "influencers," I have been mindful of the way in which focusing on one aspect of their lives—the texts that survived them—does full justice neither to their times nor to them. In the case of Jerome and John Chrysostom, the texts selected here represent only a minor proportion of their prodigious literary output, though it is clear in their oeuvre that both regarded Judaism as a threat to the flourishing of Christianity despite the post-Nicene church's newfound power in the Roman Empire.

The lens through which I examine their writings is a decidedly contemporary refraction: The church's relatively recent recognition of its need to correct its acutely distorted relations with Jews and Judaism over much of church history. That it took the church so long to recognize how its teachings misrepresented Judaism is nothing short of tragic. Even more horrifying are the consequences Jews endured. The point is not to deride these early leaders of the church but to use their writings as a necessary context for understanding where and why Christianity took such a terrible turn.

Jerome's vision about the fundamental importance of working with Hebrew as the primary original language of *Tanakh*/Old Testament was a transformative insight, even if it took centuries for his prescient acumen to be realized. So, too, was his determination to delve more deeply into the historical layer of texts by insisting that their spiritual dimensions be derived from explorations into their originating contexts. It is no accident that the first presentation in a single volume of historical–critical Catholic biblical scholarship appeared in 1968 as *The Jerome Biblical Commentary* (Brown, Fitzmyer, and Murphy 1968) and then in an updated second edition in 1990 by the same editors (Brown, Fitzmyer, and Murphy 1990). A third fully revised edition appeared in 2022 as the *Jerome Biblical Commentary for the Twenty-First Century* (Collins, Hens-Piazza, Reid, and Senior 2022). I think it would honor Jerome that among the four editors are two women (Hens-Piazza and Reid) and that women are prominent among the various authors of the articles. While the ideals of asceticism in the fourth century are not ours today, Jerome's mentoring of the widows Marcella, Paula, Eustochium, and others was a rare recognition in late antiquity of women's scholarly potential.

If Jerome made his mark primarily through his literary sensibilities, John Chrysostom inspired his audience through the elegance of his oratory. One of his most profound contributions was his commitment to the poor, manifest not only through his sermons but in the simple way he lived and the ascetic ideals he enforced, much to the ire of clergy, the rich, and imperial authorities when he was bishop in Constantinople. His reforming ways ultimately led to his exile, not once but twice; he died during his second exile while on a forced march to the Black Sea in bitter weather. Nevertheless, Chrysostom gained "posthumous fame as a fearless martyr bishop who saw his task as the defense of the poor against the depredations of the rich" and achieved significant theological importance "for ensuring the enduring impact of the Syrian theological tradition in developing Byzantium" (McGuckin 2017, 531–32).

What becomes readily apparent, however, is the extent to which these two scholarly churchmen had internalized a construction of Judaism that promoted an adversarial position. In one sense, Jerome's perspective was more insidious, insofar as it was obscured by his commitment to the "Hebrew *veritas*" and his contact with Jewish teachers. Subtlety, however, was not characteristic of Chrysostom's rhetoric; his vehemence against Judaism and those who practiced its traditions is blasphemous. Even more appalling is that their deformed construction of Judaism and vilification of Jews has had a very long afterlife. Their texts were passed down and commended as Christian classics, fueling the church's theological antisemitism that infected many with the "teaching of contempt" for Jews and Judaism.

Perhaps Jerome was so committed to demonstrating the truth of Christianity that even as he sought to learn from his Jewish teachers, he was unable to probe into the riches of Jewish tradition beyond language and interpretive modes. Yet Jerome at least did ask Jews how they were reading texts—and his asking was in a receptive, if limited, frame of mind. In this respect he moved beyond the more limited mode of most others who, like Justin, were so eager to refute Jews that there was no need to seek elucidation. In this respect, I am afraid, Justin typifies the Christian stance—and not solely in mid-second century but even to the present.

To those who gave shape to early Christian thought, including the writers who figure prominently in this chapter, it seemed unimaginable that Jesus remained a Jew. Their construct, forged out of the perceived need to explain and validate their belief in Jesus the Christ, had no space for incorporating a Jewish Christ, particularly after the Council of Nicaea's formulations in 325 CE. They seemingly could not imagine another way of interpreting Israel's Scriptures other than as God's covenantal promise to Israel now fulfilled in Jesus and his Way. Given their expertise in the prized art of argumentation and the intricate interconnections with Jewish ways of life complicating establishing borderlines of identity, their proclivity was, understandably, to emphasize difference even to the point of caricaturing Judaism. In claiming the superiority of Christianity to Judaism, early Christian writers tended to speak of Judaism as homogenous, frozen in time, and thus obsolete. And, having essentially characterized the Law of Moses/Torah as superseded by the Way of Christ, they belittled Jewish practices that embodied observance of the Torah, characterizing them as literalistic and flesh-bound rather than as spirit-filled.

The theological term for the way much of early Christian literature depicted its relation to Judaism is supersessionism, the noun form of the verb supersede. For much of the church's history, supersessionism implicitly served as a template for how many Christians perceived and treated the Jewish people. Tragically, the template contributed to a sense of superiority and dominance, including demeaning treatment of Jews, often in the expectation that they would convert to the truth of Christianity. Further, as historian Magda Teter documents, once Christianity became a political power, supersessionism shaped law and policy (Teter 2023, 3).

While supersessionism is a useful term in accounting for the ways that Christian self-understanding was articulated in relation to Judaism, as an analytical category, however, it is problematic because of its imprecision. Terence Donaldson has proposed an analytic framework, identifying five types of supersession, along with numerous subtypes. He does see one type as representing "supersessionism proper" in which Israel is seen as an "old entity that has been displaced and rendered obsolete by the church, a new entity in which any distinction between Jew and Gentile no longer has any fundamental significance" (Donaldson 2016, 18). Because in many cases it is not pastorally appropriate to make Donaldson's scholarly distinctions, I think it crucial to identify the specific ways in which a given author or perspective portrays Christianity as superseding Judaism. Not only does this mitigate to some extent the imprecision of the term, it also uses the more familiar verb *supersede* rather than the abstraction of the noun form *supersessionism* with which few people are familiar.

There is typically little subtlety in how many Christians have heard Judaism presented, particularly in their religious education and experience of liturgy. To draw from my personal experience as a child in the pre–Vatican II period, church teaching was "translated" into the question-and-answer mode of a catechism, most notably in the so-called *Baltimore Catechism*, composed in 1885 and revised in 1941. Both editions list Q. 391:

> **Q.** Why did the Jewish religion, which up to the death of Christ had been the true religion, cease at that time to be the true religion?
>
> **A.** The Jewish religion, which, up to the death of Christ had been the true religion, ceased at that time to be the true religion because it was only a promise of the redemption and figure of the Christian religion, and when the redemption was accomplished and the Christian religion established by the death of Christ, the promise and figure were no longer necessary (*A Catechism of Catholic Doctrine Prepared and Enjoined by the Third Plenary Council of Baltimore, No. 3*, 79).

This is not one of the questions and answers most Catholics raised on the *Baltimore Catechism* recall—and as it was nearly the four hundredth question of that catechism, most of us would not have encountered it. Moreover, its tedious, wordy style made memorization difficult; how much actual effect this particular question-and-answer had is difficult to assess. Nevertheless, it is disheartening testimony to how many US Catholic children in the 1950s would have been taught that with the coming of Christ, Judaism had become obsolete and the "Christian religion established." Thus, in effect, Judaism was no longer necessary.

The *Baltimore Catechism* has largely been relegated to history since Vatican II and replaced by textbooks that present a more adequate account of Christianity's relation to Judaism. But supersessionism lingers in liturgy in more subtle ways. Consider, for example, these examples taken from recent experiences in Catholic worship on Holy Thursday, which celebrates the "Last Supper" of Jesus (see John 13) and the Easter Vigil, a service at night preceding Easter Sunday.

On Holy Thursday, the congregation often sings (whether in Latin or English or both) a traditional hymn attributed to Thomas Aquinas from the thirteenth century, "*Pange Lingua*" (Sing, O Tongue), during a contemplative procession. The final verse is quite familiar to Catholics of a certain vintage but also frequently sung today:

> *Tantum ergo Sacramentum*
> *veneremur cernui*
> *et antiuquum Documentum*
> *novo cedat ritui*
> *praestet fides supplementum*
> *sensum defectui*

> Thus, such a great Sacrament
> We venerate in prostration
> And the old testament
> Yields to the new rite
> Faith supplies aid
> To the defects of the sense.

Then, during the Easter Vigil, the presider (or cantor or choir) sings the ancient *Exsultet*:

> For this is the Passover feast,
> When Christ the true lamb of God, is slain,
> Whose blood consecrates the homes of all the faithful.
> This is the night when first you set
> > the children of Israel free:
> You saved our ancestors from slavery to Egypt
> and led them dry shod through the sea.
> This is the night when you led your
> > people by a pillar of fire:
> with your light you showed them the way
> and destroyed all the darkness of sin.
>
> It is truly right and good, always and everywhere,
> with our whole heart and mind and voice, to praise
> > you, the invisible,
> almighty and eternal God, and your only-begotten Son,
> Jesus Christ our Lord; for he is the *true Paschal*
> > *Lamb, who*
> *at the feast of the Passover paid for us the debt of Adam's*
> *sin, and by his blood delivered your faithful people.*
> (Emphasis added)

The *Pange Lingua* reveals how Christian Eucharistic rituals of their time superseded the rites of the "old testament." The faith of Christians supplants the flesh-bound, literalistic defects of Jewish beliefs. The *Exsultet* is an even older liturgical poem, originating in the late fourth century with at least nine complete versions extant. Given this history of variant compositions, it is time to add another variation—an understanding of Easter in relation to Passover that acknowledges the connection for Christians of the two feasts while respecting the ever-unfolding meanings of Passover for Jews.

Here's my contribution toward a new version in this section of the *Exsultet*:

> This is the night
> of remembrance and rejoicing.
> We remember
> The pillar of fire by which God's presence
> shone through Israel's darkness long ago,
> and whose light still shines through every darkness.
> We rejoice
> in the Exodus made ever new
> in the journey from slavery to freedom,
> in each movement from desolation to light.
> On this night of our Passover feast,
> we remember the Jewish people
> celebrating Passover in every age.
> Sharing in this feast,
> we give thanks for
> the abundance of God's redeeming power.

Christian supersessionism is a theological binary that functioned as a key hermeneutical tool in Christian interpretation of Scripture and provided the basis for differentiating Christianity from Judaism. It decisively shaped Christian theology until the late twentieth and early twenty-first centuries. Given the context in which Christianity emerged in late antiquity, its logic was reasonable: It may not have been possible, given the historical–cultural context, for early Christians to have articulated a more nuanced self-understanding of their relationship to Judaism.

Supersession depended on a seriously flawed construction of Judaism. It is an artifact of antiquity that can no longer be theologically justified.

What, then, would a Christian theology of Judaism look like if it were premised on the claim that the Way of Christ neither diminishes nor lessens the Way of Torah because both are pathways to God? To begin to address this question, Christians need a fuller and more adequate understanding of Judaism, which the next chapter addresses in part.

# 4

# Early Judaism

## Resilience, Reorientation, and Reinvention

A participant in the Catholic–Jewish Colloquium in the early 1990s remarked that after the coming of Jesus, Judaism seem to disappear from her theological radar screen. Once there was Jesus and the church, she said, Judaism simply receded into the distant past. In part, this may be because Judaism became principally a foil against which Christianity defined itself. Or using the metaphor of Chapter Three, the early church in essence "constructed" what it believed Judaism to be and formulated its own developing identity in contrast, thus occluding Judaism on its own terms. This is frequently the problem when homilists and teachers portray Jesus in opposition to Judaism rather than as immersed in it. One consequence is that Christians generally think of Judaism as the religion of the Old Testament and thus as a relic of the past.

In hindsight, we recognize that a fundamental problem in the early church was the failure to seek understanding from Jews themselves about their tradition—about what they understood Judaism to be, to learn about their rituals and what they meant to those who observed them. For example, when Trypho responded to Justin that the Christ follower's interpretations of the prophets "do not prove what you want them to prove" (Slusser 2003, 51:1), Justin did not ask him how he as a Jew understood and read the prophets. Rather, he simply continued in his testimony to the Christ. For Justin and many of his successors, Judaism in all its diversity was given little, if any, consideration. Had they inquired, the writers of nascent Christianity would surely have received a variety of responses, particularly since Judaism did not then nor does it in the present have a single normative body to uphold one particular teaching as official. But Jewish life, contrary to Christian assumptions, was very much alive in the second century and beyond, beset with crises yet forging new ways of forming community that continue to shape contemporary Judaism.

In the 1980s, theologian and Episcopal priest Paul Van Buren pioneered in creating a three-volume theology of the people Israel. In the second volume, he observes that the church today is obliged to *ask* Jews about their Judaism rather than assuming what Judaism is. Van Buren emphasizes the church's obligation to *ask*:

> A Christian theology of Israel *asks*.... Israel has something to say which the church needs to hear. The church has always believed that Israel *had* something to say worth hearing, namely, what Israel said in the Scriptures which make up our Old Testament.... [W]e shall be raising the further question, whether living, postbiblical Israel has something more to say, either in its way of interpreting its Scriptures, or in its further reflections arising out of its continuing history in the covenant with God. (Van Buren 1983,18)

As the writings cited in the previous chapter bear witness, the church's theology arose out of its imposed understandings of Judaism. Early church writers constructed their critiques on tropes of Jewish infidelity, legalism, and obsolescence.

These writers based their claim on the assumption that what Israel had to say was totally eclipsed by Christ, that its Scriptures spoke only a word of promise, not the message of fulfillment that came only with Jesus and his church. The church's task in the present, however, is, as Van Buren argues, to pay attention to how *living Israel* interprets its sacred texts. And when the church does this, Van Buren maintains, it will adhere more closely to the "Torah-faithful Jew Jesus" (Van Buren 1983, 238).

Replacing the fundamentally flawed portrait of Judaism as a homogenous relic of the past and replacing it with a sense of *living, postbiblical Israel* is the major aim of this chapter.

So, if many in the church today think of Judaism as locked in the past—invisible on our theological radar screens—it may well be in large part because the heritage bequeathed to us by early church writers was based on the assumption that the truth of Christianity invalidated that of Judaism: Christ superseded the Torah; God's promises to Israel were fulfilled in Christ and the church. Our deeply committed ancestors in faith may not have been able to imagine otherwise, given the cultural and religious currents of their day. One consequence is that many in the church today, who often have no experience of Jewish communities, assume that Judaism was indeed merely preparatory for Christianity. The sensibilities and presuppositions of the time within the fragile, embryonic church prized argument over dialogue. That stance seemed to them the only possibility. The light of Christ illumining his followers somehow cast shadows on Judaism as a legalistic religion whose vengeance contrasted with the loving God preached by Jesus. That the church has been unbearably slow to learn the power of asking has had tragic consequences.

It took the Catholic Church, for example, until 1965 to speak in its decree from Vatican II, *Nostra Aetate*, of the church as "wild olive branches" grafted onto the "good olive tree" of Judaism. In 2015 the church's Commission on Religious Relations with the Jews, issued a more extensive reflection for the fiftieth anniversary of *Nostra Aetate* that emphasizes the significance of situating Jesus in his Jewish context. Titled *The Gifts and Calling of God Are Irrevocable* (see Romans 11:29) and authored by the Pontifical Biblical Commission, it includes this central claim: "*One cannot understand Jesus' teaching or that of his disciples without situating it within the Jewish horizon in the context of the living tradition of Israel; one would understand his teachings even less so if they were seen in opposition to this tradition*" (n.14; my emphasis). Said more forthrightly, What Jesus and the early disciples (e.g., Paul) taught must be understood *within* the matrix of Judaism. To set their teaching in opposition to Judaism distorts both traditions.

In a Christological title the early church writers could not have imagined, *Gifts and Calling* speaks of Jesus Christ as "*the living Torah of God*" (n. 26; my emphasis)—a claim in vivid contrast to the long history of the church speaking disparagingly of the Torah by categorizing it as obsolete, abrogated by Christ. As Justin phrased it, "The law promulgated at Horeb is already obsolete and was intended for you Jews only, whereas the law of which I speak is simply for all men. Now a later law in opposition to an older law abrogates the older; so, too, does a later covenant void an earlier one" (Slusser 2003, 11.2). Earlier generations of Catholics and Christians more generally formed in Justin's understanding, could not have imagined these recent claims. And many today would find them difficult to understand. For most in the early church and even to the present, Judaism has been the moon to Christianity's sun, its practices well-intentioned but futile, its law revealing bondage to the flesh rather than a Spirit-filled life in Christ. In short, the oppositional imagination. Or, to borrow a term from the art world, many claims among the early church writers made abundant use of *chiaroscuro*, a technique that emphasizes contrasts between dark (Judaism) and light (Christianity).

The early church writers faced a particular challenge because Judaism was widely respected as a tradition from antiquity. Christianity, in contrast, was regarded as a low-status movement until the late fourth century. In response to that reality, early church writers devoted considerable energy to formulating beliefs in clear and compelling ways to articulate Christian teaching vis-à-vis adherents of Greco–Roman traditions ("pagans"), others who taught variant accounts of Christian belief ("heretics"), and Jews. They excelled above all in making a case against Judaism—but in so doing, badly mischaracterized it. Their legacy depicted a Jesus in opposition to Torah and thus of Christianity in contrast to Judaism. We are still living with the consequences of that misrepresentation.

In this chapter, however, we will see that Judaism followed its own path of maturing by virtue of its *resilience, reorientation*, and *reinvention*. *Resilience* in the face of crushing military defeats, expulsion, and loss of civil rights. *Reorientation* by way of replacing the sacrificial cult with communal commitment to the Torah and to prayer and liturgy. *Reinvention* by virtue of the development of rabbinic thought. These three characteristics of post-70 CE Judaism in the wake of the tragic devastation of Rome's military vanquishment testify to a very different understanding of that tradition that many in our church know: They arise from *asking* what we might learn from Jewish history and from contemporary Jewish communities that help to enlarge our imagination about the tradition that formed Jesus and continues as a vital force today.

If the "influencers" handed on a portrait of Christianity in opposition to Judaism, then what did the proverbial man or woman on the street think? Social historians hold that Jews and Christians interacted with their neighbors in their everyday lives, though we have little indication about what they might have discussed together. What if, however, we were to imagine other followers of Christ committed to this new movement but less inclined to theological disputation?

Let us stipulate that at least some were curious about their Jewish neighbors, and vice versa. Having heard in their assemblies that Christ offered a new law, perhaps they asked their Jewish friends about what the Torah was. Maybe their inquisitiveness led them to inquire about why some of their fellow villagers rested on Saturdays instead of working while everyone else did. Or why they didn't buy pork at the marketplace? And what did Jews do in a synagogue?

What if, in turn, the Jewish interlocutors asked Christ followers about Jesus? We might imagine that the word on the Jewish street was that he was from a small village in the Galilee, Nazareth; that he'd been circumcised, went to synagogue, and knew his Torah; and that his teaching stirred up controversy, but then weren't Jews known to debate each other? Yet they had heard that some followers of the one whom they called the messiah held some very negative views about Judaism. Why?

It's entirely possible such conversations happened on numerous occasions, especially in places like Antioch, Alexandria, and Rome, where there were significant numbers of both Jews and Christians. We do not, however, have documentation that provides details of personal encounters among the populace. Nor is there sufficient evidence to offer a historically reliable, detailed examination of how Jesus lived his Jewish life or about what the Torah observance meant in pre-70 Judaism.

We do, however, have important knowledge about Jewish life in the time of Jesus as well as in the early centuries of the Common Era: The expansion of Jewish life in the diaspora, gradual emergence of the synagogue, the emergence of the rabbinic movement, and the development of a new genre of commentary all assume a prominent place among the most salient developments in post-70 Judaism. Each of these is complicated, with many details of their origin difficult to discern conclusively, given that they are shrouded by the passage of time. Nor is this chapter in any way meant to be a thorough summary and analysis of these developments, which would be impossible because of their complexity and the immense body of literature from this period. Yet, even a sketch of post-70 Judaism has the potential to help Christians locate it on their radar screens as a living tradition adapting to new realities and developing new modes of self-understanding. Also absent from the view of most Christians is the process by which the church gained power and prominence at great cost to other traditions, a topic also taken up in this chapter. The consequences of the Christianization of the Roman Empire shaped history in ways too seldom acknowledged today and bear particular relevance in the present when many are promoting Christian nationalism.

### Judaism Beyond the Borders of the Land of Israel

Judaism is associated with the Land of Israel, and more specifically with Judea, as it is from this tribal name that the term Judaism eventually evolved. In fact, however, when we think of Jewish life in the first four or so centuries of the Common Era, we must widen the scope of the landscape throughout the Mediterranean area as well as parts of Mesopotamia and Asia Minor. In terms of urban areas, this includes Rome, Alexandria, Antioch, Byzantium (Constantinople; later Istanbul), as well as the sites of Paul's letters, such as Corinth, Thessalonica, Galatia, and Philippi. And by the late 20s, Rome had become the superpower of the West. It encompassed sixty to seventy million people and extended from the Upper Nile to the English Channel, from Jerusalem to Lisbon. Jews were dispersed throughout the Roman Empire. Jews settled in Babylonia in the late first century, adding to the number of Jews who had remained after the Exile in 587 BCE; Babylonia became a second major site of learning, complementing that of the Land of Israel.

Greek had become the widespread *lingua franca*, along with the Northwest Semitic language Aramaic; Hebrew remained the sacred language for Jews while Aramaic was the widespread spoken language, albeit in variant dialects. Although the account in the Acts of the Apostles (2:5) that there were "devout Jews from every nation under heaven living in Jerusalem" during the pilgrimage feast of *Sukkot* (Gk., *Pentecost*) likely overstates the case, it does not seem far-fetched to imagine the scene Luke depicts of the far-flung diaspora:

> Amazed and astonished, they asked, "Are not all these who are speaking Galileans? And how is it that we hear, each of us, in our own native language? ⁹Parthians, Medes, Elamites, and residents of Mesopotamia, Judea and Cappadocia, Pontus and Asia, Phrygia and Pamphylia, Egypt and the parts of Libya belonging to Cyrene, and visitors from Rome, both Jews and proselytes, Cretans and Arabs—in our own languages we hear them speaking about God's deeds of power." (Acts 2:8–11)

Given the extent of geographical distribution, it is obvious that Jewish life comprised a diversity of cultures yet were held together by key institutions. It was the study of the Torah that constituted the core of Jewish learning, with academies for study developing in Israel and in Babylon for intense discussion of the Oral Law, resulting in the Talmud of Israel (or of Jerusalem, the *Yerushalmi*) circa 400 CE and of Babylon (the *Bavli*) at least a century or more later. Synagogues offered the space for Jews to gather in community.

## The Synagogue

Evidence—archaeological, literary, and epigraphical (i.e., inscriptions)—on precisely when and where the first synagogue appeared is sparse. Among the earliest would seem to be a "prayer house" (*proseuchē*, in Greek) in the third century

BCE during the Ptolemaic dynasty (305–330 BCE). In the Land of Israel, where worship pre-70 CE was oriented to the Temple, synagogues likely emerged during the late Hellenistic/ early Roman period. The earliest evidence for a synagogue in Jerusalem prior to the destruction of the Temple is an inscription written in Greek on limestone discovered by French archaeologist Raymond Weill in 1913–1914. Though its exact date cannot be determined, most experts date it to the first century CE. In translation it reads as follows:

> Theodotos, son of Vettrenos, priest and *archisynagogos* [likely the head of the synagogue and leader of a Jewish community], son of an *archisynagogos* and grandson of an *archisynagogos*, built this synagogue for the reading of the Torah and teaching the commandments, and as a hostel with chambers and water installation to provide accommodation for those who, coming from abroad, have need of it, which [i.e., the synagogue] his fathers, presbyters and Simonides founded. (Martin 2002, 162)

The precursor to the synagogue seems to have been the city gate, a town's gathering place for community activities as well as its marketplace and site for meeting with rulers. With the development of other ways of fortifying urban areas, a separate building assumed similar functions. The synagogue—literally a gathering place—functioned as a multipurpose community center with a wide variety of activities, including collecting charitable donations, housing communal archives, assembling for social and political functions, holding court and administering punishment, and studying the Torah. More comprehensive than comparable Greco–Roman institutions, it eventually became central to Jewish life. The community in the Judean desert from whom we have the Dead Sea Scrolls has texts indicating communal

# Early Judaism 133

prayer. But whether they prayed together in a building designated as a synagogue is unclear. The synagogue gradually assumed more importance in the wake of the defeat of the Jewish uprisings, culminating in the destruction of Jerusalem and its Temple, and, following Bar Kokhba, expulsion from Judea. It functioned differently from the Second Temple cult in which priests assumed leadership and participants silently offered sacrifices according to cultic norms. The early synagogues were lay-led; participants recited prayers and the Torah was read and discussed. Increasingly, the synagogue assumed a prominent role in Jewish life. The Temple was never rebuilt and the offering of physical sacrifices never resumed. Given the importance of the Temple to Jewish life before 70 CE, the ways in which synagogues came to assume important yet distinct aspects of the Temple is a remarkable example of Judaism's reinvention.

There is a fascinating link between the terms translated as "synagogue" and "church" in the New Testament: Etymologically, the terms are largely synonymous. A word of explanation. In the Hebrew Bible, or *Tanakh*, two of the terms used to indicate a communal gathering were *qāhāl* (community) and *bet Knesset* (house of gathering). In the Septuagint, the Greek translation by Alexandrian Jews, an extensive range of terms was used for the Hebrew terms for gathering. The most frequent Greek equivalents were *synagōgē* and *proseuche*. *Synagōgē* referred both to Greco–Roman civic institutions as well as to Jewish associations, in both cases denoting gatherings of people. It was the most prominent among some seventeen documented Greek terms for a place of assembling or gathering. Another translation was *ekklēsia*, a term that occurs some 114 times in the New Testament, including fourteen times by Paul in his undisputed letters (i.e., those that came from Paul himself rather than from those who wrote in his name).

Thus, when the New Testament writers, most notably Paul and Matthew, used *ekklēsia,* they were not speaking of the institution ultimately understood as "church" in Late Antiquity as well as in the present—that is, an assembly of Christians—but rather of *a gathering of people forming a community.* Some were "Christ assemblies," that is gatherings of Jesus-oriented Jews and non-Jews, but others were more simply gatherings (Runesson et al. 2008, 328; Korner 2017, 264–65). Were our English translations of the New Testament to recognize this fluidity of language, we might be less inclined to conclude that "Christianity" was already an entity separate from Judaism in the first century CE. Or, to state it positively, to speak of Paul's assemblies of Jews and Gentiles or the Matthean community of Christ-followers acknowledges that in the first century religious border lines were permeable.

**The Rabbis**

When Trypho mentioned his teachers to Justin Martyr, they were likely not as yet rabbis in the formal sense. Although today we think of rabbis serving as leaders of synagogues, the precise connections between the rabbinate, synagogues, and liturgical prayer in the second century are not entirely clear. More clarity is possible by the fifth and sixth centuries. Thus, a brief word about how rabbis came to be and their role in reinventing Judaism.

The center of Jewish life in the Land of Israel moved from Judea to Galilee in the post-70 period, and new leadership began to emerge. In the early postwar years, sages learned in the Torah gathered small groups of students for private study. These teachers formed loose-knit networks, systems of personal alliances in which there was both cooperation and rivalry (Hezser 1997, 492–97). Out of these informal alliances, the rabbinic movement began, taking on a more organized form in the fourth century and developing into rabbinic academies in sixth-century Babylon that had become a second center of Jewish life. Although by the fifth and sixth centuries, rabbis had become the preeminent authorities in Judaism, in earlier years they contended with other Jewish groups (e.g., priests and Christ followers) for leadership. Rabbinic authority increased over time, not instantly.

Of course, Judaism no longer had the Temple, but it did have the Torah—what one of my teachers called a "portable temple." So, the focus of the rabbis was discerning how the Torah might best be lived in this dramatically new situation and in so doing establish ways of building systems of interpretation in response to the present—the interpretations known as the "Oral Torah" (*Torah shebeal*). While there are many variant ways of formulating the relationship of the Written Torah to the Oral Torah, this observation seems particularly apt: 'I said to him: My son, were these things given at Sinai? Are they not but the teaching of the Sages? Rather when the Holy One, blessed be He, gave the Torah to Israel, he only gave it as wheat to extract flour from it and as flax to make into a garment" (Hirshman 2006, 901).

### Oral Torah as Embodied in Rabbinic Literature: The *Mishnah* and *Talmudim*

Around the early third century, Rabbi Judah ha-Nasi, who was the Patriarch of Galilee, played a major role in editing the first major rabbinic commentary, the *Mishnah* (redacted ca. 220), which is a collection of teachings, predominantly legal reasoning, from the first and second centuries that reflects oral recitation and transmission. (The term "Mishnah" derives from the Hebrew stem *sh*, "to repeat.") Its six orders or anthropological categories—Agriculture, Calendar, Matters Pertaining to Women, Torts/Damages, Sacred Items/Holy Things, and Taboos/Purity—are in turn subdivided into sixty-three tractates (Visotzky 1991, 16).

Its laws reflect the community's continuing need to clarify biblical imperatives given in earlier eras. The Mishnah is an unusual commentary—even revolutionary insofar as it seems to have had no precedent in the Jewish tradition. It is the first Jewish text after the Torah that organizes a nearly comprehensive system of laws and practices, yet it is unlike the Torah in its organization and even in its Hebrew, which varies from biblical Hebrew (Osborne 2011, 159–72). It is "genuinely unique and original" and "must be understood in terms of its originality" (Kraemer 2006, 299–300).

The Mishnah codifies laws clarifying biblical imperatives of an earlier era. For example, in the order *Moed* (Calendar/Festivals), the tractate *Shabbat* lays out conditions on precisely what actions constitute work because of the commandment to "Remember the Sabbath day and keep it holy. Six days you shall labor and do all your work. But the seventh day is a Sabbath to the Lord your God; you shall not do any work—you, your son or your daughter, your male or female slave, your livestock, or the alien resident in your towns" (Exodus 20:8; cf. Deuteronomy 5:12–14). Understandably, questions arose about what exactly constitutes "work": What is the nature of the work not permitted on the Sabbath? In what specific ways must we refrain? When does a walk become more than a stroll and thus should be considered work? In order to address such questions, the Mishnah identifies thirty-nine categories of work (*m. Shabbat* 7:2), known as *melakhot*. In so doing, this tractate emphasizes the importance of fulfilling the biblical command to refrain from work on the Sabbath.

The Mishnah's order *Moed* also discusses how the Passover is to be observed (cf. Exodus 12:1–28). While numerous biblical passages discuss Passover, the tractate *Pesachim* offers further specifications for the observance of Passover, including how to eliminate leavened products, make matzah, and roast the paschal lamb. The same tractate contains numerous directions for a ritual celebration of Passover, a seder ("order"). The seder as Jews celebrate it today is based largely upon the tractate of *Pesachim*—here the Mishnah offers specific ways of fulfilling an ancient biblical command regarding observance of Passover. Today there is no end of creative seders, but it is the Mishnah that provides the basic structure.

Among the best-known tractates of the Mishnah is *Avot* (Fathers), often known as the "Ethics of the Fathers," a compendium of sayings that, among other characteristics, offers glimpses into ways the rabbinic movement articulated the desire to live the wisdom of Torah. Frequently studied on Shabbat, *Avot* complements the wisdom literature of the Bible and also has parallels with Greek philosophical schools. A concluding aphorism, attributed to Ben Bag Bag, offers memorable counsel about elucidating Torah: "Ben Bag Bag said: 'Turn it over, and [again] turn it over, for all is therein. And look into it; And become gray and old therein; And do not move away from it, for you have no better portion than it'" (*Avot* 5:22). The "it," in Ben Bag Bag's saying is, of course, Torah. Torah is everything for Israel. *Avot* 1:2 teaches that Torah has existed from the beginning of creation with God and has been the gift that makes concrete the permanence and ongoing relationship between God and Israel. The Torah does not fade away for Israel, because that which is so precious to God cannot. Because of the Torah's permanent and foundational value, the Torah can be constantly examined, or turned over, as one would a scroll (Joslyn-Siemiatkoski 2018, 273).

One of the most fascinating aspects of the Mishnah is that the rabbis cited are not necessarily in agreement with one another; it is the "earliest canonical text that preserves tradition in the form of disputes" (Zetterholm 2012, 42). From its early years, rabbinic thinking manifested an inclusion of a variety of views (Kraemer 2006, 306), as it continues to do even in the present, such as discussion during the coronavirus pandemic about ways synagogues should or should not adapt (e.g., livestreaming Shabbat services even for Jews whose Sabbath practices exclude the use of electronic devices). Moreover, there are variant "denominations" within contemporary Judaism, each of which has its own Oral Torah. Of course, the clarifications made in the early third century no longer sufficed as conditions changed. Thus, not long after the appearance of the Mishnah, another collection of rabbinic texts appeared—a "supplement," the *Tosefta*, following its predecessor's structure but considerably lengthier. This pairing served as a basic curriculum for rabbinic thought and was then amplified by the Jerusalem or Palestinian Talmud, the *Yerushalmi*, redacted circa 400 in Galilee and then amplified by the more significant Babylonian Talmud or *Bavli*, redacted circa seventh–eighth centuries in the period of the Sassanian Persian Empire.

These *Talmudim* (plural) are immense collections of biblical interpretations and legends, interspersed with folk tales, medical and astronomical observations, incantations, and theology. They are layered complexity. Metaphorically, one might think of the Talmudic literature as a sea, or in Hebrew, *yam ha-Talmud*, the "sea of the Talmud." It is "as massive and as deep as the sea. Like the sea, much of the Talmud is hidden from the eye, beneath the surface" (Katz and Schwartz 1998, 7). From its first redactions, it came to incorporate new rabbinic commentary, most famously that of Rashi (Rabbi Schlomo Yitzhak, 1040–1109), whose interpretations are written in a special script—the Rashi script. The densely layered pages of the Talmud, as established in its first print version (1520–1523), embodies the complexity of Jewish commentary, including the citation from the Mishnah followed by a citation of its supplements, then Rashi's commentary, additions to Rashi and further additions (*tosafot*), followed in turn by the commentary of Rabbi Hananel (990–1055) and references to law codes applicable to the topic under discussion; biblical references, and then references to parallel passages in the Talmud—and for good measure, an anonymous layer, perhaps a recognition that this later interpretation was less formative than commentaries from the earliest generations (Zetterholm 2012, 56). Rabbinic commentaries continue in collections of *midrashim,* anthologies of rabbinic biblical interpretations from different periods that typically expound on particular biblical books. The various exegetical moves the rabbis made differ from the current assumptions of modern biblical scholars and were in many ways shared with other commentators in antiquity. According to James Kugel, the *midrashim* reflect four assumptions the rabbis held in common. They presupposed that the Bible was (1) fundamentally cryptic so that behind apparent meanings lay an esoteric one, (2) essentially relevant, (3) perfect—and perfectly harmonious within, and (4) divinely inspired in its entirety (Kugel 1997, 1–36).

At least some of the biblical writers themselves seem to have shared the notion that the perfection of the Bible meant its various texts must harmonize. A particularly memorable example of this inner biblical interpretation involves cooking the Passover lamb. The instruction in Exodus is to roast it (12:9), whereas the writer of Deuteronomy says it should be boiled (16:7). The author of Chronicles, who retells and reshapes the historical narratives in Samuel and Kings, did not let the contradictory culinary instructions in the Torah stand. Instead, he writes, "They roasted the Passover sacrifice in fire, as prescribed, while the sacred offerings they cooked in pots, cauldrons, and pans [i.e., boiled], and conveyed them with dispatch to all the people" (2 Chronicles 35:13). One could see why the rabbis sought to clarify practices such as in this culinary dilemma.

In general, the *midrashim* reveal the rabbinic desire to seek out God's ways, particularly in interpreting the books of the Torah. There are collections of *midrashim* dating from the third century CE through the twelfth century, most commenting on a single book. Another form of commentary may be seen in the *targumin* (*targum*, sing.), translations from Hebrew into Aramaic. The *targum* most likely developed out of the world of the synagogue, where the reading of a text in Hebrew was followed, verse by verse, by the translator's rendition—and, of course, all translation is commentary. Thus, the congregation heard two voices in tandem: the rendition of the text and its translation/commentary. For those lacking knowledge of Hebrew, the *targum* offered access to the text; for those who were bilingual, the *targum* added another layer to the text.

The rabbis' influence on the synagogue has proven long-lasting, not only in the production of classic texts of commentary but in the shaping of the "synagogue Bible," that is, the lectionary and its accompanying rituals that have been and remain the primary site for Jewish encounter with the Torah (Petuchowski 1959, 142–50). As early as the Mishnah, the rabbis established the foundations of recitation of biblical texts in the synagogue (*Megillah* 3:4–4:10). The Bible of the synagogue consists primarily of the entire Torah/Pentateuch, the Scrolls (particularly the Psalms, Ecclesiastes, Esther, Song of Songs, Ruth, and Lamentations) and selections from the Prophets, primarily the later prophets. The lectionary's cycle of readings stresses the covenant between God and people, and omits many of the details of tribal conquest, the machinations of the kings, etc.

### The Rabbis, the Early Church Writers: Similar Methodologies, Differing Visions

Although rabbinic commentary is a distinctive genre with which few Christians are familiar, this way of interpreting the Bible also had features in common with the patristic writers. Both patristic and rabbinic commentators sought to offer moral wisdom for their communities, provide the grounding for theological development, strengthen beliefs, and respond to their contemporary situations (Bakhos 2024, 290). In their exposition of the Scriptures of Israel, they generally drew upon common and creative ways of reading ancient texts, sometimes with more emphasis on the literal layer, and on other occasions using more imaginative techniques like allegory and typology. Methodologically, they were in the same world.

Two fundamental perspectives of the early church writers, however, differentiated their approach from that of Jewish interpreters. Christian interpretations viewed Israel's Scriptures through a Christological lens—seeing Christ as the one to whom those Scriptures ultimately pointed—and were preoccupied by making a case against Judaism. Other minor differences may be seen as well. Early rabbinic thought was typically oral in character and handed on in various collections without specific attribution of authorship. In contrast, patristic writings exemplified somewhat more varied modes of interpretation through commentaries on biblical texts, homilies, apologia, and letters, typically by specific authors.

Today scholars are increasingly mindful that both the rabbis and early church writers were involved in a lengthy process of mutual drawing of borders and of absorption of the other's work. Rabbinic Judaism "emerged in constant exchange with and differentiation from what, during this mutual process, became Christianity" (Schäfer 2012, 19). Such mutuality, albeit with suspicions and caution, would not be the case in the disputations of the Middle Ages in Paris (1240), Barcelona (1263), and Tortosa (1413), in which church officials established formal and inequitable rules for debate between a Jewish and a Christian scholar. Somehow, the latter was always victorious.

Fortunately, the partiality and hostility that characterized the medieval debates no longer dominates. Although the path of mutual understanding has been overgrown with hostility and distrust, many have been working for the past sixty years or so to clear new ways forward. In large part, this opening is due to advances in biblical scholarship among both Jews and Christians. Particularly in my own Catholic tradition, this may be seen not only in the work of many scholars but also in the development of more nuanced thinking at the official level (Boys 2022b, 2138–45). One illustration is the lengthy monograph in 2000 from the Vatican's Pontifical Biblical Commission (2002) (an international body of approximately twenty Catholic biblical scholars) entitled *The Jewish People and Their Sacred Scriptures in the Christian Bible*. Among its numerous insights is a carefully calibrated understanding of what it means to speak of the New Testament "fulfilling" the Old Testament; one of the conclusions that follows from this reworking is the following:

> Christians can and ought to admit that the Jewish reading of the Bible is a possible one, in continuity with the Jewish Sacred Scriptures from the Second Temple period, a reading analogous to the Christian reading which developed in parallel fashion. Each of these two readings is part of the vision of each respective faith of which it is a product and an expression. Consequently, they cannot be reduced one into the other. (Pontifical Biblical Commission 2002)

Admittedly, this document is not an easy read, so its insights have as yet to make a major impact. One wishes for more forthrightness. For example, the paragraph above reflects a hesitation to say plainly that Jews have a rich history of interpretation that has inspired and sustained their community for centuries—and that Jewish ways of interpreting Scripture offer the church rich fare for dialogue. To speak of postbiblical Judaism in ways that emphasize its resilience, reorientation, and reinvention would make the abstractions of statements such as *The Jewish People and Their Sacred*

*Scriptures in the Christian Bible* come alive. It would also offer details that give specificity to, for example, phrases such as "within the Jewish horizon in the context of the living traditions of Israel" (in *The Gifts and Calling of God Are Irrevocable*). If those who engage in the challenging work of writing such documents want to help people understand new perspectives on relations between Jews and Christians, then more straightforward language is required.

### The Process and Cost of the Christianization of Roman Empire

The criticism of Judaism and Jews among early patristic writers was not uniform; Justin Martyr's cerebral arguments with the Jew Trypho in mid-second century contrasted sharply with the harsh and vehement fulminations of John Chrysostom and Ephrem of Syria's strident teaching songs in the fourth century. Moreover, the vast library of early church writings includes a spectrum of critical judgments on Judaism. Yet, the differences between Justin and Chrysostom, for example, are not merely personal or stylistic; rather, they also reflect a major cultural shift in which the church became more closely affiliated with the power class of the Roman Empire. In Justin's time the nascent church existed in a liminal status in the Empire. That is, insofar as it was seen as one of several varying ways in which Jewish life was expressed, it shared in Rome's more tolerant, if grudging and skeptical, acceptance of Judaism as a respected tradition from antiquity. Christ followers at that juncture were generally seen as one among other Jewish assemblies.

Complicating their liminal legal status was a reality that many in Roman society resented Christians for their refusal to participate in the cults of their cities; by refusing, many believed, they endangered the people's welfare: pleasing the gods meant their benevolent protection for the city. Nor were

Christians participating in the various festivals, often held in and around temples that, for them, were places of idolatry. By deviating from what was expected of the populace, Christians heightened suspicion that they threatened stability. Conspiracy theories depicted them as guilty of incest and cannibalism, and as practicing magic (e.g., signing themselves with the cross). Local persecutions broke out from time to time, including in 64 under the emperor Nero; more destructive were the empire-wide persecutions under the emperor Decius in 250 CE.

With its ethnic connection to Jewish life largely severed and its theological claims more clearly distinctive, the church's divergence from Judaism became increasingly evident—and placed the church in an even more insecure situation vis-à-vis Rome. In Justin's time Christ followers were a small minority scorned by many in the Roman Empire. By the fourth century, however, they had become far more numerous, constituting a significant proportion of the population across the empire. In certain cases, "Christians" became a threat to Roman authorities, refusing to offer sacrifice to the gods as all non-Jews were required to do. While their refusal had sometimes engendered local harassment, the scale and extent of maltreatment increased under co-emperors Diocletian (r 284–305) and Galerius, who instigated an empire-wide persecution of Christians known as the "Great Persecution" (303–312). In several waves of legislation, Christians had their legal rights rescinded. Initially, this included the banning of Christian meetings, destruction of Christian sites of worship, and denying the right to respond to legal charges. Several months later, decrees called for the arrest of clergy, followed by further laws announcing amnesty for clergy who agreed to participate in the sacrificial cult. This was an era in which many martyrs suffered death.

It was thus a momentous event when the dual emperors Licinius and Constantine promulgated the Edict of Milan in

313 proclaiming religious tolerance. Christianity was made a legal religion, thereby bringing greater stability. Constantine, who became the sole emperor in 324 after defeating Licinius in the East, seems to have experienced an affiliation with Christianity that is often referred to as his "conversion," although sources do not offer access to what this openness to the Christian life truly meant for him. Whatever his inner spiritual convictions, Constantine became a major patron of the church. For example, he exempted Christian clergy from the onerous service on city councils and, by assigning judicial authority to bishops, enabled Christians to seek justice in their courts. He also invalidated the laws against celibacy and childlessness while tightening divorce laws; he banned the gruesome gladiatorial contests and declared Sunday a day of rest. Constantine's assistance to the expanding Christian church also included offering land and buildings, assigned it the Lateran property in Rome, and built many churches in that city, including the initial construction across the Tiber of St. Peter's Basilica, as well as in what was now in Christian memory regarded as the "Holy Land," and at Constantinople (Herbst 2019, 179).

At the same time, however, within the church passionate arguments broke out. One question involved whether those who had capitulated to Diocletian should be welcomed back within the church—the so-called Donatist controversy in Carthage. While personally reluctant to arbitrate an innerecclesial debate, Constantine resisted two calls for his direct intervention. Yet he capitulated to the third request, ruling against the Donatists' appeal. Having settled one crisis, Constantine seemed to regard it as a precedent: When the next controversy arose, his approach was "far more interventionist" (Leadbetter 2017, 1004). Constantine's patronage significantly assisted the church's status as a major entity in the empire. It also made clear the extent to which Christianity had become a tradition riven by conflict. And emperors were wary of conflict.

Another, even more charged debate involved the Alexandrian priest and the popular preacher Arius who taught that Jesus should be understood as subordinate to the transcendent God whom he addressed as "Father." His bishop, Alexander, led the opposition to Arius in arguing for Jesus's divine status. Despite various attempts at mediation and calls for Arius to submit to his episcopal authority, the debate became more disruptive. So, this time Constantine took the matter in hand and summoned all the bishops in the empire to meet at Nicaea in 325, about sixty miles from Constantinople (modern Istanbul). The emperor, however, did more than merely convene the bishops. He covered the costs of transportation, extended hospitality to the bishops in an imperial building, and implored them to reach agreement—likely less because of his own theological convictions, but rather because the conflict that had begun in the city of Alexandria was no longer confined there. In his perspective the fragile unity of his vast empire was at stake.

Complete agreement among the bishops was beyond the bishops at Nicaea. A strong majority, however, did issue a creed affirming Jesus as "one in being" (*homoousios*) with the Father; Jesus was "begotten not made, of one substance with the Father through Whom all things came into being, things in heaven and things on earth"—a claim central to the Nicene Creed, which received its final wording at the Council of Constantinople in 381. Little space was given for dissent after the majority also voted to condemn Arius and his followers as "accursed and separated from the church."

But the Arians were not deterred, and controversy raged throughout the empire. Complicating the situation was Constantine's decision as the convener of the Council of Nicaea to enforce its ruling. The emperor's involvement in theological disputes meant that the church's judgment about teachings considered "orthodox" doctrine became subject to political enforcement. Every Roman emperor after Constantine, with one exception (Julian 355–363), similarly became a patron of Christianity, offering considerable benefits to the expanding church. In 380 Emperor Theodosius I (379–395) issued the decree *Cunctos populos*, establishing orthodox Christianity as defined by the Council of Nicaea as the only legitimate form of the faith, which the Theodosian dynasty upheld by favoring orthodox bishops, removing privileges from non-Christians, and sanctioning those Christians considered "heretics" by the standards of Nicaea. Despite the weight of imperial and episcopal authority upholding theological orthodoxy, unity was elusive: "Orthodoxy could never outpace heresy, unity could never erase division, and piety and obedience required rigid and constant enforcement" (Jacobs 2022, 104).

The political enforcement of orthodoxy from Constantine in the first quarter of the fourth century to Justinian in the mid-sixth century resulted in legislation that significantly affected the status of Jews and others. This legislation may be found in two compendia of Roman Laws: The Theodosian Code of Theodosius II (438) and the larger *Corpus juris civilis* of Justinian. The laws concerning religious traditions in the two collections suggest a totalizing Christian Roman Empire in which the (orthodox) church would no longer be subject to persecution, but other religious ways—even that of dissenting Christians— were proscribed. Legally, Judaism was now regarded as a *secta* (subgroup), a *religio* (a community of obligation), a *superstitio* (a scrupulous and idiosyncratic *religio*), a *natio* (community of common birth), and a *feralis secta* (a beastly subgroup). These laws affected Jews economically, socially, and religiously and were intended to facilitate "total legal subjection of Jews as Jews" so that the Jewish "other" might be integrated into "Christian Rome" (Jacobs 2022, 114, 116).

By way of context, it is crucial to recognize the extensive effect of the legal rulings. First, the legislation had greater effect on the eastern empire; the western empire came under the aegis of Visigothic rulers in the early fifth century who were generally Arian Christians and thus less inclined to enforce Nicene orthodoxy. Second, the legislation not only impacted the status of Jews but resulted in the suppression and eradication of all traditional religious practice except that of Jews and Samaritans. Temples and other places of cultic expression were closed, with severe consequences (e.g., banishment, confiscation of property) for those who sought to enter them. The legislation so decimated traditional Mediterranean religious practice that it never recovered. Moreover, the orthodox Christians (i.e., those who upheld Nicene teaching) tyrannized Christians whose theologies and practices they considered heretical (Kraemer 2020, 402–3).

The legislation under the Nicene emperors and bishops and the actions it justified exacted a terrible cost. As Ross Shepard Kraemer summarizes, it resulted in the loss of traditional practices, the destruction of cultic sites, and the disruption of social relations. More specifically, it prohibited social relations between Jews and Christians; restricted Jewish occupations so as to reduce Jews to poverty and incentivize conversion; banned Jews from medical, legal, and educational professions; and forbade Jews from employing Christian servants. She concludes that "for all interests and purposes, these laws laid both the legal and the practical groundwork for centuries of particular forms of repression" (Kraemer 2020, 37–38).

### Reflection

But of what "gain" to Christianity? Without question, it profited from the state's support, achieving a considerable degree of stability and political and economic dominance. In some perspectives, this period marks the "triumph" of Christianity. Certainly, in relation to its earlier persecution, the church needed no longer fear the empire, and the support of the political order enabled building projects that responded to the increased need for places for worship.

But in my view, it was no triumph: Christianity paid a cost to its own moral integrity. Too many bishops looked away from (or even incited) mob violence that destroyed synagogues and harmed Jews. In the desire to assure its official teachings were adhered to, the church justified mistreatment of those who were "other," particularly Jews who refused to acquiesce to Christian beliefs. In accepting not simply the legitimation of the state but also its enforcement of doctrine, it compromised its own freedom to function beyond what the political order mandated. Failing to hear the offense in its rhetoric of vilification, it became unable to stanch the demonization of Jews in the Middle Ages and beyond, for which they paid with their lives.

But that is to go beyond this book; the libraries are full of fine works that trace the long arc of the church's theological antisemitism; I have offered one such narrative in tracing the effects of its accusation that the Jews were responsible for the crucifixion of Jesus in *Redeeming Our Sacred Story: The Death of Jesus and Relations between Jews and Christians* (Boys 2013).

The present year, 2025, will mark the 1,700th anniversary of the Council of Nicaea. Various academic societies will observe the year with new studies of its history and teachings. The anniversary also provides a teachable moment for reflection on the consequences of fostering close ties between church and state—a particularly auspicious moment to assess the dangers of the current advocacy of various forms of Christian nationalism with support from the Trump administration.

And having begun this chapter with a call for the church to ask about Judaism, I conclude with a brief exercise in imagination in which I think out loud about Justin Martyr's "Dialogue with Trypho" as a conversation in which Justin *asks* Trypho to share what Judaism meant to him. After all, it is unlikely that the *Dialogue with Trypho* was a rendition of Justin's actual encounter with a Jew named Trypho. So, too, might we take some liberty with this literary encounter in the second century and suggest how a real dialogue—an interaction between two people intent on engaging each other as human beings—might go? Of course, I confess this is unfair to Justin Martyr, as I'm imposing a twenty-first-century perspective on him. But perhaps we Christians have learned something in our time—finally—about the value of dialogue over disputation.

So, what might Justin—and we—learn from this earnest and learned Jew Trypho, whose final word in their "dialogue" was hope that they might "meet more frequently and continue our study of the Scriptures" (Slusser 2003, 142.1)? And in this imaginative exercise, we can build upon facts and theories scholars have discovered about key events and developments after the death of Jesus (ca. 33 CE) and point to ways in which they contributed to modern Judaism, thereby not restricting ourselves to the mid-second century.

A previous work of scholarship, Timothy J. Horner's *Listening to Trypho: Justin Martyr's Dialogue Reconsidered* (2001), has ventured along similar lines, albeit with a more historical, analytical lens intended for an academic audience. Focusing on the disparity between the chapters in which Trypho actually speaks (in some 40 percent of the *Dialogue* and then 60 percent in which Justin is the lone speaker), Horner argues that the *Dialogue* in its present version is based on an earlier "Trypho Text" in which we have the exchanges between Trypho and Justin. Only later (ca. 160), Justin reworked the *Dialogue* in its present form to include his extensive discourses regarding biblical citations that he regarded as proving his convictions. In analyzing the Trypho Text, Horner concludes that Trypho's Jewish knowledge suggests he was a Jew from Asia Minor consistent with what is known about second-century Judaism in that location. He was a "Jew of the

Diaspora who was curious, astute, philosophically trained and committed to Judaism" (Horner 2001, 188). By separating the Trypho Text from the longer and more meandering array of Justin's assemblage of biblical proof texts, Horner concludes that Trypho illumines how at least some second-century Jews in Asia Minor understood their tradition in relation to nascent Christianity—thus providing us with a viewpoint not readily available from extant sources

Horner's book is a well argued and original perspective. I am indebted to him for his careful listening to Trypho in his second-century world. In my own exercise, however, I am, admittedly, leaving behind early antiquity to read the *Dialogue* through a contemporary lens shaped by an acute awareness of how harmful has been the Christian failure to ask Jews about their tradition—and to listen attentively to their responses. And while I am particularly mindful of this particular failure of my own Catholic Christian tradition, the consequences of the failure to ask far transcend any one tradition. Our world has been deeply scarred by the inability to differentiate without disparaging. History—if only we were to learn from it—bears witness to the immense danger of the evil of interreligious conflict, fueled in large part by ignorance, misunderstanding, authoritarian personalities, bigotry, and conspiracy theories.

Thus, my imaginative foray into Justin's work from one conscious of the long history of Christian animus toward an unjust treatment of Jews ...

Had Justin been more interested in learning from Trypho, he might first have asked more about what his Jewish interlocutor had shared in introducing himself as a "Hebrew of the circumcision" who was a "refugee from the recent war" (Slusser 2003, 1.3). A war refugee; surely that deserved a hearing. Even if Justin didn't pursue this, we can in the present.

Trypho was referring to the Jewish revolt led by Shimon bar Kosiba ("son of the star"; see Slusser 2003, 14:17–18), vainly fought in the Judean countryside between 132 and 135. Not only had Trypho survived this war, but a previous revolt against Roman imperialism fought some sixty years earlier between 66 and 70 shaped the circumstances of Jews both in and beyond Israel, which was called Syria-Palestine after the Bar Kokhba war. The devastating effects of these two wars affected Jewish life significantly. Yet, despite all the tragedy involved in the wake of the devastation wrought by two wars, it became a prelude to the reinvention of Judaism.

Ever since the imposition of Roman rule in 63 BCE, Jews for the most part had lived peaceably if precariously in Israel for about a hundred years. That situation changed when Gaius Caligula became emperor in 37 CE and demanded that his life-sized statue be placed in Jerusalem's Temple, a mandate that struck at the cultic center of Jewish life and signaled a new willingness of Roman authorities to interfere in Jewish life. The strains of living as a Roman colony intensified; for some Jews, they became intolerable and fomented a rebellion that broke out in 66, often termed the "Great Revolt." But nothing was great about it—except Roman military prowess. For Jews the consequences were devastating: numerous soldiers were killed, maimed, or taken captive; there was extensive displacement of the populace; a new tax was imposed, the *Fiscus Judaicus*; there was Roman production of coins boasting *"Judah captiva"*; and the Temple's treasures were plundered.

Most distressing of all was the five-month siege of Jerusalem in 70 that resulted in the destruction of the Temple and the city. The Temple, itself a replacement for Solomon's Temple razed by the Babylonian king Nebuchadnezzar in 587 BCE, had been magnificently expanded and enhanced by an extensive, eighty-year reconstruction begun in 20 BCE under Herod the Great. This Second Temple had "made Jerusalem a spectacular metropolis" (Meyers 1992, 365). But in 70, both the city and its preeminent symbol lay in ashes—a devastation mourned ever since and observed each year in the Hebrew month of Av, its destruction dated to the ninth day of that month (August 30, 70 CE). The poignant poetry of the Book of Lamentations mourning the first Temple's destruction nearly six hundred years earlier took on new dimensions in wake of the loss of the Second Temple

> How she sits alone,
> the city once great with people,
> She has become like a widow.
> Great among the nations,
> mistress among provinces,
> reduced to forced labor.
> She weeps on through the night,
> And her tears are on her cheek.
> She has no consoler
> from all her lovers.
> All her friends have betrayed her,
> have become enemies to her.
> Judah is exiled in affliction
> and in hard labor.
> She dwells among the nations,
> she finds no rest.
> All her pursuers overtake her
> in straits.
> (Lamentations 1:1–3; Alter 2019 translation)

It is highly likely that Trypho was aware of at least some of the tragedies that had befallen Jerusalem and its Temple in the war of 66–74. The second-century Bar Kokhba war may have displaced Trypho, as he told Justin he was presently living in Corinth (Slusser 2003, 1.3). But it was the prior war that above all signified Jewish displacement: its symbolic city and its heart demolished, its sacrificial worship abolished, its beauty defaced, its pilgrim songs silenced.

And Trypho would not have been alone in mourning the destruction of the Second Temple. The date of its destruction, August 30, 70 CE, that is, the ninth day in the Hebrew month of Av—*Tishah B'Av*—took on new layers of meaning over the course of the generations even to the present. The Ninth of Av is seen as the date that absorbed Jewish tragedy, both before 70 CE and after it. This can be seen around the late second to early third century in the Mishnah, the first major collection of Jewish Law and commentary compiled circa 200 CE, which lists five disasters that befell their ancestors (see *Mishnah Ta'anit* 4) on the Ninth of Av. So, too, do subsequent calamities continue to be mourned on *Tishah B'Av*. It is a "sponge for our sorrows," writes Rabbi Dalia Marx. It is the date that "absorbed the memory of many disasters other than the First and Second Temples as the centuries passed." For herself, she writes, "*Tisha B'Av* is a day on which I give thought to the holy site that was destroyed, the sanctity that was violated, and the suffering of innocents among the Jews and in the family of humankind at large" (Marx 2023, 305–6).

So had Justin followed up Trypho's admission that he was a "refugee from the recent war," he might have learned not only about his interlocutor's experience of loss and displacement but also about the importance of Jerusalem and the Temple—and perhaps also gained some sense of how deeply Jews were affected by this tragic loss. Trypho might even have told him how Jews were reconstituting themselves and mentioned that he found a new connection to Jewish tradition through a synagogue in Corinth.

Perhaps, by listening more carefully to Trypho, Justin might have realized that following Christ was *not* "the *only* sure and useful philosophy" (Slusser 2003, 8:1; my emphasis). Just as we Christians today might come to realize that what was "promulgated at Horeb" took on deeper resonances as the generations passed and Jews followed the imperative of the

Mishnaic tractate *Avot* to "turn [the Torah] again and again, growing old and gray over it, for everything is in it."

Were Christians to understand and appreciate Judaism's resilience and its capacity to reorient and reinvent, we may perceive it on our theological radar screens quite differently from Trypho. Through a "respectful and blessed exchange" that has fostered a rediscovery of our common humanity, we are now able, in the words of Cardinal Walter Kasper, to see Judaism as "a sacrament of every otherness that as such the Church must learn to discern, recognize and celebrate" (Kasper 2002).

Justin's utter conviction of Christ as the "only sure and useful philosophy" impeded his vision of the other. He was unable—as have so many in the church over the ages—to have foreseen a Christianity hospitable to Judaism as a "sacrament of otherness" by virtue of a "respectful and blessed exchange." It has taken us nearly two thousand years to learn that dialogue means that Judaism "has something to say which the church needs to hear" (Van Buren 1983, 18). Let us continue to ask, to listen, and to act.

5

# Recovering the Jewish Jesus and Rediscovering Judaism

When I first pondered this book, I did not envision giving such a prominent role to Justin Martyr's *Dialogue with Trypho* (Slusser 2003). Without question, it is a valuable text. The *Dialogue* provides the earliest extensive view of how an articulate, second-century follower of Christ understood his teaching in relation to Judaism. Yet, written some 1,800 years ago, it's little known today. For the vast majority of Christians, it's an abstruse text from a remote time. It doesn't show up in sermons. It lacks a presence on social media. Likely Justin has few, if any, followers.

As a philosopher deeply affected by the "one sure and useful philosophy" of Jesus Christ, Justin shares a sincere attempt to persuade another thinker of the truth he experienced in Christ. His "dialogue partner," the Jew Trypho, hears him out. Despite Justin's passionate advocacy of interpreting Israel's Scriptures fulfilled in Christ, Trypho responds that he understands his Scriptures differently. Unpersuaded by Justin's arguments, Trypho tells Justin that he finds Judaism to be a cogent way of life. That response, however, does not deter Justin in his zeal to persuade Trypho.

Working with his ancient text enhanced my respect for the magnitude of Justin's attempt to elucidate the meaning of

Jesus Christ as the fulfillment of Israel's hopes. The *Dialogue* established a pattern for Christian thinking about its relationship to Judaism that ultimately served as a foundation for centuries of church writings. It marks a pioneering insight in the history of Christian thought, albeit one in which the dialogue did not prove persuasive to its interlocutor, Trypho.

Had the two philosophers left it there, agreeing to disagree about their respective interpretations of Israel's Scriptures, Christians might have developed a different theological sensibility. But Justin, skilled in the style of Greco–Roman rhetoric, wasn't the sort of philosopher satisfied with agreeing to disagree. Moreover, he was so utterly convinced of his position that Trypho's perspective seems not to have truly penetrated his awareness. So committed was Justin to his convictions that he apparently could not imagine a connection between Jesus and Judaism other than as the one who fulfilled the hope of Israel's prophets. And in the conventions of debate, the other's position must be countered. Thus, Justin presents Jesus not only as the fulfillment of Israel's prophecy but as one who stands in opposition to Judaism and whose presence in effect rendered it obsolete. It is as if Justin saw Christ's coming as the erasure of Jewish belief and practice. And yet, there stands Trypho, unconvinced by the argument and persuaded by his experience of Jewish life. Yet Justin seems unable to hear his respectful rejection of Christ as the fulfillment of Israel's hopes.

Therein lies the problem: Justin tells without asking and testifies without inquiring. It's more than just one philosopher's inability to heed the other's perspective. It's that his interpretive pattern was essentially flawed. He and many in successive generations of church writers who took up this pattern assumed theirs was *the* true and certain way of reading Israel's Scriptures. How Israel itself read its sacred texts was irrelevant: "We read your Scriptures more truly than do you." That this perspective had lamentable effects on actual Jews was disregarded, particularly beginning in the fourth century and continuing through the twentieth century. And, despite some breakthrough understandings in the past sixty or so years, the theological antisemitism it helped to foster has not disappeared. Within the church, at least five unintended consequences resulted from this pattern that continue to affect the church even in the present:

- The church lost sight of the Jewishness of Jesus, his early generations of disciples, and his Jewish milieu.
- The New Testament texts were seen as "Christian," without awareness that they originated "within Judaism."
- Judaism became a homogenous and obsolete "other" against which Christianity would be favorably compared.
- While Justin himself did not develop at length Jewish culpability for the crucifixion of Jesus, many other early church writers heightened this claim considerably. The intensification of this claim was the key element in the subsequent vilification of Jews. In ensuing centuries, portraying Jews as culpable for the crucifixion of Jesus served to justify violence and contempt for Jews as perfidious "Christ killers" (Boys 2013).
- Justin's conviction that Israel's Scriptures, which eventually became the church's Old Testament, should be read as proof texts for Christ, which helped to undermine the importance of the Old Testament for the church. The church for the most part also lost sight of the depth of Jewish interpretation of their Scriptures.

From this Catholic's perspective, only one of the above five consequences has been the *focus* of teaching in the contemporary church: *Nostra Aetate*'s insistence that neither the Jews of the past nor of the present were to be blamed for the crucifixion of Jesus. This teaching of Vatican II in the mid-1960s has been followed by subsequent documents, updated religious textbooks, and numerous studies at both the popular and academic levels. Thus, many people have at least some awareness that the "Christ killer" charge is incompatible with contemporary church teaching. I often wonder if congregants at the Good Friday liturgy take note of the tension between the solemn reading of the passion account in John's Gospel in which "the Jews" bear principal responsibility for Jesus's death and this significant teaching of Vatican II in which Jews do not bear culpability. This tension deserves explanation.

Along with declaring Jews innocent of Jesus's death, recovering the Jewish Jesus will have a significant effect. But this recovery must be presented in a way that resituates him in the fuller biblical and theological context, particularly on the meaning of "Jewish" in the first centuries of the Common Era and on the way in which Judaism is embedded in the New Testament. Thus, in this chapter I will first identify the factors that led to the relatively recent recognition of, and appreciation for, the Jewishness of Jesus. The second section will illuminate what scripture scholars mean by claiming that the New Testament should be interpreted "within Judaism," including one study that offers a theory about "the Jews" in John's passion narrative. A concluding section will briefly explore three metaphors that open up possibilities for deeper reflection on the Jewishness of Jesus: Jesus as "other," as "living Torah," and as Wisdom. A brief reflection concludes the chapter.

## Rediscovering the Jewishness of Jesus

Lacking comprehensive knowledge of the vast storehouse of Christian texts over the centuries, I cannot claim that the Jewishness of Jesus was totally lost to the church until the past fifty years or so. Yet, it was neither emphasized nor readily apparent. What does stand out as an explicit *denial* of his Jewishness is the prominence of the claim that Jesus was Aryan (as distinguished from the "Arian Jesus" promulgated by Alexandrian priest Arius, whose teaching the Council of Nicaea denounced in 325 CE). The Aryan Jesus from Galilee was the white, Christian Jesus of the Nazis who stood in opposition to Judaism—and most certainly to Jews (Heschel 2008). A 1941 German catechism, *Ein Deutsches Glaubensbuch*, claimed that the message and behavior of Jesus stood in stark opposition to Judaism; the bitter struggle between him and "the Jew" caused his crucifixion: "Thus Jesus cannot have been a Jew. Until this day the Jews persecute Jesus and all who follow him with unreconcilable hatred.... He became a savior of the Germans" (cited in Boys 2013, 120). At the implicit level, the Jesus preached in contemporary Christian Nationalism in the United States is also depicted as a white Christian—and certainly not as a Jew.

Christian theologians were slow to awaken to potential connections between the church's representation of Jesus as the (Christian) "founder" of Christianity and the widespread failure of the churches to oppose the persecution of the Jews that culminated in the Nazi genocide during the Shoah. Artists, however, took notice, often in ways that shocked traditional renderings of Jesus, such as in Marc Chagall's "White Crucifixion," in 1938, following *Kristallnacht*. A few years later, Chagall depicted a Jewish Jesus surrounded by a disturbing image of a synagogue on fire in *The Yellow Crucifixion* (1943). Of this painting, German theologian Jürgen Moltmann (2015, xxii) wrote,

> In front of me hangs Marc Chagall's picture *Crucifixion in Yellow*. It shows the figure of the crucified Christ in an apocalyptic situation: people sinking into the sea, people homeless and in flight, and yellow fire blazing in the background. And with the crucified

Christ there appears the angel with the trumpet and the open roll of the book of life [Revelation 14.6]. This picture has accompanied me for a long time. It symbolizes the cross on the horizon of the world, and can be thought of as a symbolic expression of the studies which follow.

What Chagall envisioned in the late 1930s, biblical scholarship would eventually emphasize. Particularly in the early 1970s, studies depicting a more nuanced, contextual depiction of the Jewish Jesus began appearing. The most salient aspect of their depiction is an augmented knowledge of a period now given the nomenclature "Early Judaism," that is, often dated from the late third to early second century BCE to 135 CE. It is Early Judaism, as the final phase of Second Temple Judaism, that has now become a crucial context for interpreting the New Testament (Collins and Harlow 2010) and thus an essential context for understanding Jesus. "Early Judaism" contrasts with the terminology previously used, "Late Judaism," which Christian scholars had used as a way of describing a desiccated, legalistic, and homogenous Judaism after the prophetic era—an "Israel that mourns in lonely exile," as the hymn "O Come, O Come Emmanuel" phrases it. "Late" in this context meant that Judaism was in its senescence, whereas "early" implies that Judaism, as it has come to be in the present, was in an initial phase of development, on the brink of the rabbinic era.

The Dead Sea Scrolls, discovered in 1947, and further manuscripts unearthed from the Judean desert proximate to the Dead Sea opened a new world of complexity of Jewish life prior to the Jewish Revolt against the Romans that ended in the fall of the Temple in 70 CE. Teams of Jewish and Christian scholars painstakingly reconstructed the manuscripts, many in fragments and varied in genre (biblical texts and commentaries, hymns, legal texts, a manual of community life, etc.).

These manuscripts revealed details about how a particular group of Jews with a distinct view of their tradition interpreted sacred texts and applied them to their communal life, regarded the Temple and its priesthood, and saw themselves vis-à-vis other Jews. The increase in knowledge of Judaism that the Dead Sea Scrolls catalyzed has been monumental. The manuscripts provided access to the *self-understanding* of one way of living Jewishly, often understood to be that of the Essenes, although that identity appears more complicated than originally thought. But whatever the name(s) of those groups gathered in the region of the Dead Sea, we know how they interpreted the Scriptures of Israel; we also have an understanding of how they lived communally. What we've learned about them contrasts to the better-known Pharisees, from whom we have—at least as yet—no documents we can attribute to them directly. We have only the judgments *about* Pharisees in Josephus and the New Testament and in a few other sources; these views have generated numerous hypotheses and a voluminous literature but no primary sources from the Pharisees themselves except for Paul's self-identification.

The discovery of the Scrolls also increased attention to other Jewish literature from roughly the same era, both the apocryphal books (included in the canons of the Catholic and Orthodox churches, but not in the canon of Judaism or Protestantism) and an extensive collection of varied texts categorized as Pseudepigrapha ("writings falsely attributed"). Many of these latter works were attributed to figures of the Jewish Bible/Old Testament or even to non-Jewish figures of antiquity. Together with the Scrolls, this literature has provided a substantial and complex textual basis for expanding knowledge of Early Judaism that is fundamental to rectifying the distorted and polemical portrayal of the Jewish world of Jesus that has characterized much of Christian literature for centuries and that still lingers in the present. Also of great importance is early rabbinic literature as redacted in the Mishnah circa 220 CE.

New Testament scholar E. P. Sanders (1937–2022) played a vital role in upending the stereotype of Judaism as legalistic in his *Paul and Palestinian Judaism* (Sanders 1977) in which he argued for the centrality of "covenantal nomism" as an assumption common to most extant Jewish literature from 200 BCE to 200 CE. In contrast to scholarship dominated by the Reformation's characterization of Judaism as a religion of "works righteousness" and thus as a religion of "self-redemption," Sanders countered that Jews understood their "works" as acts of obedience within the framework of their covenant with a gracious and merciful God. It is God who called them to be bonded by covenant and to follow the "Law" as the way by which they maintained their belonging to that covenant. When they failed to live according to the covenant, they restored their belonging among the covenanted people through acts of atonement. In a more recent essay, Sanders, who spent years in intensive study of Jewish primary sources, concluded, "My fondest hope is that judgmental Christians should look at Jewish literature the same way they look at their own, since it, too, is based on the idea of God's gracious choice" (Sanders 2009, 55).

Another challenge to the stereotype of Jewish legalism came through a study of Paul by the Swedish Lutheran scholar Krister Stendahl (1921–2008). Stendahl claimed that large sectors of the Western church, particularly the churches of the Reformation, interpreted Paul as being preoccupied by the same existential question that had gripped Luther: "How can I find a gracious God?" Because human beings could never live up to the demands of the Torah—simplistically equated with Jewish Law—their efforts to save themselves were fruitless. Following the Law entailed a futile attempt to earn divine love through good works. Luther had discovered that one could be saved from the "penetrating self-examination" that constituted the "introspective conscience of the West" through justification by faith and without the works of the Law. Christ alone saved one from sin and meaninglessness.

Quite to the contrary, Stendahl first argued in 1960 that Paul possessed a "robust" conscience, unlike Luther, and was not preoccupied with questions of forgiveness. Nor was Paul concerned with *Jewish* observance of the dietary laws and the rite of circumcision—it was the *Gentile* observance of these Jewish boundary markers that he criticized. Thus, when the Apostle to the Gentiles spoke about justification, he did so to *Gentiles* to defend Christ following Gentiles as full heirs to God's promises to Israel (Stendahl 1962, 261–65). Further, as Stendahl argued in a lecture in 1963, Paul's mystical encounter on the Damascus Road was a "call" rather than a "conversion," a new mission rather than a change of religion from Judaism to Christianity. He hadn't "converted" from being a hopeless works-righteous Jew into a joyful, justified Christian. *His was a call, not a conversion.* Paul understood himself as an "Apostle of the one God who is Creator of both Jews and Gentiles (cf. Romans 3:30); (Stendahl 1976, 15).

Sanders and Stendahl exemplified a commitment to transcend Christian depictions of Judaism as mired in law and thus a religion of "works righteousness," a major legacy of the perspective of the Reformation. Both scholars were enormously influential, Sanders with his extensive documentation drawn from Jewish primary sources, and Stendahl with his more plainspoken and deeply learned communication through numerous lectures and positions as Dean of Harvard Divinity School and Bishop of Stockholm (Boys 2016, 281–93).

Amplifying the work of Sanders and Stendahl on the Jewish world of Jesus, many published works situating Jesus in his Jewish context appeared in the 1970s and beyond, including the following volumes in English by both Jewish and Christian scholars: *Jesus the Jew* (Vermes 1973), *The Jewish Reclamation of Jesus: An Analysis and Critique of Modern Jewish Study of Jesus* (Hagner 1984), *Jesus and Judaism*

(Sanders 1985), *The Historical Jesus: The Life of a Mediterranean Jewish Peasant* (Crossan 1991), *A Marginal Jew* (Meier 1991–2016 [5 volumes]); *The Religion of Jesus the Jew* (Vermes 1993), *Jesus of Nazareth, King of the Jews: A Jewish Life and the Emergence of Christianity* (Fredriksen 1999), *Jesus: A Jewish Galilean: A New Reading of the Jesus Story* (Freyne 2004), *The Misunderstood Jew: The Church and the Scandal of the Jewish Jesus* (Levine 2006), *The Jewish Jesus: Revelation, Reflection and Reclamation* (Garber 2011), *Jewish Jesus Research and Its Challenge to Christology Today* (Homolka 2016). While each differs in methodology, conclusions, and style, even this incomplete listing suggests the proliferation of recent studies on the topic—not to mention numerous articles.

And while I have stressed the role of biblical scholarship, a few works have approached the Jewishness of Jesus through the lens of systematic theology, the most prominent being the three-volume *A Theology of the Jewish-Christian Reality* (Van Buren 1980, 1983, 1988) and the recent *Jesus the Jew in Christian Memory: Theological and Philosophical Explorations* (Meyer 2020).

In my experience, this rich scholarship has yet to make an impact on church teaching, preaching, and liturgical life. Among many church leaders and laypeople, Jesus and the first generations of his disciples are regularly assumed to be Christians. Judaism is mentioned primarily in the context of the Old Testament and as a monolithic religious tradition of the past. Occasionally, mention may be made of Jews celebrating Rosh Hashanah or Passover, though I've yet to hear even a mention of the rich spirituality surrounding the observance of those holidays—the deep spirit of repentance in the Days of Awe leading up to Yom Kippur and the keen sense of identity with their ancestors in recounting the Exodus event at a seder. Homilists would do well to enhance their understanding through resources such as Irving ("Yitz") Greenberg's excellent volume *The Jewish Way: Living the Holidays* (Greenberg 1988), which interprets Judaism through the living of its key festivals, and for those who live in areas with Jewish communities to inquire what meanings their celebration of the holidays holds for them personally and communally.

Recovering a Jewish Jesus reorients our understanding of the New Testament, as I explain in the following section.

### Situating Early "Christian" Texts "within Judaism"

A related school of thought is emerging as reading the New Testament "within Judaism." This development reflects a keener focus on the Jewish world from which those texts emerged before the rabbinic movement reshaped Judaism, and Christianity became a distinct entity. It is characterized by peering more deeply into first-century Judaism in which "different Jews enacted Jewishness differently" (Fredriksen 2022, 368). Or, to change the metaphor, interpreting texts "within Judaism" requires listening to early texts on their own terms, accompanied by a willingness to silence familiar understandings and heed specific voices in "Jewish polyphony" (Konradt 2024, 125). In other words, we are challenged to allow ourselves to enter into the unfamiliar so that we might begin to read the New Testament writings as "expressions of Judaism," constituting part of a diverse trajectory "embodying Jewish ancestral customs in the pre-rabbinic, Second Temple period" (Runesson 2023, 299).

"Within Judaism" differs from traditional theoretical perspectives that assume an early separation of Christianity from Judaism or that presuppose merely a "Jewish background" for the New Testament. Situating New Testament texts "within Judaism" may mean the text itself, the author, or the intended audience—or all of these variables. Further, "Judaism" as an ethnicity might be seen as a specific instance of common attributes of ethnic groups, including a common proper name, a myth of common ancestry, shared memories of a common past, elements of a common culture (e.g., religion, customs, language), link with a common homeland, and a shared sense of solidarity. "Within Judaism" involves "seeing Judaism as having an enduring significance for the meaning of texts" (Van Maaren 2023, 268–79). Situating Paul within Judaism, while it contravenes centuries of conventional interpretation, can be more readily understood. Paul is forthright in describing himself in his letter to the community at Philippi in northern Greece as one "circumcised on the eighth day, a member of the people Israel, of the tribe of Benjamin, a Hebrew born of Hebrews; as to the law, a Pharisee; as to zeal, a persecutor of the church; as to righteousness under the law, blameless" (Philippians 3:4b–6). Similarly, in writing to the Galatians in central Asia Minor, Paul rehearses his past as one "zealous for the traditions of my ancestors" who "violently persecuted the church of God" until his encounter with Christ and subsequent call to preach to the Gentiles (Philippians 1:13–16). Paul's call to preach to the Gentiles did not displace his own Jewish identity, as Krister Stendahl and E. P. Sanders argued in the 1960s and 1970s. Recent years have seen a surge of articles and books further exploring Paul's Judaism, including the 2015 collected essays in *Paul within Judaism: Restoring the First-Century Context to the Apostle*, edited by two of the leading scholars on this topic, Mark Nanos and Magnus Zetterholm. The title of Pamela Eisenbaum's *Paul Was Not a Christian: The Real Message of a Misunderstood Apostle* (2009) aptly conveys the overturning of the common view of Paul as the convert to Christianity.

For many, resituating Paul within his Jewish context can be disconcerting. For those who view Paul as a "founder" of Christianity and/or as a foremost exemplar of Christian thought, seeing him as *both* a faithful Jew and as a follower of Jesus Christ, the "power and wisdom of God," may initially be disturbing. The resulting disequilibrium may be related to the familiar tendency to impose our modern assumptions upon antiquity. So, it is understandable to see Paul as a significant figure in "Christianity," as has been traditionally taught. In Paul's world, however, to be a passionate advocate of Christ while living in fidelity to Judaism was not a contradiction. His mission was to the Gentiles—and the Christ he preached was a Jew from Nazareth in whom God had spoken a new Word. Yes, he believed other Jews should also turn to the Christ, but that did not mean he intended to have them "convert" to "Christianity," which did not then exist as a separate entity. Paul was not a convert to "Christianity" but a Christ-following Jew passionate in following his call to preach to the Gentiles.

Grappling with a Jewish Jesus and a Jewish Paul and a Jewish Peter and Paul, a Jewish Mary and Magdalene means allowing ourselves to set aside assumption as creatures of modernity:

> Any first-century person, pagan or Jew, should seem unfamiliar to us. Ancient people lived in a geocentric universe teeming with nonhuman and posthuman agents large and small. Their impurities were physical states that could have cosmic consequences. They honored deity through offerings, while deity communicated with them through dreams, texts, weather, and animal viscera. They pleased deity through loyalty (*pistis, fides*) and scrupulous attention ... to enactments of ancestral custom. Paul thought and acted much more like any ancient pagan than like any modern Christian—or, like any modern Jew. To rephrase: an ancient Jewish Paul is no less unfamiliar to a modern Jew than he is to a modern Christian—or to a modern anyone. (Fredriksen 2022, 380)

As a historian, Fredriksen understands the importance of revealing the "unfamiliarity ... to create that space between ourselves and our historical subjects where the past becomes radically foreign" (Fredriksen 2022, 380). Her "defamiliarized Paul" neither preached a "law-free gospel" nor considered Jewish Law the antithesis of the gospel. Though he insisted that his Gentiles—pagans—cease from living "paganly" by worshiping the God of Israel exclusively, that did not mean that Paul himself stopped living Jewishly. Moreover, "Paul was not a Christian. He did not found churches. He established charismatic assemblies, for which neither he nor his people expected a *longue durée*" (Fredriksen 2022, 375).

While the approach "within Judaism" has predominantly involved studies on Paul, more recently there has been an emphasis on much of the New Testament and later texts. I turn now to a reading of the Gospel of John within Judaism.

### Reading the Gospel of John "Within Judaism"

First, some context. The Fourth Gospel is replete with condemnation of "the Jews" (Gk. *hoi Ioudaioi*). It poses the most significant moral issues for Christians mindful of a history in which Christians' vicious rhetoric and vile, inhumane acts against Jews have had unspeakably tragic results. Obviously, John's Gospel is not the sole cause, but history shows that its many passages seemingly condemning Judaism have inspired and justified antisemitism.

A careful reading of John's Gospel reveals that the collective noun "the Jews" is used in varying ways. Other characters in John's narratives are obviously Jews yet not identified as such (e.g., his disciples; Jesus's friends Mary, Martha, and Lazarus; the Pharisees, the high priest Caiaphas, and the chief priests). Nevertheless, even a careful reader—and not all who peruse John are discerning readers—is mindful that throughout this gospel "the Jews" are associated with opposition to Jesus, including the desire to kill him. Consider the following examples (boldface added):

- The man went away and told **the Jews** that it was Jesus who had made him well. Therefore **the Jews** started persecuting Jesus, because he was doing such things on the Sabbath. But Jesus answered them, "My Father is still working, and I also am working." For this reason **the Jews** were seeking all the more to kill him, because he was not only breaking the Sabbath, but was also calling God his own Father, thereby making himself equal to God (John 5:15–18).
- After this Jesus went about in Galilee. He did not wish to go about in Judea because **the Jews** were looking for an opportunity to kill him (John 7:1).
- Again **the Jews** were divided because of these words. Many of them were saying, "He has a demon and is out of his mind. Why listen to him?" Others were saying, "These are not the words of one who has a demon. Can a demon open the eyes of the blind?" (John 10:19–20).
- **The Jews** took up stones again to stone him. Jesus replied, "I have shown you many good works from the Father. For which of these are you going to stone me?" **The Jews** answered, "It is not for a good work that we are going to stone you, but for blasphemy, because you, though only a human being, are making yourself God" (John 10:31–32).
- Many of **the Jews** therefore, who had come with Mary and had seen what Jesus did, believed in him. But some of them went to the Pharisees and told them what he had done. So the chief priests and the Pharisees called a meeting of the council, and said, "What are we to do? This man is performing many signs. If we let him go on like this, everyone will believe in him, and the Romans will come and destroy both our holy place and our nation." But one of them, Caiaphas, the high priest that year, said to them, "You know nothing

at all! You do not understand that it is better for you to have one man die for the people than to have the whole nation destroyed." He did not say this on his own, but being high priest that year he prophesied that Jesus was about to die for the nation, and not for the nation only, but to gather into one the dispersed children of God. So from that day on they planned to put him to death (John 11:45–53).

- Jesus therefore no longer walked about openly among **the Jews**, but went from there to a town called Ephraim in the region near the wilderness; and he remained there with the disciples (John 11:54).
- Caiaphas was the one who had advised **the Jews** that it was better to have one person die for the people (John 18:14).
- Jesus answered [Pilate], "My kingdom is not from this world. If my kingdom were from this world, my followers would be fighting to keep me from being handed over to **the Jews**. But as it is my kingdom is not from here" (John 18:36).
- After he [Pilate] had said this, he went out to **the Jews** again and told them, "I find no case against him. But you have a custom that I release someone for you at the Passover. Do you want me to release for you the King of the Jews?" They shouted in reply, "Not this man, but Barabbas!" Now Barabbas was a bandit (John 18:38b–40).
- Pilate went out again and said to them, "Look, I am bringing him out to you to let you know that I find no case against him." So Jesus came out, wearing the crown of thorns and the purple robe. Pilate said to them, "Here is the man!" When the chief priests and the police saw him, they shouted, "Crucify him! Crucify him!" Pilate said to them, "Take him yourselves and crucify him; I find no case against him."

- The Jews answered him, "We have a law, and according to that law he ought to die because he has claimed to be the Son of God" (John 19:4–7).
- From then on Pilate tried to release him, but the Jews cried out, "If you release this man, you are no friend of the emperor. Everyone who claims to be a king sets himself against the emperor" (John 19:12).
- When Pilate heard these words, he brought Jesus outside and sat on the judge's bench at a place called The Stone Pavement, or in Hebrew Gabbatha. Now it was the day of Preparation for the Passover, and it was about noon. He said to the Jews, "Here is your King!" They cried out, "Away with him! Away with him! Crucify him!" Pilate asked them, "Shall I crucify your King?" The chief priests answered, "We have no king but the emperor." Then he handed him over to them to be crucified (John 18:13–16).
- After these things, Joseph of Arimathea, who was a disciple of Jesus, though a secret one because of his fear of the Jews, asked Pilate to let him take away the body of Jesus (John 19:38).
- When it was evening on that day, the first day of the week, and the doors of the house where the disciples had met were locked for fear of the Jews, Jesus came and stood among them and said, "Peace be with you" (John 20:19).

Moreover, one of the most problematic passages is ostensibly addressed to "the Jews who believed in him" (John 8:31). From the context, however, it seems far more likely to be addressed to "the [unbelieving] Jews." In this notorious exchange, Jesus says "to them," "You are from your father the devil and you choose to do your father's desires. He was a murderer from the beginning and does not stand in the truth because there is no truth in him." This hateful accusation is among the most provocative and polemical passages in the New Testament, an issue compounded by its placement in a complex and confusing narrative. Over the years numerous learned commentaries have grappled with this now widely recognized issue. One comment in particular from the Jewish New Testament scholar Adele Reinhartz has stayed with me since I read it shortly after its publication nearly twenty-five years ago: "My heart still sinks every time I open the Gospel of John to 8:44 and read that the Jews have the devil for their father" (Reinhartz 2005, 167).

In her more recent book *Cast Out of the Covenant: Jews and Anti-Judaism in the Gospel of John*, Reinhartz develops her ethical criticism at greater length. She argues that John's rhetoric invites its audience into the family of God through a rhetoric of affiliation. Yet that invitation *excludes* those Jews who do not believe in Jesus as the divinely sent Messiah. By their unbelief they have forfeited their status as God's covenanted people. Thus, they testify to the reality that "one cannot simultaneously be a child of God (1:12) and a child of the devil (8:44)." Consequently, the gospel's rhetoric of disaffiliation means they are displaced from their covenant relationship with God and replaced by those who believe in the Way of Christ (Reinhartz 2018, xii).

Reinhartz is an astute analyst of Johannine rhetoric whose work speaks to me because of her deep scholarship, and her insightful reading of texts complemented by her candid grappling with what this gospel means for her as a Jew. As a Catholic Christian—and thus in the gospel's perspective, one belonging to the community of those reborn in Christ—I find *Cast Out of the Covenant* a substantial work of scholarship and an astringent read. Her rendering of John's rhetoric of disaffiliation for the *Ioudaioi* raises many questions for Christians. Certainly, Reinhartz is a trustworthy scholar; if we follow her conclusions, then what is the appropriate response? Should this canonical text that has proved deeply meaningful for Christians be set aside? Yet, insofar as it is in the canon of Christian sacred texts, that is not an option. Then what? I suggest we consider our response on two levels, one pertaining to biblical interpretation itself and the other to the obligation of Christians to listen with the "ears of their heart" to the obligation to resist dehumanizing or deprecatory views of the other that have found their way into biblical texts. In the Reflection that concludes this chapter, I wrestle with the challenge of dealing with "troubling texts" in the pastoral context, including what it means in the liturgical context to proclaim biblical texts—especially troubling ones such as John's characterization of "the Jews"—as God's Word. Without being mindful of what we are responding to, we may seem to endorse as sacred odious charges against an entire group of people, past and present: Jews.

One way to think about this dilemma of honoring our sacred texts without affirming their problematic claims is to situate Reinhartz's scholarship in relation to that of other interpreters. One such interpreter is Wally V. Cirafesi, who is explicitly in conversation with Reinhartz. Moreover, he has expressed a deep appreciation for her work and acknowledges the impact she has made on his professional development.

In his 2022 book, *John within Judaism: Religion, Ethnicity, and the Shaping of Jesus-Oriented Jewishness in the Fourth Gospel,* Cirafesi offers an alternative argument through analysis of ways in which Jewish identity was negotiated in the late first century. Key to his work is understanding the role ethnicity plays in John—and not simply in this gospel account but in understanding Judaism in antiquity. In his view, ethnicity refers to related characteristics that form identity, such as peoplehood, ancestral laws, land, and national cult. Ethnic identities are not fixed but relational and dynamic. In the case of the Jewish *ethnos*, there was a high level of internal variation throughout the Mediterranean world as Jews in disparate places formed their identity through their beliefs, practices, and material cultures. In contrast to those who argue that the term "religion" is anachronistic in terms of antiquity, Cirafesi also proposes that the ways Jews lived their beliefs and practices revealed how they worked out their ethnicity. So, Judaism is thus best understood as an "ethno-religion" in antiquity. Insofar as it "cohered around processes of meaning-making involving the concepts of peoplehood, law, land, and national cult, then the many lived interpretations of these categories generated its diversity" (Cirafesi 2022, 42, 51).

In his analysis of Jewish diversity, Cirafesi suggests two contrasting positions along a spectrum of first-century Judaism. At one end is what he terms "priestly-oriented Judaism" that emphasizes peoplehood based on genealogy and male initiation into the covenant by virtue of eighth-day circumcision. Priestly oriented Judaism considers Jewish law as constitutive, holds a territorial understanding of the land of Israel, and prioritizes the centrality of the Jerusalem Temple as the site where Israel's God interacts with the Jewish people. At the other end is "diasporic-oriented" Judaism—diaspora referring to the widespread loci of Jewish communities beyond the land of Israel. This mode of Jewish life, however, is not solely geographical, but rather involves living under foreign rule, whether actual or ideological. It rests on a cultural approach that emphasizes behavioral norms of Jewish belonging rather than genealogy. So, it is amenable to the inclusion of Gentiles, relates to Jerusalem and the land through metaphor and the imagination, and envisions a transformed Temple sanctuary democratizing access to the God of Israel. Jewish ethnic identity along the diasporic pole provided the ideological infrastructure for visions of Jewishness without a national and cultic center (Cirafesi 2022, 51–68).

Moreover, as might be anticipated, other Jewish groups occupied a middle ground such as some communities living outside the land of Israel who, though drawn to a priestly orientation, established their own temples rather than looking to Jerusalem's Temple. Cirafesi places the community at Qumran in the middle of the spectrum. They had their own priests, yet held distinctive understandings of genealogy and practices in the assembly. There were also others who broke entirely with Judaism (see 1 Maccabees 1:11–15), thereby rejecting their own ethnic group and associating with another ethnicity altogether (Cirafesi 2022, 66–71).

By implication, Cirafesi's spectrum opens up the complexity of *Ioudaioi*, pointing to the heterogeneity seemingly hidden behind John's use of the term. His work, along with other studies highlighting the diversity of Second Temple Judaism/Early Judaism, makes it conceivable that when John is using *Ioudaioi*, he does so in a specific way: *Ioudaioi* are those Jews who are "decidedly on the priestly-oriented side of the spectrum, as they put a premium on genealogical exclusivism in their understanding of Jewishness." Jesus in John's Gospel is not arguing against *the Jews as a people* "but rather against Jewish identity bound up with the priestly politics of the Second Temple period, a mode of Jewishness that, according to John, was hostile to Jesus and that Jesus heavily criticized" (Cirafesi 2022, 119).

*John within Judaism* is a richly detailed, scholarly study to which my brief summary does not do justice. Cirafesi himself recognizes that many will find his argument unpersuasive or at least inadequate to account for the way the Fourth Gospel characterizes the *Ioudaioi*, the Jews. Some may judge his efforts as simply an attempt to absolve John of the problems his text poses or consider that Cirafesi is merely being "politically correct." Likewise, Jews may be offended; Cirafesi's thesis that *this* gospel is a Jewish text may well be difficult to absorb when John has been used to disparage Judaism and inspire or justify hostility to Jews. Similarly, some Christians, particularly those with little awareness of the problems in John, may take umbrage at Cirafesi's claim that John envisions "a life lived Jewishly as a presupposition and a prerequisite for salvation" (Cirafesi 2022, 286). Nonetheless, by postulating the complexity of the *Ioudaioi* in the late first century, Cifafesi opens a new lens on a gospel account that has been a source of antisemitism and continues to disturb those Jews and Christians sensitive to its deeply troubling history. In the next chapter I will offer some suggestions about teaching or preaching the Gospel of John in educational and pastoral contexts "within Judaism."

Appreciative though I am of Cirafesi's distinctive reading of John, it doesn't seem to account sufficiently for the rhetorical intensity of the Fourth Gospel's animus toward the *Ioudaioi*. As a follower of the Way of Christ, I instinctively resist Reinhartz's conclusion that the rhetoric of this gospel consistently and stridently places the *Ioudaioi* beyond the borders of the Johannine community and, therefore, outside the circle of the children of God. And yet, her reading seems not only to accord with the literary style of John but also seems entirely possible, given the tendency in the history of religious groups to vilify others whose faith is deemed insufficient or heretical.

Ultimately, the more pressing question to church leaders is this: Given the rhetorical style of the Gospel of John in which "the Jews" are consistently portrayed as the principal opponents of [the Jewish] Jesus, will you forthrightly address the problematic characterization of "the Jews" in the Gospel of John? In the case of Catholicism, in which its Pontifical Biblical Commission has issued significant statements on biblical interpretation, now is the time to draw upon the principles in these documents in light of recent scholarship on the Fourth Gospel to promulgate a teaching document that will serve as an illuminating and useful guide to preaching and teaching. Even if, as Reinhartz argues, the Gospel of John endeavors to persuade the followers of the Christ that their faith requires rejecting that of the *Ioudaioi,* cannot the church today speak a new word? Can it not confess that reading this gospel in light of the long history of Christian disparagement of Judaism and its hostility toward and persecution of Jews that it has a moral imperative to reject this gospel's portrayal of the Ioudaioi as unfaithful and unbelieving? Can it, sixty years since *Nostra Aetate* inaugurated theological and pastoral rethinking of its relationship to Jews and Judaism, now be candid? The Gospel of John, beloved by so many over the course of centuries, offers wisdom about the life and meaning of Jesus Christ. Its depiction of "the Jews," however, was tragically flawed: It was not that Jews were *unbelieving* but that their belief did not accord with that of those who believed Jesus was the Christ of God. It has taken the church far too long to recognize that a faith that is different from the church's does not render it unfaithful to God but simply different. And that we have much to learn from those whose paths to the Divine differ from the church's.

### Jesus and the Early Community within Judaism: Three Possibilities

In our time we are fortunate to have many works exploring the "Jewishness of Jesus," which I see as consonant with those advocating for reading the New Testament "within Judaism." In this brief section, I propose several possibilities for further thought, each of which might profitably be developed at great length.

### Jesus as Other

Sometimes I'm startled by a claim that is obvious but to which I've been oblivious. High in its startling effect is Barbara Meyer's assertion that "Jesus the Jew remains as Other for contemporary Christians with regard to his embodiment of

Torah and bodily practice of the commandments" (Meyer 2020, 149). Of course! Jesus lived by the patterns of Jewish life: worship of the One God, heeding the obligations of its holy texts to "be holy as I am holy" and to "love the stranger as yourself, for you were strangers in Egypt," and to observe Sabbath rest and participate in the rituals of festivals and of Jerusalem's Temple. Nothing surprising there. Except that as a Christian (i.e., as a Gentile) I do not live by precisely those same patterns, but rather by those ways of life that while grafted onto Jewish life, are nonetheless distinctively Christian. I pray in the name of the Jewish Jesus and aspire to live by the Way, which is passed down by his disciples. The Jew Jesus is an other to me, a non-Jew.

For many of my Gentile ancestors in faith, following the Jewish Christ meant denying his Judaism—and, as history reveals so clearly, demeaning it—to uphold the superiority of Christianity as the "one true and sure philosophy." To affirm Jesus's otherness in our time involves seeking to situate Jesus in the particulars of a Jewish life lived in the land of Israel in the early first century as best we might understand that time so distant from us. If as Meyer shows, Jesus lived a "Torah-bound" life, then in what ways might my own understanding of the Torah become more capacious so as to live out discipleship as followers of the Way? And what does that mean for how I live out my own commitment to the One God manifested for us as "Father," "Son," and "Spirit"—metaphors that open up new ways of imagining divine life and yet also metaphors grounded in Israel's life?

Reflection on the otherness of Jesus also contributes to an openness to see Paul, the "Christ-believing Pharisee," who is also other to us—as one passionate about God's call to non-Jews while himself living Jewishly. So, too, was the earliest generation of disciples, Jews drawn to the Christ. Contrary to the conventional portrait of the Twelve as Christian apostles, they, too, were Jews committed to Jesus. Consider the possibilities of this title for a sermon: "The Twelve Apostles: Jewish followers of Christ."

To follow the Way of the Jewish Jesus comes with a theological responsibility to move beyond the shallow and simplistic depiction of Jesus as one who stands in opposition to Israel's law (Hesslein 2015, 188). Yet the dominance this depiction has even in contemporary church life suggests the difficulty of transcending the constricted portrait of Jesus against Jewish legalism. One potential pathway lies in exploring the connections between Jesus and the Torah—even Jesus as the "living Torah."

### Jesus as the "Living Torah of God"

Over the course of the nearly sixty years since the promulgation of the Second Vatican Council's decree *Nostra Aetate* in October 1965, various officials and offices in the Vatican have published a succession of documents refining and developing the claims of section 4 (on relations with Jews). For the celebration of its fiftieth anniversary in 2015, the Vatican's Commission on Religious Relations with the Jews issued a lengthy and densely written theological reflection, "The Gifts and Calling of God Are Irrevocable (Rom 11:29)," summarizing ways in which *Nostra Aetate*'s legacy has advanced. While the document is not beyond criticism, it nonetheless has value both for the historical background it summarizes and for new insights (Moyaert 2017, 24–43; Gregerman 2018, 36–59).

One insight stands out as notably thought-provoking: "Christians affirm that Jesus Christ can be considered as '*the living Torah of God*'" (my emphasis). To situate this startling assertion within the document, prior sections discuss God's revelation to humankind through the Word—for Jews to be learned through "the Torah and the traditions based on it.... Whoever observes the Torah has life in its fullness."

Citing Pope Francis, the Commission writes that the "Christian confessions find their unity in Christ; Judaism finds its unity in the Torah. Christians believe Christ is the Word of God made flesh in the world; for Jews the Word of God is present above all in the Torah. Both faith traditions find their foundation in the One God, the God of the Covenant.... Christians turn to Christ as the fount of new life, and Jews to the teaching of the Torah."

To speak of Christ as "God's Living Torah" is an astonishing assertion. It is a striking reversal of centuries of Christian disparagement of Judaism's "Law" as legalistic, its strictures superseded by the freedom found in Christ's love. If the Commission's assertion is to have meaning, then the capaciousness of the term *Torah* must be explored, including its place in worship. The Torah connotes the chain of tradition as manifested in the exposition, expansion, and commentary known as the Oral Torah. A text is not kept alive simply by preserving the text but by interpreting it in new situations and discovering hitherto unknown possibilities in a different age. As the sages formulated the process of transmission in one of the earliest accounts, the Mishnaic tractate *Pirkei Avot* (Ethics of the Fathers) begins,

> Moses received the Torah at Sinai and he transmitted it to Joshua and Joshua to the elders, and the elders to the prophets and the prophets transmitted it to the Great Assembly. The men of the Great Assembly [those who innovated in ways that kept tradition alive and adaptive to changed circumstances] said three maxims: Be measured in the legal process: raise up many students; make a fence for the Torah. (Greenberg 2016, 7)

It is the Oral Torah that shapes the understanding of the (Written) Torah; thus, rabbinic commentaries may be seen as comprising scripture as well, although they do not play the same formal role in the synagogue. For many Jews, the study of rabbinic texts—the Mishnah, the *Talmudim* (of Jerusalem and of Babylon), and the *midrashim* (interpretations)—is also an act of learning and devotion. One way of understanding the importance of the Oral Torah is to recognize the distinction between the books that constitute the Jewish Bible and "Scripture" as the more expansive term that connotes the interpretive process beyond the canonization of the biblical books.

Although I do not know precisely what the authors of "The Gifts and Calling" meant by appending "living" to the Torah, to me the addition of this adjective draws upon the understanding that the Torah is not simply a precious artifact from antiquity but an animating source of life for the Jewish people, its umbilical cord to the Divine. By analogy, the Jesus Christ who is for Christians "the image of the invisible God" (Colossians 1:15a) reveals by his teaching and actions what it means to live in the ways of God. Raised from the dead by divine power, Christians are called, according to Gerard Manley Hopkins in his poem, "The Wreck of the Deutschland," to follow the Way of Christ so as to

> Let him easter in us, be a dayspring for the dimness
> of us, to be a crimson-cresseted east
> (Hopkins 1995, 113)

So, then, what meanings might we Christians discover in contemplating Christ as our "living Torah"? Matthew's Gospel can be helpful here. More than the other evangelists, he depicts Jesus as one whose very being is harmonious with the Torah. Matthew portrays Jesus not simply as one who interprets the Torah in a distinctive manner but also one who embodies the Torah through his life-giving teaching and in his willingness to live those teachings even at the cost of his life.

Living a Torah-inspired life implies action; what it teaches is meant to be lived out, not merely treated as an abstraction. Mary of Nazareth, the mother of Jesus, is not a central figure in the gospel accounts because of her motherhood, but because she lives in accord with God's Word. This is evident in Mark's account of an encounter that at first glance appears to be a jibe at Jesus's own family:

> Then his mother and his brothers came and standing outside, they sent to him and called him. A crowd was sitting around him, and they said to him, "Your mother and your brothers and sisters are outside, asking for you. And he [Jesus] replied: "Who are my mother and my brothers?" And looking at those who sat around him, he said, "Here are my mother and my brothers. Whoever does the will of God is my brother and sister and mother." (Mark 3:31–35)

Mary, formed by the Torah, is a "doer of the Word," not merely a hearer, as the Letter of James would express it (James 1:22). The gospels portray her as a disciple, formed by walking in the Torah's pathway.

Envisioning Jesus as the "living Torah of God" challenges Christians to reorient their understanding of Judaism. To open new horizons on Judaism also reorients our understanding of Christianity.

**Jesus as Wisdom**

In the fourth and final week of the liturgical season of Advent that precedes the Christmas–Epiphany season, a verse composed in Latin is chanted or recited at Vespers (the evening Liturgy of Hours) prior to the recitation or chanting of the Magnificat (Luke 1:46–55), as is traditional at the close of Vespers. These seven verses, an inheritance from the medieval church of the sixth or seventh century, are known as the "O Antiphons." The first evokes Wisdom as the context in which we Christians understand Christ:

> *O Sapientia, quae ex ore Altissimi prodiisti, attingens a fine usque ad finem, fortiter suaviterque disponens omnia: veni ad docendum nos viam prudentiae.*
>
> O Wisdom of God, proceeding from the mouth of the Most High, from end to other end reaching with mighty strength, yet tenderly with loving care disposing all things: O come! Come to teach us and to guide us in the right way of Wisdom's path. (Dietz 2023, 375)

Similarly, despite its mischaracterization of Israel as a captive in mourning, the Advent hymn , "O Come, O Come Emmanuel," evokes Wisdom in its first stanza:

> O come, thou Wisdom from on high,
> who orders all things mightily;
> to us the path of knowledge show,
> And teach us in her ways to go.

These touchstones in Christian liturgical life evoke the way the earliest generations of Christ followers drew upon passages and motifs from the Wisdom literature of the Old Testament in Greek translation. Texts such as these offered images and vocabulary that enabled them to give voice to developing understandings of the meaning of Jesus Christ. Of particular importance was Wisdom (Greek, *sophia*; Latin, *sapientia*), as they saw Jesus as one who incarnated divine Wisdom. As disciples of Jesus, they were recipients of his wisdom (Wisdom of Solomon 6:17). Through his instruction they experienced one who was the "reflection of eternal light," "breath of the power of God" and "friend of God and prophet" (Wisdom of Solomon 7:25–27). As for his origins:

> I came forth from the mouth of the Most High ...
> Among all these I sought a resting place,
> in whose territory should I abide?
> Then the Creator of all things gave me a command,
> And my Creator chose this place for my tent,
> He said, "Make your dwelling in Jacob,
> and in Israel your inheritance."
>
> Before the ages, in the beginning he created me;
> and for all ages I shall not cease to be....
> Thus, in my beloved city he gave me a resting place,
> And in Jerusalem was my domain.
> (Sirach [Ecclesiasticus] 24:9, 11)

Wisdom invites:

> Come to me, you who desire me,
> And eat your fill of my fruits....
> Those who eat of me will hunger for more
> And those who drink of me will thirst
> for more. (Sirach 24:19, 21)

Wisdom is another way of expressing Torah:

> All this is the book of the covenant
> of the Most High God,
> The law [nomos/Torah) that Moses commanded us
> as an inheritance for the congregations
> of Jacob. (Sirach 24:23)

For Paul, Christ is the "power of God and the wisdom of God" (1 Corinthians 1:24), the one "through whom all things are and through whom we exist" (1 Corinthians 8:6). And in the tradition of Paul, the author of Colossians speaks of Christ as the "image of the invisible God, the firstborn of all creation, for in him were created all things.... For in him all the fullness of God was pleased to dwell" (Colossians 1:15–20).

### Reflection

Many years ago. I made a retreat focused on the Gospel of John led by someone deeply moved by its insights into Jesus. Yet there was no awareness about issues with the gospel's characterization of "the Jews." Somehow, despite the gospel's seventy-one occurrences of "the Jews," many depicting them as unbelieving opponents of Jesus, no mention was made of possible problems linked to their portrayal. It's difficult to believe the presenter didn't take note of at least some of the passages. Perhaps it was not knowing what to say. Or that the gospel's negative characterization of "the Jews" was seen as largely irrelevant in the present. Not many Christians know the history of antisemitism, nor do they see themselves as personally affected when an antisemitic act, screed, or demonstration takes place. It's not so different from the apathy that many of us who are white show toward racism; after all, it doesn't have a personal impact on our lives, or so we rationalize.

That general indifference toward antisemitism and its theological dimensions is evident in the church as well, including within Catholicism. That is not to deny the serious commitment in sectors of the Catholic world to continue what began at Vatican II with the promulgation of *Nostra Aetate*, but those efforts now seem overall to have too little visibility and influence. While many church authorities maintain courteous and cordial relations with Jewish leaders—a welcome contrast with much of the history between our traditions—beyond the polite exchanges I sense disinterest in addressing the troubling issues that lodge in many New Testament texts.

A recent example comes to mind. In 2024 The Australian Bishops Conference issued a statement, "Truth and Peace: A Gospel Word in a Violent World." Without question, the document has some exemplary insights. In addressing the prevalence of a "crisis of truth," it criticizes the role of misinformation and disinformation in many societies and calls for a "culture of dialogue" characterized by a "lively awareness of our relations" to one another. It points to the significance of Jesus as the Word (*logos*), as in John's prologue: "In the beginning was the Word, and the Word was with God, and the Word was God" (1:1). Jesus is not only the Word but also the Dialogue, the one who brings the "dialogue that began in the creation of the world to completion." Moreover, Jesus is both the "truth of God" and the "peace of God" beyond the "atrocities of Calvary, the dark mountain on which all the violence of the world and all its lies are gathered." The bishops continue,

> John 8:39–45 shows Jesus in heated exchange with those who will send him to the Cross, those who will choose the way of lethal violence. His opponents who will call for his death say to him: "Abraham is our father", to which Jesus replies, "If you were Abraham's children you would be doing what Abraham did. But now you seek to kill me, a man who has told you the truth that I heard from God. This is not what Abraham did. You are doing what your father did". They then say to him, "We have one father—God". To which Jesus replies, "If God were your father, you would love me, for I came from God. You are of your father, the devil, and your will is to do your father's will. He was a murderer from the beginning, not

holding to the truth, because there is no truth in him. When he lies, he speaks his native tongue, for he is a liar and the father of lies. But because I speak the truth, you do not believe me."

Following the citation from John, the writers suggest that this exchange epitomizes the "conflict between the divine truth to which Jesus gives witness" and "those who become murderers like the father of lies." Thus, they conclude, the "link between lying and death, untruth and violence, could hardly be clearer" (Australian Catholic Bishops Conference 2024, 16).

I applaud the bishops' call for Australians to become truth-seekers and peace-makers. Yet, the (mis)use of John 8:39–45 in support of their message is deeply disturbing, even if many readers were untroubled by its inclusion. I find it disheartening and unsettling that those involved in the writing and publication of this statement in 2024 of the Bishops Conference have failed to explicitly acknowledge that John 8:44 is one of the most notorious passages in the New Testament. It has been the principal text used to fuel accusations of the connection between Satan and Jews. It also furthers the "Christ killer" charge with phrases such as "those who will send him to the Cross, those who will choose the way of lethal violence." In John it is clear that it is indeed "the Jews" who are portrayed as "those who will call for his death." Even Catholics who know very little about the New Testament will think of Jews in this regard; they have only to recall the cries of "the Jews" in response to Pontius Pilate: "Away with him! Away with him! Crucify him" (John 19:15), proclaimed with great solemnity in the Good Friday passion account.

Or, perhaps someone at the Conference took note of the problems with using John 8 and decided to frame the passage in such a way that it obscures the identity of those Jesus is addressing. Yet it is evident from the full context in John 7 and 8 that "they" are "the Jews."

Whatever the circumstances behind the use of John 8 in their statement, it is symptomatic of a problem at the level of the church's episcopal leadership. At least in my experience in the United States, our bishops are generally approving of greater knowledge about Judaism and improved relations with Jews. They are opposed to antisemitism, yes. They are desirous of good preaching. But as for a deep understanding of theological antisemitism for which the church must be accountable or of a substantive critique of movements like Christian nationalism, there is little evidence of this at the level of the Bishops Conference itself. Of theological developments in interreligious relations more generally, I see far more wariness than involvement. The late Rabbi Leon Klenicki spoke with some frequency about many Christian encounters with Jews as consisting of "tea and sympathy." His observation, sadly, still rings true. I detect little investment in the US hierarchy, theologically or financially, in substantive engagement with scholarship on Judaism in its relation with Christianity, past and present. Nor do I sense that as a body the bishops are committed to promoting biblical scholarship at all levels of the church.

October 2025 marks the sixtieth anniversary of *Nostra Aetate*. Will its observance be limited to repeating its most important claims—or to investment in possibilities for continuing its development and implementation? The resources are substantial. In Chapter Six I will point to ways in which local leaders can teach and preach that draw from the wellsprings of recent scholarship. How we preach and teach texts about Jews is crucial to a church committed to justice.

Finally, a word about the way in which thinking about the first-century world of Jesus, the disciples, and the evangelists "within Judaism" holds implications for interreligious dialogue. In a recent column in the *New York Times*, "The Shock of Faith: It's Nothing I Thought It Would Be," the writer and commentator David Brooks tells the story of his gradual movement from agnosticism to a belief in God (Brooks 2024). A Jew, raised in a Jewish home, he describes his upbringing and earlier adult life as "religious but not spiritual." He kept a kosher home and sent his children to Jewish schools, but his "proximity" to religion did not lead to being a person of faith. Over the years, however, Brooks experienced transcendent moments that illumined life's meaning: being in the mountains, in Chartres Cathedral, even in a New York subway car where "I had this shimmering awareness that all the people in it had souls ... that gave them infinite value." Then, while hiking alone in the mountains of Colorado, he ventured upon a lake in a magnificent setting. Stopping to take in the stunning beauty and, being the bookish type, he pulled a volume of Puritan prayers from his backpack that included

> Let me learn by paradox the way down is the way up.
> That to be low is to be high.
> That the broken heart is the healed heart,
>    That the contrite spirit is the rejoicing spirit,
>    That the repenting soul is the victorious soul.

The logic of this prayer struck Brooks as "startling, revolutionary and astonishingly beautiful"; it was a "contact with radical goodness, that glimpse into the hidden reality of things," a realization of a moral order in the universe—approaching God without explicitly "encountering God." Looking back over the lengthy, gradual process of coming to faith, Brooks writes,

> Today, I feel more Jewish than ever, but as I once told some friends, I can't unread Matthew. For me, the Beatitudes are the part of the Bible where the celestial grandeur most dazzlingly shines through. So these days I'm enchanted by both Judaism and Christianity. I assent to the whole shebang. My Jewish friends, who

have been universally generous and forbearing, point out that when you believe in both the Old and New Testaments, you've crossed over to Team Christian, which is a fair point.

The journey Brooks describes is distinctively his own. Respecting the integrity of his account, it nevertheless seems to me that as a Jew he has no need to "unread Matthew." In fact, it may be that is why Matthew speaks to him *precisely as a Jew*. Of the four canonical gospels in the New Testament, Matthew's is the most recognizably "within Judaism." Matthias Konradt delineates four principal elements suggestive of Matthew's Jewish matrix: his portrayal of Jesus's Davidic ancestry, his extensive use of Israel's Scriptures, the centrality of the Torah for living ethically, and a view of the church as co-existing with Israel rather than as a substitution for it. Konradt also points to Matthean features that contributed to the gradual movement of a "gentile-Christian movement that increasingly defined itself through its distinction from Judaism" (Konradt 2024, 132).

So, with respect for Brooks's Jewish friends, finding the Beatitudes deeply meaningful and even being attracted to a Jewish Jesus whom he characterizes as a "total badass," does not necessitate Brooks becoming a Christian. That Brooks has found the teaching of Jesus to be *a* compelling way of being drawn to the Torah need not draw him away from Judaism. Both Jews and Christians may find the Gospel of Matthew speaks deeply to them—albeit in different ways. I, too, find Jesus's Torah teaching compelling. The difference is that I see Jesus as incarnating the Torah, of being "the living Torah of God" as I *have learned it through the life of the church*—that is, in the graced experiences of its community, both living and dead; in its Scriptures and interpretative traditions; in its sacramental life and powerful rituals; and in its legacy of teachings. To be sure, some of the church's doctrines as defined in the categories of the early centuries require reinterpretation and reformulation in our time. Not every experience of the church's sacramental-ritual life is uplifting. Its exclusion of women is deeply alienating, its misogyny scandalous. The riches of its Scriptures are too often hidden by superficial preaching and teaching. But it is in the messiness of the church's life—including in its interreligious commitments—that I experience Jesus's Torah teaching.

But that David Brooks and I, a Jew and a Christian in the Catholic tradition, would read Matthew in similar ways speaks to the potential of interreligious conversation in our respective readings of the New Testament "within Judaism." The New Testament is a capacious text over which both Jew and Christian—and other traditions—might (and in some cases do) converse and discover both deep commonalities and sharp differences. In my experiences, such conversations are encounters with the Divine in our midst.

# 6

# The Past Is a Foreign Country

## *A Guide for Traversing Its Terrain*

Often when I'm listening to a sermon, I'm mentally coaxing the preacher/homilist: "Open up what this means. Show us why it's important and suggest what we might take home to ponder and act on." Similarly, over the years I've given many workshops for teachers who understandably expect they will learn something they can take with them to their own classrooms. Their expectation heightens my preparation and increases just enough anxiety to produce a shot of new energy.

Now it's the reader's turn to say the same: "What might we take with us for our own consideration? How will what you've written make a real difference in my teaching or preaching?" Those who are simply interested in learning more about their religious tradition likely come with an analogous question: "So what? What difference will the knowledge conveyed in these pages make to the ways I interpret and live the Scriptures?"

In short, what implications for the present might be derived from thinking differently about Christian origins in relation to Judaism? What might we ponder further and act on?

I begin with some more general reflections. The first explores the significance of committing to a deepened understanding of Christianity's relation to Judaism—and of Christians' relation to Jews. The second focuses on study of

Scripture in our time, and on the complexities of the lectionary in forming our impression of Judaism, emphasizing the particular challenge of the lectionary in the Roman Catholic tradition. I then turn to more specific considerations, typically but not exclusively formulated in terms of recommendations, including suggested resources—not an exhaustive list, but some essential texts that provide reliable, valuable information in a time when our world is awash with misinformation and disinformation even in the religious sphere.

### The Importance of Christianity's Relation to Judaism— and of Christians' Relations with Jews

#### Christian Origins

However obvious it may be, it needs to be said repeatedly: We cannot understand Christianity without reference to Judaism. Traditionally, this has involved pointing to Judaism as the predecessor to Christianity, as the tradition into which Jesus was born, as the "root" of Christianity. Each of these has a certain truth, but those formulations are misleading because they typically rest on the assumption that Christianity "fulfills" Judaism: Judaism was the promise to which Jesus and the church are the fulfillment. This leaves the impression that Judaism is a religion of the past, superseded by Christianity. What the church has unintentionally communicated is that Judaism is in effect obsolete—an artifact of the past.

To the contrary. As Chapters Four and Five establish, Judaism was and is a resilient tradition, reorienting and reinventing itself in the face of defeat and diminishment. It developed a dynamic tradition of commentary on Torah not only in extensive texts but in rituals, spirituality, music, and the arts across many cultures. The commentary tradition in the present includes podcasts, videos, and online publications. The website Sefaria: A Living Library of Torah (https://www.

sefaria.org/texts) offers an extensive, reader-friendly open-source library of Jewish texts and interpretations in Hebrew and English translation.

Scholarly sources make clear that the church has failed over the centuries to communicate Judaism as it is. Rather, it has largely relied on earlier constructions from the second through fourth centuries reflecting a period when Christian identity formation seemed to necessitate presenting Judaism as its inferior antecedent. Given the knowledge that provides a far more accurate portrayal of Jewish life in the past, we are obliged to tell that account as truthfully as possible. This is not simply because the church has passed on an inadequate perspective on Judaism but because its "oppositional imagination" developed in ways that led to real harm to Jewish communities over the course of many centuries.

This is a truth that makes many Christians uncomfortable. It should.

None of us, whether as individuals or as members of a society or tradition, welcomes learning about the moral failures of our ancestors, as the current struggles of this country to face its racial history illustrate. The difficulty notwithstanding, the church is obliged to be truthful about its less-than-edifying history. "The Church is not afraid of history," Pope Francis remarked on the occasion of the opening of the Vatican's archives for the period of 1939–1958 (i.e., during the papacy of Pope Pius XII). But he seemed to be speaking of an aspiration of the contemporary church rather than the reality of the church of the past—even the recent past—that has too readily taken refuge in rationalizations. Moving beyond "tea and sympathy" remains a major challenge in our time, namely, to welcome what we learn from history, despite the vulnerability it involves.

A church that speaks more truthfully about its relationship with Judaism in the past and commits to honor how Jews themselves understand their tradition in all its diversity has something to say to our world in which religious difference continues to be divisive. And speaking as a Catholic, if our church were to be more transparent in its obligation to do justice to its relation to Jews, then it might model how to relate to other traditions as well. How the church uses its power and resources is a vital dimension of its commitment to justice.

**Scripture**

We live in a time when unparalleled resources for the study of Scripture are available. Some studies are highly technical and difficult to follow. But even more important than exegesis of texts is a firm grasp of the interpretive process. I often wonder about principles of interpretation in homilies in Catholic liturgies. I am aware that most seminaries in the United States have well-educated biblical scholars on their faculties who are learned in the historical, literary, and sociocultural contexts of texts. So how is it that so many of their former students interpret the gospel accounts in a way that seems to assume what the gospel accounts say accords completely with what happened? Typically, the homily seems to rest on the assumption that there are few, if any, differences between and among the gospel accounts, that Jesus and his disciples were Christians, that the church was "born" on Pentecost—or even, as I heard a few years ago, that "Jesus founded a new religion." I was so startled by this assertion, repeated a second time for emphasis, that I looked around to see how others reacted. No discernible response. Or, as I mentioned in the second chapter on the Pharisees, preachers often emphasize their negative portrayal in the gospels despite the abundant scholarship that offers a far different view. It's not just the preachers. I have a quite good sense of what my New Testament colleagues emphasize in their courses, but when I hear their students preach, they too often fall into the tired, old stereotypes, such as the oppressive purity laws of Judaism and their patriarchal oppression of women. Protestants and Catholics alike fall prey to stereotypes of Jews in the New Testament.

My intuition suggests that many preachers know that the interpretations they are presenting to a congregation don't accord with what they were taught. But to do differently brings risks. Will people think the Bible isn't true if a homilist suggests it is not factual in the modern sense of history? Will protest ensue? So, it's safer to stay with the tried—even if it's not accurate. But at least it won't upset people. And in many churches there are few educational opportunities these days that would provide a fuller understanding.

If this is indeed the case, I can sympathize. After all, teaching necessarily involves dealing with disequilibrium, revealing the problems of faulty conceptualizations and one-dimensional assumptions in order to offer more adequate knowledge. So, in preparing to teach in such a situation, it is necessary to anticipate discomfort or objections and to design class sessions that allow time to process the reasoning and to offer more substantive understandings. In our present polarized nation, the pedagogical challenge of presenting ideas contrary to certain assumptions has become freighted with conflict. Witness the verbally violent sparring at school board meetings, the conflict between librarians and those who wish to censor a library's holdings, the tension between a teacher's grasp of complexities and that of some parental groups who object. Or the tension of some parental groups mindful of complexities objecting to a teacher's shallow presentation of an issue.

Yet my experience in teaching in theological settings has been different. Granted, my work has principally been in private higher education. As I have included new modes in interpreting Scripture in my work, I've seldom had anyone object, neither in the classroom nor in settings in the churches nor in more public forums. My experience has been more to the contrary—primarily because the new understanding seems to offer perspectives on the text that *allow it to come alive in new ways*. Perhaps this is in part related to my own belief that the perspective I'm presenting has potential for awakening a fresh view of an ancient text, even if in the end it may not prove quite as insightful as it might seem. When a teacher—or a preacher—believes there's real potential in looking at a text (or film, painting, etc.) from a different angle, that conveys a crucial element in learning: energy.

Teaching and preaching, although different in important respects, seem to have two crucial aims in common: to awaken and to edify. Providing new lenses on an issue or event arouses interest. Replacing conventional approaches with more creative ones as appropriate stimulates more interest. Showing that one's own understanding is enhanced by the new idea or approach similarly stirs interest.

"Edify," I have learned from the *Online Etymological Dictionary* (https://www.etymonline.com/word/edify) is no longer a trendy word—likely, I surmise, because of its moralistic connotation as synonymous with sanctimony or a smug piety. The term, however, denotes a stronger reality of building or constructing. For a teacher or preacher, what better goal than to build up, to help someone construct knowledge by offering some key fact, concept or viewpoint? To "edify" comes from the Old French *edefiier*, which in turn originates in the Latin *aedificare*, "to build, construct." As theologians, teachers, and preachers, we contribute to people engaged in constructing their understanding of faith—even as we continue building our own. We do so in order that the practice of this faith might contribute to constructing a world more reflective of its just and merciful Creator. And the etymological dictionary also says that in Late Latin (developed in the third to sixth centuries), *edify* apparently took on the connotation of "improve spiritually." That certainly seems a worthy goal, as long as one doesn't confuse spirituality with sanctimony.

So, a few comments with preachers particularly in mind. First and foremost, preaching has a crucial role to play in worship. I often feel that homilists are insufficiently aware that they have a privileged opportunity to say something that matters to people's lives. It's a teachable moment too easily squandered by poorly prepared sermons. In many cases, it's the only time that a congregant, often largely unfamiliar with the Bible, has an opportunity to gain an insight from the readings. When homilists offer merely a passing glance at the texts on the way to saying something bland, the congregant often tunes out because the sacred text that has just been proclaimed seems disconnected with life. Congregants are neither awakened nor edified.

Not every homilist is verbally gifted or as knowledgeable as desired. But when preachers show they've *worked at discovering meanings* they are eager to share, most congregants will be attentive. That requires a commitment of time and the use of reliable resources on a regular basis and a determination to say something the homilist has thought about and finds meaningful. Clergy often must rearrange their schedules in the face of a congregant's crisis, so some leeway needs to be built in to allow for contingencies. There is no substitute for study—preferably with a study partner or study group. When a preacher seems unprepared, that sends a message about their disinterest in Scripture and in the lives of their congregants.

It's necessary to think ahead of time when a presentation or homily will be offering facts and/or concepts that complicate or clash with traditional understandings. So, consideration of the congregation's prior knowledge can be useful. What views might people be holding that potentially complicate learning a new fact or concept? If, in preparing to preach, new information seems significant but is still not firmly grasped, it is wise to seek help from someone who might serve as a reliable resource and sounding board. A new understanding typically requires work in formulating; when left to improvisation, it generally will not be the Spirit speaking. And if the homilist doesn't feel ready to tackle a new insight-not-quite-fully-formed, it's better to pause for another opportunity to come along. But with a new insight forming, it would be a contradiction to repeat a worn-out, misleading understanding. Suggest that the text has layers of meaning still to be explored. People will be grateful to know that homilists can admit that the Scriptures have depths still to be explored. And that some texts are puzzling! After all, remember that the writer of the Letter of Second Peter admitted he found the Apostle Paul confounding: "So also our beloved brother Paul wrote to you according to the wisdom given to him, speaking of this as he does in all his letters. There are some things in them hard to understand" (2 Peter 3:15b–16a). If a biblical author could frankly confess he didn't grasp all of what Paul meant, then preachers might similarly admit that some texts don't reveal their meanings easily.

### The Lectionary

I belong to a church for which the lectionary is an essential component of liturgical life. It has many advantages, particularly because it offers an array of biblical texts for reflection and commentary. It challenges those who preach to work with a variety of texts rather than self-selecting passages they might prefer to speak on. It complements the liturgical seasons, linking season with sacred texts. Many church traditions throughout the world use a lectionary, that is, biblical texts specified to be proclaimed as part of a cycle of readings during worship. Here I will work principally with the Catholic Lectionary for the Mass for Dioceses of the United States for Sundays, since it serves as a case-in-point of the lingering perspective on the relation of the Old Testament to the New that is a legacy of the early church.

This lectionary originated out of the vision of Vatican II: "Access to sacred scripture ought to be widely available to the Christian faithful" (*Dei Verbum* [Constitution on Divine Revelation], no. 22; Flannery 2014, 110). Prior to this Council, readings at Mass consisted of excerpts from the New Testament's letters and from the four gospels, proclaimed in Latin while congregants followed translations in their missals. The Old Testament simply did not figure in readings before the advent of the lectionary. The current lectionary first appeared in 1969 as the work of a commission of liturgical and biblical scholars. Some relatively minor edits have been done since 1969, but the overall organization of texts has remained essentially the same. The Sunday readings are organized in a three-year cycle, each emphasizing one of the synoptic gospels: Year A, Matthew; Year B, Mark; and Year C, Luke. The Gospel of John appears periodically on various occasions, especially in Lent and Holy Week as well as the Sundays after Easter.

In many respects, the lectionary has advanced biblical literacy and implicitly required those who preach to respond to a wide swath of biblical texts rather than taking comfort in familiar inspiring passages. Yet, for all its contribution to enhancing the role of the Bible in Catholic liturgical life, its lectionary requires a comprehensive revision of its selection of texts if it is to do justice to the complex relationship between the testaments and, ultimately, to the church's relation with Judaism. As presently arranged, it does not do justice to the complex relationship between Old and New Testaments. (As to the inclusion of women, one would hardly know they played any role, with the exception of Mary of Nazareth. But this is a topic for another occasion.)

The lectionary, however valuable, complicates comprehension of biblical books. Unless congregants have a sense of the narrative arc of the Scriptures, it is particularly difficult to gain a sense of the "big picture" of the Old Testament. What story is Genesis telling? How do its stories relate to those of the Exodus or the oracles of the Prophet Ezekiel—or to the letters of the Apostle Paul? In my experience, very few of even regular churchgoers have a grasp of the major events and narratives that constitute the Bible, an anthology of books whose principle of coherence is far from obvious. Lacking a sense of the overall structure and emphases, let alone key interpretative principles, most people understandably are somewhat mystified by the lectionary, though they are often intrigued by particular texts.

In one sense the Catholic lectionary is organized in such a way as to help people recognize the connections between the Testaments. According to the section Liturgy (https://www.usccb.org/offices/new-american-bible/liturgy) on the website of the United States Conference of Catholic Bishops (USCCB), the first reading (of the three Sunday lections) is "usually from the Old Testament [and it] reflects important themes from the Gospel reading." In other words, the gospel text determines the reading from the Old Testament. The commission of scholars who assembled the pattern of readings for the lectionary considered it important for the readings to emphasize the unity of the Old and New Testaments, thus bringing out God's "plan" of salvation. On a number of occasions, this works by way of comparison and contrast: the first reading reveals an inadequate understanding that the gospel selection in essence corrects. In establishing this contrast—the inadequacy of Israel now rectified by the ministry of Jesus—the legacy of the early church writers who saw the Old Testament as the inferior promise of salvation to that fulfilled by Jesus the Savior—is reinforced. Further, most homilists in my experience accentuate its inferiority by referring briefly—if at all—to the Old Testament reading. Ignoring or merely mentioning the Old Testament in passing in essence teaches people it's not important. And by seldom, if at all, referring to the role those Scriptures play in Judaism and its rich interpretative traditions, the impression is given that Judaism is an obsolete religion—of historical significance to Christianity but a homogeneous religion of the past.

Michael Peppard offers a fine critique of the present arrangement of Old Testament texts in the lectionary. Perhaps most significantly, he finds the lectionary's depiction of the God of Israel to be inadequate and misleading: "With limited examples of God's acting through law or narrative history, the Old Testament lections lead the listener to believe that God's primary activity in the ancient past was to predict an ancient future, namely to prepare for the coming of Jesus" (Peppard 2024, 63). In so doing, the lectionary propagates stereotypes of Judaism and fails to emphasize that the Old Testament is a book we share with Jews, albeit with some differences in canonical books and in the overall order of books.

There is another difficulty in my view: Because the lectionary ranges widely over the Scriptures in seeking texts corresponding to the liturgical seasons, the narrative of the biblical books is easily lost. One week it may be Genesis, then the next week Deuteronomy, and another week Isaiah. This leaves many a hearer wandering in the wilderness of incomprehension. Because the liturgical season is more determinative of what biblical texts are chosen, when the gospel texts of Matthew, for example, are being read each Sunday, a particular feast may interrupt the continuity. I understand the reasoning, but am aware of how it interrupts a congregant's sense of the gospel's overall narrative. For the vast majority of congregants whose sense of Scripture is largely inchoate, it is difficult to "get" the Bible through the lectionary's lens. This is all the more reason for the church to redouble its commitment to making the Bible "more widely accessible to the Christian faithful" by giving far more emphasis to biblical study. Widening accessibility means prioritizing the teaching of Scripture, which parishes need to provide and support on a regular basis, and dioceses need to subsidize financially.

My hope is that those who preach and teach the Old Testament will deepen their own relationship with its richness and complexity so as to compensate for the lectionary's lacks.

### A Religious Critic of the Bible: Approaching the Scriptures with a Critical Eye

Those whose professions necessitate their presentation of Scriptures to others need to be clear why they are doing so. Dutiful expositions of biblical texts are deadening. They also mislead by implying these texts no longer say something vital. To preach or teach a biblical text means to be engaged with it—to be seeking its meanings and to communicate its aliveness.

Having the privilege of drawing from the Bible's wells in my own work and personal life, I wish to make explicit the concepts and methods foundational to my interpretation of the Bible, a perspective I share in large part with many other scholars. I approach the Bible to discern—from the Greek *krinein,* "to judge, distinguish"—meanings of texts that Christianity, as I understand it, holds sacred. Playing on that Greek verb, I am a religious *critic* of the Bible. A "critic" in this sense emphasizes the art of discerning meaning, not as delivering a negative judgment. A critic respects a biblical text in its situatedness—in the particularities of its time, place, events, and persons from whom the writings came and how they have been understood over the ages. Just as a food critic needs a love of food and a broad knowledge of various foods, their chemical make-up, etc., so one who approaches the Bible critically requires love for its wisdom and knowledge as expressed in its religious, historical, literary, and cultural backgrounds.

To be a critic is requisite because its texts, primarily composed in ancient Hebrew and Greek, originated in ages and cultures long past. This means we moderns are always entering the foreign land of the past, and so we must enter as strangers taking care to let the past speak on its own terms. Uncritical, fundamentalist interpretations, no matter how sincere, fail to take the originating contexts seriously. Fundamentalist readings can and often do have adverse consequences. Consider, for example, the fate of those whom societies executed as witches in obedience to the scriptural imperative "You shall not permit a female sorcerer to live" (Exodus 22:18). Or consider the effects on women in abusive marriages who are counseled to remain in their relationship out of fidelity to the biblical command: "Just as the church is subject to Christ, so also wives ought to be, in everything, to their husbands" (Ephesians 5:24). And history is replete with evidence that Jews as a people suffered many tragedies because Christians concluded from certain New Testament texts (e.g., John 19:6–7; Matthew 27:25; 1 Thessalonians 2:14–16) that Jews were "Christ killers."

Scripture is replete with problematic passages. Writer and Presbyterian minister Frederick Buechner (1926–2022) wryly characterized the Bible as "a disorderly collection of books which are often tedious, barbaric, obscure and teem with contradictions and inconsistencies." It's a "swarming compost of a book, an Irish stew of poetry and propaganda, law and legalism, myth and murk, history and hysteria ... hopelessly associated with tub-thumping evangelism and dreary piety, superannuated superstition and blue-nosed moralizing; with ecclesiastical authoritarianism and crippling literalism" (Buechner 2004, 43).

But there's more, because Buechner saw the Bible as encompassing the sublime as well as the unspeakable, and in its seeming disorderliness we glimpse life as it really is—and of God's engagement with humans who are flawed yet graced. It witnesses to the divine presence, yet that presence is an elusive one (Terrien1978). Buechner's droll description highlights the Bible's inclusion of customs and beliefs strange to modern ears as well as the ways in which peoples in many times and places have used their understanding of texts to judge others—or even to justify violence against them. The past may be foreign territory, but many are heedless; they are strangers, mindless tourists trampling through territory dense with culture, history, religious constructs, and literary forms. So, to be a critic necessitates respecting the complexity of texts in their contexts, involving study under knowledgeable mentors and participation in the community of scholars. To situate texts contextually entails using analytic tools framed under the broad category of "historical-critical methods."

Yet I am also a critic who is a member of a Christian religious tradition—Roman Catholicism—and who thus looks to the Bible as a source of divine wisdom and inspiration. God "speaks" through the medium of Scripture, among other modes through which we come to understand who we are called to be by the Holy One who created us and whose presence surrounds us in ways we cannot fully comprehend. But God's "voice"—so magnificently depicted in Elijah's encounter on Mount Horeb in 1 Kings 19:12 as the "sound of sheer silence"—can appropriately be conveyed only in poetic terms. Divine utterances transcend human understanding yet can only be conveyed in human language. In the formal language of Catholic teaching, the Scriptures "express in human words bearing the stamp of their time the historical revelation communicated by God in various ways" (*The Interpretation of the Bible in the Church 1993*).

Recent Catholic statements on biblical interpretation offer a significant formulation: the Bible is the *word of God in human language*. This ostensibly simple formulation implies the necessity of situating biblical texts in the context of their history and culture:

> The historical-critical method is the indispensable method for the scientific study of the meaning of ancient texts. Holy Scripture, inasmuch as it is the "word of God in human language," has been composed by human

authors in all its various parts and in all the sources that lie behind them. Because of this, its proper understanding not only admits the use of this method but actually requires it. (*Interpretation,* 1993, IA)

The implications are profound. Human language encompasses far more than merely a particular linguistic system such as Hebrew or Greek, although their distinctiveness and complexity are vital for comprehension. "Human" language implies the finitude of our creaturely condition, including the limitations of each perspective; the distortions, biases, and complicity in evil that characterize the human condition, the varied literary devices and genres of languages, and the historical and cultural contexts in which language is embedded. God's word does not float down ethereally from the heavens but is incarnate in and through the human experience. Its meanings must be discerned amidst the quotidian realities of existence.

So as a critic, I am searching for what those human words conveyed in their time and place, and how those words relate to other human words in that extensive and diverse anthology we call the Bible. As a religious critic, I am discerning what those words might mean for life in our world today, seeking to fathom the "ineffable God" whom Elizabeth Johnson, drawing on Karl Rahner, speaks of as "incomprehensible holy mystery" who calls forth and sustains the human spirit (Johnson 2007, 37). This is the God Moses encounters at the burning bush and on Sinai when God's goodness passes in front of him: "And so when My glory passes over, I shall put you in the cleft of the crag and shield you with My palm until I have passed over. And I shall take away My palm and you will see my back, but My face will not be seen" (Exodus 33:21–33; Alter 2019 translation). This is the God Jesus experiences at the Jordan River and in Gethsemane, the God of Paul's encounter on the road to Damascus.

The Bible we study is a human document through which we discern God's desires for creation, composed in particular times and places by persons and communities with particular experiences, perspectives, and beliefs. Those who composed, edited, and chronicled their communities' experiences had only a partial vision, distorted by their narrow-mindedness and prejudices, impaired by sin and self-interest, and subject to the constraints of their culture. So, too, is our own vision limited, constricted by finitude and the ease with which we also get drawn into evil, whether by our actions or failures to act. In the Bible the religious critic also becomes the subject of criticism, seeing oneself through the gaze of "*'Ehyeh-'Asher-'Ehyeh*, I-Will-Be-Who-I-Will-Be" (Exodus 3:14; Alter 2019 translation).

### The Bible as Scripture

Although most persons equate the Bible and Scripture, the two are distinct. Scripture is the more comprehensive term, denoting works that various religious peoples regard as mediating the sacred, as facilitating access to transcendent truths that offer meaning and depth to human existence. We might say that religious traditions "scripturalize," that is, they recognize a depth dimension latent in their community's texts that calls them to transformation; not every Scripture, however, is written, particularly in traditions in the East. *The sacredness lies not in the texts themselves as in the human process of seeking to plumb the mystery, the "more than" of life.* So, a text becomes Scripture when a community regards it as powerful and authoritative, as a privileged witness to divine self-disclosure (Graham 2005, 8195; Green 2006, 82). What Scripture proffers, Wilfred Cantwell Smith wrote in his classic *What Is Scripture?*, is "transcendent truth. The words that we read are 'deep in mystery,' and present us with a mystery that we must struggle to explain" (Smith 1995, 32).

*The Past Is a Foreign Country* 209

Both Jews and Christians share certain texts that constitute much of the Bible (Greek *ta biblia*, "the books") but our two traditions do not share the same Scripture. A word of explanation is necessary, particularly because most Christians assume Judaism is the religion of the "Old" Testament. Jews, writes poet Marge Piercy, are people of the book "traveling with our words sewn in our clothes/and carried on our backs" (Piercy 2007, 134). But the book Jews travel with is not the Old Testament, which in Christian Bibles precedes the New Testament. Rather, it is an anthology of twenty-four books in Hebrew (with a few Aramaic passages) ordered in tripartite fashion (*Tanakh*: Torah, Prophets, and Writings) and understood in distinctive ways. Many Christians are aware that we share this collection of books in large measure (Boys 2024b) but lack understanding of the extent and profundity of Jewish interpretation in both rabbinic and historical–critical traditions.

### The Bible's Old and New Testaments

The Old Testament is a distinctly Christian designation for a vast anthology of texts constituting Israel's sacred history. Its texts—written in Hebrew (with some use of Aramaic in later books)—are shared with Jews, although there are differences in the ordering of books and, in the case of the Roman Catholic and Orthodox churches, in the number of books included. For Jews the texts are not termed the "Old" Testament but *Tanakh* that constitute the Jewish Bible. The capacious term *Torah* may also refer to the writings of the Jewish Bible.

The New Testament consists of a canon of twenty-seven books written in Greek that Christians hold sacred. Together with the Old Testament, it forms the Christian Bible. Yet, although today we naturally think of the New Testament as the normative anthology of Christian sacred texts, *its origins and development lie within Judaism*. The events recounted and the issues addressed come from a Jewish world; its ways of interpreting earlier texts, its principal concerns, teachings, and arguments arose out of Jewish life in the Roman Empire. Jesus and the earliest generations of disciples were Jews who typically and primarily interacted with other Jews. Interpreting the New Testament requires situating its writings in the complex of diverse Jewish texts, teachings, practices, and rituals. Thus, the significance of the recent publication of *The Jewish Annotated New Testament*; a third edition is in press, with publication anticipated for November 2025.

Both Jews and Christians have extensive traditions of biblical interpretations; in many instances, Jews and Christian scholars share methods of interpretation, even as they also draw upon modes of commentary characteristic of their respective communities. One of the blessings of contemporary scholarship is the collaborative work done by Jewish and Christian biblical scholars.

### Judaism and Christianity in Relation

Because the temptation of anachronism is ever present, most Christians assume that Judaism and Christianity were related in the past much as they are today as two different religions. As a consequence, there is a general lack of knowledge about the lengthy and contentious process of differentiation by which Rabbinic Judaism and Christianity took on largely separate identities with distinctive institutional structures, beliefs, and practices. What must be stressed, however, is that Jewish life of the early centuries of the Common Era was the matrix—the womb—within which Christianity developed. And not just Judaism in general, but Early Judaism with its crises and its complexities. To take Jesus's Jewish identity seriously means seeking the particulars of Jewish life of his time. It also involves situating the evangelists within their worlds, likely forty to sixty years after Jesus. When, for example, Matthew portrays Jesus criticizing Pharisees, he is most likely depicting a debate about Torah among Jews, some of whom had become Christ followers. When Paul tells the Galatians (3:1) they are "foolish" for seeking circumcision or keeping the dietary laws, he does so as a Christ-following Jew telling Gentiles that such observances are for Jews; Gentiles are called to live their faith differently.

To read the New Testament in our time involves a radical change. For centuries, Christians approached it in ways that portrayed Jesus as the critic of Judaism par excellence. Now, however, largely because of the breadth and depth of biblical scholarship, we are able to situate Jesus in his Jewish world of the first centuries of the Common Era. Making the Jewish Jesus come alive for congregations and students is the privilege and obligation of those who preach and teach. The more we learn about Jesus in his Jewish life, the more we begin to understand his humanity and the radical significance of the Incarnation.

One effective way to emphasize the emergence of Christianity within Judaism is to allow Jesus and his early generations of disciples to be Jews, not Christians. It is more accurate to speak of those early disciples, certainly including Paul, as Christ followers rather than as Christians, since there was as yet no institutional entity "Christianity." It should be made clear that borders were fluid, even after the Council of Nicaea. The process by which Christianity differentiated from Judaism was lengthy and complicated.

Appreciating that the New Testament arose within Early Judaism also involves explicit acknowledgment that the anthology of books Christians term the "Old Testament" is complex and profound. Far more than a mere forerunner to the New Testament, the Old Testament offers compelling, captivating, and complicated stories of a people's journey into a relationship with an ineffable God. It's imperative that Christian teachers and homilists discover the Old Testament anew, and learn of the vital tradition of commentary and intense observance of festivals, which animates Jewish life. Judaism originated in antiquity, has a complex history, and continues in ever new ways far beyond its simplistic depiction as the mere "root" of Christianity.

## Texts Too Easily Used to Disparage Judaism

### The "Jews" in John's Gospel

It is important that Christians *notice* the ways in which the fourth gospel's use of "the Jews" functions to characterize them as people of bad faith who oppose Jesus. This negative valence is particularly evident when passages are proclaimed in the liturgical context, concluding with the affirmation, "The Gospel of the Lord." Yet I have never heard a homilist in a parish context sufficiently explain John's use of his frequently used term "the Jews." Even as I write this, I'm shocked by the omission of important scholarship.

On a historical level, the negative resonances of "the Jews" most likely arose out of conflicts within Judaism (see the discussion in Chapter Five). This explanation, while helpful, does not go far enough. That Jews in the late first century might have engaged in derogatory characterization of other Jews can easily be grasped. People in the churches should have no problem understanding how rancorous, even malicious, intramural denunciation can be—it's an all-too-common and destructive trait of humankind. What also needs explanation is the long history of John's Gospel being used to demonize Jews as "perfidious" and as "Christ-killers." This is a "teachable moment" for congregants and students to learn both how over the centuries the church's disparagement of "the Jews" helped to fuel antisemitism and how churches today are committed to healing the wounds they caused by their misuse of the gospel. Even in our time, John's term, "the

Jews," should not be proclaimed without explanation. Antisemitism is resurgent and the church has a responsibility to counter it.

The fourth gospel's prologue is also a wonderful source of understanding ways in which the wisdom tradition of the Old Testament became a way of meditating on Jesus, the *Logos*.

### Judas

Judas, one of the Twelve whom Jesus called, is one of the most maligned figures in history, regarded as "the one who betrayed Jesus" in Mark, Matthew, and John, and as the "traitor" in Luke. Mark has a relatively sparse account in comparison with later gospel texts. Matthew adds memorable details: the thirty pieces of silver, the "blood money" associated with his infamous depiction of the assembled crowd crying out "His blood be upon us and on our children" (27:25). Matthew has Judas dying by suicide whereas Luke's more grisly account in Acts of the Apostles (1:15–20) depicts Judas dying in a fall so terrible that he splits open, his bowels gushing out. Luke (22:3–4), and John (13:2) both associate him with Satan or the devil. In short, for the evangelists, Judas is a shadowy figure, a thief according to John (12:5–6). Judas is remembered as the one who betrayed Jesus, yet less so Peter who betrays Jesus three times (John 18).

Meager reliable historical information exists about Judas. Nature abhorring a vacuum, it may well be the case that this lack allowed memorable additions about Jesus's arrest to heighten the tragedy of his passion and death. There is also ambiguity about the meaning of the Greek verb *paradidomai* describing how the authorities captured Jesus. The verb may mean simply "handed over" or it can mean "betrayed." There is quite a difference. So was Judas simply one of those forced to hand Jesus over, or did he betray Jesus to the authorities? We will never know. What is little acknowledged, and deserves to be widely known, is that Judas—the only one of the Twelve whose name evokes Judaism—became synonymous with Jewish perfidy. This occurred, even though Peter famously betrayed Jesus three times. And the name Judas is the only one among the Twelve that clearly links to a Jewish identity, though all of the Twelve are Jewish. The move from Judas as a figure in the passion accounts to the demonizing of Jews has had—and continues to have—tragic consequences for Jews. Whatever the history behind Judas, no generalizations associating Jews with evil can be justified. So also the association of Judas with alleged Jewish attraction to money.

### Purity Laws

One of the curiosities for modern readers of the Bible is the attention given to codes of purity, such as those found at length in Leviticus and Numbers. Numerous New Testament stories include references to, for example, the impurity of corpses; of those with scabrous diseases (e.g., "leprosy"); and with bodily emissions (especially of blood). Norms about purity involved both the moral and ritual spheres. The former concerned the polluting nature of sin and ways in which sin defiled persons. Ritual purity was related to actions, especially states of contagion that could be incurred involuntarily through bodily functions. Both were connected to Israel's sacrificial system, but it is ritual purity that is the focus here because modern Christians have misinterpreted this latter category in ways that disparage Judaism.

Purity laws are relevant here primarily because the default interpretation many Christians offer is one of contrast: Jews had these strange laws about purity that exemplified the outmoded legalism that Jesus abolished. This mode of interpretation, I regret to say, has also fueled certain feminist and womanist readings of Scripture, including the memorable story about the woman with the unceasing hemorrhage (Mark 5:24–34). Her impurity by virtue of her flow of blood had in effect made her an outcast in her community. In some modern perspectives, she becomes a symbol of women's oppression—punished for the particularities of her body—and Jesus is portrayed as the one who abrogated such unjust laws. Biblical scholars have decisively critiqued such perspectives, but they continue nonetheless, especially in popular and pastoral readings. What follows is a brief word about two of the well-known gospel stories concerning purity that also appear in the lectionary (Schuller 2013). It concludes with some observations about how Christians might more accurately speak about this particular aspect of Judaism in antiquity.

Judaism's putative legalism in its norms of pure/impure along with the dominance of patriarchy seems to provide a handy contrast with Christianity—but it is an erroneous one. Judaism of antiquity was indeed patriarchal, as were all cultures then. To indict Judaism for patriarchy without pointing to its pervasiveness in antiquity reflects the all-too-familiar tendency to set Judaism in opposition to Christianity. Add to that the tale of a woman seemingly condemned by her community as impure because of a flow of blood, the stage is set for the entrance of the liberating Jesus. In many interpretations he represents Christianity's freedom in contrast to Jewish legalism. But Leviticus 15 speaks of the impurity of both male and female emissions—and provides remedies for the restoration of purity (see Leviticus 15:13–32). Mark's story, however, centers not on impurity but on the healing of a woman in ill-health (Haber 2003, 171–92). That the persistent flow of blood had also made her impure is part of the story because it explained her reluctance to approach Jesus directly. Yet, believing in God's power in Jesus, her faith empowered her daring touch of his garment and then her approach to Jesus "in fear and trembling" (Mark 5:33). Medicine had not helped this woman, but through Jesus the power of God had healed her.

Jesus's encounters with "lepers" offer even more familiar passages regarding purity laws. Luke's Gospel recounts two such encounters, 5:12–15 (a "man covered with leprosy," with parallels in Matthew 8:1–4 and Mark 1:40–45) and 17:11–19, in which Jesus healed ten lepers. Leviticus 13–14 and Numbers 12:9–15 provide the legal backdrop of how the community should deal with persons afflicted with scabrous diseases, which in fact were not leprosy in the modern sense (Hansen's Disease) but a broad category called in Hebrew *tzara'at*, a term for various kinds of scaly skin eruptions. As with the hemorrhaging woman, those afflicted with such skin eruptions were impure; in their case, the afflicted were to be sent to the priest, since among the priestly roles in Israel was helping persons move from an impure state to a pure one. Notably, in Luke's first account, Jesus cleanses the "leper" and instructs him: "Go and show yourself to the priest, and as Moses commanded, make an offering for your cleansing for a testimony to them" (Luke 5:14). That is, Jesus here follows Leviticus 13. Hardly a Jesus who abrogates the purity codes.

So, then, some general observations about how to frame the purity laws. First, purity codes require viewing through an anthropological lens. However strange they may seem to moderns, purity concerns were widespread in antique cultures, not simply in Judaism. Understanding them in the twenty-first century requires us to be mindful of L. P. Hartley's dictum: "The past is a foreign country; they do things differently there." Israel's particular laws were a reminder of God's holiness, of God's otherness. Second, in view of the numerous ways in which impurity could be incurred, most people were frequently in an impure state—for which there were simple remedies, principally purification by means of water, observing some sort of interval from community life, and often also by sacrificial offerings. Being impure precluded entrance to the Temple, but then most people lived far from this holy site in Jerusalem.

The various purifications involving washing account for the relatively numerous *mikvaot* (*mikvah*, sing.; pools for ritual cleansing) archaeological expeditions have found in ancient Israel. Third, it would appear that Jesus took purity rules for granted as a part of everyday life in faithfulness to the God of Israel. Fourth, the purity laws affected everyone: "The fussiest Pharisee, the highest high priest, would be neither more nor less impure after sexual intercourse than the scruffiest Galilean fisherman" (Fredriksen 1999, 201).

The purity codes should serve as a reminder that Jesus was a Jew of the early first century CE who "took them for granted as fundamental to the worship of the God who had revealed them" (Fredriksen 1999, 203). They were a part of his religious world and part of ancient cultures, even if not of ours.

While there is a considerable amount of secondary literature on various passages concerning purity codes, two resources offer excellent background information. *The Jewish Study Bible*, 2nd ed., includes fine commentaries on the relevant chapters of Leviticus and Numbers as well as an article on "Concepts of Purity in the Bible" (Berlin and Brettler 2014). *The Jewish Annotated New Testament*, 2nd ed., has excellent notes on the passages from the gospel on the healings of the woman with the hemorrhage and of the leper; see also the essay on "Bearing False Witness: Common Errors Made about Early Judaism" that includes a short but pithy analysis of misconceptions about purity laws (Levine 2017, 761).

### Reflection: "Words Like That Grow Legs and Walk Out of Their Context."

A number of years ago, I was invited to give a lecture in Stockholm, Sweden, that annually honors the great Swedish biblical scholar Krister Stendahl (Boys 2016). Preparing for this lecture provided the impetus to delve more systematically into Stendahl's work. To my delight, I discovered that his insights could be found not only in academic journals but also in the form of unpretentious lectures. His genius lay in part in the ability to make the riches of scholarship accessible in a down-home manner. The saying that heads this section arises in the context of Stendahl's argument in a 1992 lecture that certain New Testament texts typically used as warrants against religious pluralism can and should be read differently. He cites three texts to serve as a case in point:

- Acts 4:12: "For there is no other name under heaven given among human beings, whereby we must be saved."
- John 14:6: "I am the way, the truth, and the life: no one comes to the Father except through me."
- Matthew 28:19: "Go therefore and make disciples of all the nations, baptizing them in the name of the Father, and of the Son, and of the Holy Spirit."

Then he observes: "But words like that grow legs and walk out of their context." The lecture, "From God's Perspective We Are All Minorities," is widely available and certainly worth a read (Stendahl 2004). He addresses the question of how Christians formed by biblical texts "can come to think about God's whole menagerie and the place of the Christian church and the Christian religion in the midst of it." Stendahl reminds his audience that in God's eyes all religious traditions are minorities. How then, he asks, "Do I sing my song to Jesus with abandon without telling negative stories about others?"

And many texts such as the three he cited involve how we Christians today read our New Testament vis-à-vis Judaism and the Jewish people. In particular, I think of the problems posed by texts that give rise to negative views of Jews and Judaism. In the Gospel of John, for example, "'the Jews' are connoted with virtually everything negative in that Gospel: fear, murmuring, murderous intent, diabolical origins, blindness, darkness, and death" (Sheridan 2012, 45). Arguably, of all the words that grew legs, the one that grew the largest and most destructive is this: "Crucify him!"

Rereading Stendahl's lecture brought to mind a recent essay by David French, an opinion columnist for *The New York Times*. A lifelong evangelical Christian whose own church turned against him as he became more critical of the evangelical zeal for Donald Trump and his MAGA movement, French wrestles with the provocative question, "Why are so many Christians so cruel?" (French 2024). Perhaps we might ask more specifically, Why have so many Christians over the centuries demonized Jews and condemned them as unfaithful to God? Yes, some New Testament texts, such as the Gospel of John, placed blame for the crucifixion of Jesus on "the Jews." But even if this charge could be validated as historical fact, which it has not been, those accused were "the Jews" of Jesus's time in Jerusalem. Jesus himself was crucified as a Jew, and those identified as standing vigil at the foot of the cross, such as Mary of Nazareth, Peter, and the other women also named Mary (in variant traditions) were all Jews. How could Christians aware of the teaching of Jesus, including the centrality of the one prayer he taught his disciples, continue for centuries to disparage Jews and collaborate in violence against them? In short, why over time have so many Christians been so contemptuous of Judaism and so cruel to Jews?

Many reasons come to mind, though none suffice. Might it not be in part because church leaders failed to convey the heart of the gospel? Because their reading of the New Testament allowed Christians to claim theological superiority? And, further, because Christians' majority status in many societies fostered a sense of supremacy upheld by society's structures and institutions (Teter 2023)? Likely all these readings and more. But ought not our history vis-à-vis Jews heighten awareness that some of the New Testament's words have indeed grown legs and traveled far beyond their context—so far, in fact, that they've blasphemed their source.

I happened to be working on this section on the eightieth anniversary of the liberation of Auschwitz as well as the day of the annual observance of Holocaust Remembrance Day. Following the day's events, my thoughts turned to my visit to Auschwitz in August 2004 in the company of Jewish educator and my colleague in dialogue Sara Lee and my friend in community Lesley Sacouman. Cruelty does not suffice to name the unspeakable inhumanity to which every inch of Auschwitz bears witness—the starvation cells of Block 11; the Wall of Death; and, in Auschwitz–Birkenau, the gas chambers where 4,400 prisoners, nearly all Jews, were exterminated each day.

Cruelty, of course, is not exclusive to Christianity. It's a mark of human brokenness, arising in part from our tribalism, our desire for vengeance, our susceptibility to violence, our complicity in evil. Cruelty is manifest in every religious tradition that suggests, as French phrases it, that those who "hold eternal truths are entitled to rule" and that "right deserves might." Cruelty is palpable in the demeaning and dehumanizing language increasingly used of immigrants and migrants, as well as sexual minorities. In 2025, a political party that has embraced Germany's Nazi past, *Alternative für Deutschland* (Alternative for Germany, AfD), continues to gain adherents. On the weekend preceding the eightieth anniversary of the liberation of Auschwitz, this far-right German political power gained the endorsement of the world's richest man, Elon Musk, who is now closely allied with the newly elected president of the United States. Nationalist movements are gaining in the West, and Christian Nationalism in the United States is emboldened by the new administration. Antisemitism surges throughout the world, fueled in part by social media, particularly on "X," formerly Twitter. There is new meaning in "Right deserves might."

Thus, how the church reads the Bible in our time is ever more critical. What will we learn from Jewish interpretations of the Torah that might give depth and breadth to our understanding of Jesus's reading of the Torah? How the church reads the Bible in our time is ever more critical. What will we learn from Jewish interpretations of the Torah? What will we learn from the riches of church tradition and from laying aside remnants of that tradition no longer life-giving (if ever they were)? What will we learn from those whose Scripture scholarship awakens and edifies us?

If there is one term we might keep in mind, I suggest that recommended by Krister Stendahl: Holy envy. "Holy envy," he frequently said, "is when we recognize something in another tradition that is beautiful but is not in ours, nor should we grab it or claim it.... Holy envy rejoices in the beauty of others" (Stendahl 1993). To rejoice in the beauty of others involves getting to know the other. For early generations of Christ followers, discovering the beauty of Judaism seemed unimaginable, incompatible with their new identity. Today, however, we have the opportunity to reorient Christianity's relation with Judaism—and with Jews.

In our time we are privileged to have opportunities and resources to encounter the beauty and wisdom of Judaism, past and present. And in so doing, we Christians will encounter Jesus Christ, "the living Torah of God" (*The Gifts and the Calling of God Are Irrevocable*, 3.26). This is a blessing of a new dawn.

# Epilogue

"Of the making of books," says Ecclesiastes, "there is no end, and much study is a weariness of the flesh" (11:12). The writing of this book is nearing its end after many years of having a keen sense of what I wanted to publish, but there was some "weariness" in deciding how best to go about it.

In the first chapter I claimed that "this all began" with an essay I wrote in 1981. That statement is true but not the full truth. In fact, for many years before I had the opportunity to study, I had been drawn by Christianity's relation with Judaism. While I can point to a few influences—growing up in a family with a warm and long-standing relationship with a Jewish friend, being in a Catholic high school during the years of the Second Vatican Council, and reading Abraham Joshua Heschel's book *The Prophets* while in college—there was no definitive moment when I decided to explore the Christian–Jewish relationship more intensely. It happened along the way of deepening my own understanding of Christianity and in the process of theological explorations—and perhaps even more through friendships with Jews in graduate school and then in my experiences teaching at Boston College and Union Theological Seminary. "Interreligious friendships," I am convinced, are invaluable, and I am immensely grateful for how they continue to grace my life.

As to the "no end" of making books of the weary Ecclesiastes, I thought this book of mine would have been finished at least two years ago. But the writing process wouldn't conform to my calendar—or even more to my thought processes. As it happens, however, its publication will coincide with the sixtieth anniversary of *Nostra Aetate* in October 2025. While I hadn't planned that overlap, it is appropriate. This brief and modest document, hotly contested at Vatican II, has opened areas of study and relationships its writers could not have dreamed possible. In retrospect, I see how what began through this 1965 decree is woven into my professional and personal life.

Sixty years is both a blink in time and yet a distant past. In reality, most Catholics have little if any awareness of *Nostra Aetate,* especially section 4 that focuses on relations with Judaism. Many clergy seem at best to have a vague sense of it, and its insights, refined and deepened over the years, seem to lack salience except among a few. Yes, its impact has been phenomenal on one level; the hostility toward Jews and Judaism has largely receded in Catholic circles. As for understanding its deeper significance, I fear that the decree is largely obscure except to a few. It is my hope that this book will contribute not so much to knowledge of *Nostra Aetate* itself as to the ways in which it serves as a catalyst in reorienting the Catholic Church—and many other Christian traditions—in ways that do justice to their relation with Jews and Judaism. I, in collaboration with many Christian scholars, consider doing justice to that relationship to be a sacred obligation.

So let my concluding words be an attempt to articulate what a revised *Nostra Aetate,* section 4, might say at sixty. I write it as a Catholic, drawing upon subsequent Catholic documents that refine and nuance Vatican II's decree. I hope that in writing in the particularity of my own tradition, others will draw upon their theological legacy in formulating a statement that might serve to reenergize dialogue.

In a departure from the foregoing style of this book, I have chosen to include footnotes in the following section as a way of showing that my text, while my own, is shaped by ecclesial documents and theological developments. I hope it might serve as a stimulus for discussion and refinement; a draft can be a useful discussion starter. The learning is as much in the challenging process of formulation and the conversations it engenders as in the final statement.

## Nostra Aetate at Sixty: A Revised Version

Sixty years ago, the Second Vatican Council (1962–65) initiated a reassessment of the relationship between the Catholic Church and the Jewish people with its declaration *Nostra Aetate* (Declaration on the Relation of the Church to Non-Christian Religions). Despite the decree's brevity and modest conclusions, section 4 of *Nostra Aetate,* awakened a new commitment on the part of many in the church to repair injustices, engage in dialogue with Jewish communities, and deepen its interpretation of Scripture.

The commitment to dialogue included seeking a greater knowledge of Judaism, particularly how Jews themselves understand their tradition in its complexity and diversity.[1] This commitment led to a new awareness of the *continuing* covenant between God and the Jewish people.[2] It also revealed how over

---

[1] "On the practical level in particular, Christians must therefore strive to acquire a better knowledge of the basic components of the religious tradition of Judaism; they must strive to learn by what essential traits Jews define themselves in the light of their own religious experience." See the Preamble to the 1974 Guidelines, available on the Council of Centers on Jewish-Christian Relations (CCJR) website, https://ccjr.us.

[2] St. Pope John Paul, in a speech in 1980, referred to Jews as "the people of God of the Old Covenant, never revoked by God, the present-day people of the covenant concluded with Moses." Similarly, in 1987, he spoke of Jews as "partners in a covenant of eternal love which was never revoked." Full texts in Eugene J. Fisher and Leon Klenicki, eds., *Pope John Paul II: Spiritual Pilgrimage; Texts on Jews and Judaism* (Crossroad, 1995), 13–16 and 105–9.

the centuries inadequate and flawed understandings of Judaism had developed in the church that compromised its moral principles by misrepresenting Judaism and misusing its power. Learning with and from Jewish and other Christian scholars in the past sixty years has brought new insights revealing the complexity of Christian origins in the matrix of Judaism. From their origins as interwoven vines whose shoots had grown out of biblical Israel, Christianity and Judaism emerged as distinct institutional entities by the fourth and fifth centuries. Rivalry based on competing claims about whether Torah or Jesus offered the truer path to God had characterized this relationship in its early centuries. But rivalry too often developed into hostility. As the church gained political power, its claim to theological superiority fostered dominance over Jews. By the Middle Ages, the church's hostility to Judaism was manifested in stereotypical representations and harsh treatment of Jews. The Crusades unleashed violence against both Muslims and Jews. Christian spiritualities became focused on the suffering of Jesus in ways that included emphasis on Jewish perfidy. Conspiracy theories, such as the blood libel, justified persecution of Jews, who were portrayed as a perfidious people responsible for the death of Jesus and thus as unfaithful to God.[3] In many respects, the church characterized Judaism as theologically obsolete. And in the Shoah, the Nazis, with far too little resistance from the church, sought to make Jews cease to exist.

*Nostra Aetate* marked a new beginning for the church: a reckoning with its relationship with Jews over nearly two

---

[3] On June 13, 1960, French historian Jules Isaac met with Pope John XXIII to present his research about the portrayal of Judaism in Christian texts; he termed this the "teaching of contempt." See Jules Isaac, *The Teaching of Contempt*, trans. Helen Weaver (Holt, Rinehart, and Winston, 1964); also, his earlier *Jesus and Israel*, trans. Sally Gran (Holt, Rinehart, and Winston, 1971).

millennia and a reassessment of its teachings about Judaism. It inspired the church to grapple with its responsibility for a "tormented history" with Jews, including the painful and difficult realization that church teachings provided a fertile seedbed for the Nazi genocide in its silence in the face of the Nuremberg Racial Laws, *Kristallnacht*, and the concentration and death camps.[4] To remember the *Shoah* "is to become fully conscious of the salutary warning it entails: the spoiled seeds of anti-Judaism and antisemitism must never again be allowed to take root in any human heart."[5]

What began at Vatican II must continue if the Catholic Church, mindful that the Spirit continues to inspire, is truly committed to eradicating its theological antisemitism, including the "teaching of contempt" for Jews. Its teachings today must be animated by the ethical obligation to characterize Judaism accurately. Living into this obligation requires making clear that New Testament texts that depict Jews negatively, particularly in the Gospel of John, must be understood as a vestige of conflictual situations. The hostility to "the Jews" reflected in this gospel account, with echoes in

---

[4] "In the judgment of historians, it is a well-proven fact that for centuries, up until Vatican Council II, an anti-Jewish tradition stamped its mark in differing ways on Christian doctrine and teaching, in theology, apologetics, preaching and in the liturgy. It was on such ground that the venomous plant of hatred for the Jews was able to flourish. Hence, the heavy inheritance we still bear in our century, with all its consequences which are so difficult to wipe out. Hence our still open wounds." Catholic Bishops of France, Declaration of Repentance (1997), available on the CCJR website.

[5] "We Remember: A Reflection on the Shoah," available on the CCJR website. See also Pontifical Commission on Justice and Peace, "The Church and Racism: Toward a More Fraternal Society", no. 15 (1988), available on the CCJR website: "Among the manifestations of systematic racial distrust, specific mention must once again be made of antisemitism."

other biblical texts, should be read as a polemical portrayal reflecting intense rivalry rather than as a historically reliable characterization of Judaism.

Complementing this more honest—if painfully acquired—confrontation with its history vis-à-vis Judaism is the church's renewed commitment to interpretation of Scripture. The past six decades have witnessed an astonishing increase in the depth and breadth of biblical scholarship, including extensive new research into the New Testament and its complex relation to the Old Testament. Insights from church documents such as *The Jewish People and Their Sacred Scriptures in the Christian Bible* must be made widely accessible, clearly communicated, and adapted for pastoral use.[6] Although different religious perspectives shape how Jews and Christians interpret the sacred texts they share, both readings epitomize their respective traditions and provide rich resources for more profound dialogue.

Developments in the study of the New Testament shed new light on the crucifixion of Jesus, the Pharisees, and on the Apostle Paul. Such studies offer new depth of understanding about *Nostra Aetate*'s significant statement that "neither all Jews indiscriminately at that time [of the crucifixion of Jesus], nor Jews today, can be charged with the crimes committed during his passion." While the gospels appear, in varying ways, to place principal responsibility for the death of Jesus on Jews, contemporary studies make clear that the passion narratives are theological reflections on the crucifixion rather than historical accounts.[7] Biblical scholarship in our time

---

[6] See *The Jewish People and Their Sacred Scriptures in the Christian Bible* (2001), available on the CCJR website.

[7] See *God's Mercy Endures Forever*, no. 23 (1988), available on the CCJR website: "It is necessary to remember that the passion narratives do not offer eyewitness accounts or a modern transcript of historical events" (See also the U.S. Bishops' Committee for Ecumen-

situates the gospel narratives in the historical context of the Roman Empire in which the power of the empire's authorities (e.g., Pontius Pilate) superseded that of Jewish authorities (e.g., the high priest). While some Jewish authorities may have perceived Jesus as a rival or as a threat, his inclusive preaching of God's Reign was a far greater threat to the cult of the emperor and to Rome's imperial order in which an elite minority ruled over the masses. Ultimate responsibility for the death of Jesus thus falls not to "the Jews," as it might seem in the Gospel of John, but to the Roman governor, Pontius Pilate, in alliance with the power class.[8] Christian reflection on the passion and death of Jesus "should lead to a deep sense of the need for reconciliation with the Jewish community today."[9]

This scholarship also resituates Paul, the Apostle to the Gentiles, as a Jew whose encounter with Christ was a call to preach the Way of Jesus to non-Jews (Gentiles), whom he saw as wild shoots grafted onto the olive tree of Israel. Following Jesus reoriented Paul's connection to Judaism. These recent insights into Paul's letters offer new lenses for understanding that what ultimately became Christianity developed within Judaism.

---

ical and Interreligious Affairs, *The Bible, the Jews, and the Death of Jesus: A Collection of Catholic Documents* (United States Conference of Catholic Bishops, 2004); "The Gospels are the outcome of long and complicated editorial work," in *Commission on Religious Relations with the Jews, Notes on the Correct Way to Present Jews and Judaism in Preaching and Catechesis in the Catholic Church*, no. 21A (1985), available on the CCJR website.

[8] See John 19:16–17. Gerard Sloyan argues that the term "power class" more properly describes the opponents of Jesus in the passion; the term points to the alliance between the high priestly families and the representatives of the Roman Empire. See Gerard Sloyan, *The Crucifixion of Jesus: History, Myth, Faith* (Fortress, 1995), 43.

[9] *God's Mercy Endures Forever,* no. 25.

If over the centuries, contentiousness and disputation too often characterized the relationship between Christians and Jews, today differences provide opportunity for study and dialogue.[10] No attempt at reconciliation with the Jewish people is as compelling as is a renewed commitment to speak truthfully and frankly about the church's tragic hostility to Judaism and to atone by learning about and respecting the profundity of the Jewish tradition.[11]

On this sixtieth anniversary of *Nostra Aetate,* we rejoice that, as a consequence of what this declaration initiated, many Christians have developed deep bonds of friendship and solidarity with Jews. We hope that these ties of kinship in the One God will deepen and broaden. May they serve as a witness to the world that those who were once enemies can reconcile.

---

[10] Jorge Mario Bergoglio, "Dialogue entails a warm reception and not a preemptive condemnation. To dialogue, one must know how to lower the defenses, open the doors of one's home, and to offer warmth" (*On Heaven and Earth*, with Abraham Skorka, trans. Alejandro Bermudez and Howard Goodman [Image, 2013]).

[11] See The Commission for Religious Relations with the Jews, "The Gifts and Calling of God Are Irrevocable" (2015), available on the CCJR website: "The first goal of the dialogue is to add depth to the reciprocal knowledge of Jews and Christians.... This profound knowledge is accompanied by a mutual enrichment whereby the dialogue partners become the recipients of gifts. The Conciliar Declaration '*Nostra aetate*' (No. 4) speaks of the rich spiritual patrimony that should be further discovered step by step through biblical and theological studies and through dialogue. To that extent, from the Christian perspective, an important goal is the mining of the spiritual treasures concealed in Judaism for Christians" (# 44).

# Resources on Judaism

### Essential Biblical Resources

Alter, Robert. *The Hebrew Bible: A Translation with Commentary*. W. W. Norton, 2019.

Berlin, Adele, and Marc Zvi Brettler, eds. *The Jewish Study Bible*, 2nd ed. Oxford University Press, 2014.

Levine, Amy-Jill, and Marc Zvi Brettler, eds. *The Jewish Annotated New Testament*, 3rd ed. Oxford University Press, 2025.

### Helpful References on Jewish Life

Greenberg, Irving. *The Jewish Ways: Living the Holidays*. Summit Books, 1985.

Held, Shai. *Judaism Is About Love: Recovering the Heart of Jewish Life*. Farrar, Straus and Giroux, 2024.

Hezer, Catherine, ed. *The Oxford Handbook of Jewish Daily Life in Roman Palestine*. Oxford University Press, 2010.

Marx, Dalia. *From Time to Time: Journeys in the Jewish Calendar*. CCAR/Reform Jewish Publishing, 2023.

### Open-Source Resources

Documents on Jewish-Christian relations may be found on numerous websites; see, e.g., Council of Centers on Jewish-Christian Relations: https://ccjr.us/dialogika-resources

*Journal of the Jesus Movement in Its Jewish Setting.* https://www.jjmjs.org/.

*Sefaria: A Living Library of Torah,* https://www.sefaria.org/texts

*Studies in Jewish-Christian Relations.* https://ejournals.bc.edu/index.php/scjr.

# Bibliography

Ashbrook Harvey, Susan, Nathaniel P. Des Rosiers, Shira L. Lander, Jacqueline Z. Pastis, and David Ullueci, eds. *A Most Reliable Witness: Essays in Honor of Ross Shepard Kraemer*. Brown Judaic Studies, 2015.

Ashbrook Harvey, Susan. "Women and Children in Syriac Christianity." In *The Syriac World*, edited by Daviel King. Routledge, 2018.

Australian Catholic Bishops Conference. "A Gospel Word in a Violent World," 2024. https://socialjustice.catholic.org.au/2024/08/25/2024-social-justice-statement-launch/.

Bakhos, Carol. "Rabbinic and Patristic Interpretations of the Bible." In *The Routledge Handbook of Jews and Judaism in Late Antiquity*, edited by Catherine Hezser. Routledge, 2024.

Ben-Johanan, Karma. *Jacob's Younger Brother: Christian-Jewish Relations After Vatican II*. Belknap Press of Harvard University Press, 2022.

Boys, Mary C. "Questions 'Which Touch on the Heart of Our Faith'." *Religious Education* 76, no. 6 (1981): 636–56.

Boys, Mary C. *Educating in Faith: Maps and Visions*. Harper and Row, 1989.

Boys, Mary C. *Has God Only One Blessing? Judaism as a Source of Christian Self-Understanding*. Paulist, 2000.

Boys, Mary C. *Redeeming Our Sacred Story: The Death of Jesus and Relations between Jews and Christians*. Paulist, 2013.

Boys, Mary C. "Feminisms and the Interreligious Encounter." In *Faith and Feminisms*, edited by B. Diane Lipsett and Phyllis Trible. Westminster-John Knox, 2014.

Boys, Mary C. "Learning in the Presence of the Other: My Friendship with Sara S. Lee." In *Interreligious Friendships after Nostra Aetate*, edited by James Fredericks and Tracy Suzuki Tiemeier. Palgrave Macmillan, 2015a.

Boys, Mary C. "What Nostra Aetate Inaugurated: A Conversion to the 'Providential Mystery of Otherness.'" In *50 Years On: Probing the Riches of Vatican II*, edited by David G. Schultenover. Liturgical Press, 2015b.

Boys, Mary C. "Turn It and Turn It Again: The Vital Contribution of Krister Stendahl to Jewish-Christian Relations." *Journal of Ecumenical Studies* 51, no. 2 (2016): 281–94.

Boys, Mary C. "Dare We Hope?" In *The Holocaust and Nostra Aetate: Toward a Greater Understanding*, edited by Carol Rittner. Seton Hill University, National Catholic Center for Holocaust Education, 2017.

Boys, Mary C. "Countering Antisemitism." In *Antisemitism and Psychiatry*, edited by H. Steven Moffic. Springer Publishing, 2020.

Boys, Mary C. "Christianity's Complicated Origins." In T*he Jews Did Not Kill Jesus*, edited by Jon Sweeney. Orbis Books, 2020.

Boys, Mary C. "Antisemitism and the Contemporary Catholic Church in America." *Antisemitism Studies* 6, no. 2 (2022a): 324–341.

Boys, Mary C. "Ecumenism, Interreligious Relations and the Bible." In *The Jerome Biblical Commentary for the Twenty-First Century*, 3rd ed., edited by John J. Collins, Gina Hens-Piazza, Barbara Reid, and Donald Senior. T&T Clark, 2022b.

Boys, Mary C. "The Flourishing of Jewish-Christian Relations: 1978 to the Present Day." In *A Documentary History of*

*Jewish-Christian Relations*, edited by Edward Kessler and Neil Wenborn. Cambridge University Press, 2024a.

Boys, Mary C. "A Christian's Reading of the Jewish Scriptures." In *Christian Perspectives on Transforming Interreligious Encounters*, edited by Peter C. Phan and Anh Q. Tran. Lexington Books, 2024b.

Boys, Mary C. "Protesting the Hamas-Israel Way: Implications for Relations Between Jews and Christians." In *Stress Test: The Israel–Hamas War and Christian–Jewish Relations*, edited by Carol Rittner and John Roth. iPub Global, 2025.

Boys, Mary C., and Sara S. Lee. "The Catholic-Jewish Colloquium: An Experiment in Interreligious Learning." *Religious Education* 91, no. 4 (1996): 421–66.

Boys, Mary C., and Sara S. Lee. *Christians and Jews in Dialogue: Learning in the Presence of the Other*. SkyLights Publishing, 2006.

Boys, Mary, and Shuly Rubin Schwartz, "Passover and Easter." In *Encyclopedia of Jewish-Christian Relations Online*, edited by Walter Homolka, Rainer Kampling, Amy-Jill Levine, Christopher Markschies, Peter Schäfer, and Martin Thurman, 2019.

Boulton, Matthew Myer. "Supersession or Subsession? Exodus Typology, the Christian Eucharist and the Jewish Passover Meal." *Scottish Journal of Theology* 66 (2013): 18–29.

Brakke, David. "Jewish Flesh and Christian Spirit in Athanasius of Alexandria." *Journal of Early Christian Studies* 9 (2001): 453–81.

Brakke, David, and David M. Guynn, trans. and commentators. *The Festal Letters of Athanasius of Alexandria, with the Festal Index and the Historia Acephala*. Liverpool University Press, 2022.

Brooks, David. "The Shock of Faith: It's Nothing Like I Thought It Would Be." *New York Times*, December 19, 2024. https://www.nytimes.com/2024/12/19/opinion/faith-god-christianity.html.

Brown, Raymond E., Joseph Fitzmyer, and Roland Murphy, eds. *The Jerome Biblical Commentary*. Prentice-Hall, 1968.

Brown, Raymond E., Joseph Fitzmyer, and Roland Murphy, eds. *The New Jerome Biblical Commentary*. Prentice-Hall, 1990.

Buechner, Frederick. *Beyond Words: Daily Readings in the ABCs of Faith*. HarperSanFrancisco, 2004.

Butcher, James. *Christian Pharisees: The Striking Similarities of America's Conservative Christians and Jesus' Earthly Enemies*. James Butcher Publishing, 2017.

Cameron, Averil. *The Mediterranean World in Late Antiquity AD 395–700*, 2nd ed. Routledge, 2011.

Cirafesi, Wally V. *John within Judaism: Religion, Ethnicity and the Shaping of Jesus-Oriented Jewishness in the Fourth Gospel*. Brill, 2022.

Cirafesi, Wally V. "John Within Judaism." In *Within Judaism? Interpretive Trajectories in Judaism, Christianity, and Islam from the First to the Twenty-First Century*, edited by Karin Hedner Zetterholm and Anders Runesson. Lexington Books/Fortress Academic, 2024.

Cohick, Lynn H. *The Peri Pascha Attributed to Melito of Sardis: Setting, Purpose, Sources*, 2nd ed. Brown Judaic Studies, 2020.

Collins, John J., and Daniel C. Harlow, eds. *Early Judaism: A Comprehensive Overview*. Eerdmans, 2012.

Collins, John J., Gina Hens-Piazza, Barbara Reid, and Donald J. Senior, eds. *The Jerome Biblical Commentary for the Twenty-First Century*. T & T Clark, 2022.

Commission on Religious Relations with the Jews. "We Remember: A Reflection on the Shoah." *Origins* 27, no. 40 (1998): 669–75.

Commission on Religious Relations with the Jews, "The Gifts and Calling of God Are Irrevocable: A Reflection on Theological Questions Pertaining to Catholic-Jewish Relations on the Occasion of the 50th Anniversary of *Nostra Aetate* (no.4). 2015. https://ccjr.us/dialogika-resources.

Crossan, John Dominic. *The Historical Jesus: The Life of a Mediterranean Jewish Peasant.* HarperSanFrancisco, 1991.

Crossley, James G. "Matthew and Torah: Jesus as Legal Interpreter." In *Matthew within Judaism: Israel and the Nations in the First Gospel,* edited by Anders Runesson and Daniel M. Gurtner. Society of Biblical Literature Press, 2020.

Cunningham, Philip A. "The Sources behind 'The Gifts and Calling of God Are Irrevocable (Rom 11:29)': A Reflection on Theological Questions Pertaining to Catholic-Jewish Relations on the Occasion of the 50th Anniversary of Nostra Aetate (No. 4)." *Studies in Jewish Christian Relations* 12, no. 1 (2017): 1–29.

Cunningham, Philip A. "A Textbook Case—The Pharisees in Catholic Religious Textbooks." In *The Pharisees,* edited by Joseph Sievers and Amy-Jill Levine. Eerdmans, 2021.

Den Dulk, Matthijs. *Between Jews and Heretics: Refiguring Justin Martyr's Dialogue with Trypho.* Routledge, 2018.

de Wert, Chris, and Wendy Mayer, eds. *Revisioning John Chrysostom.* Brill, 2019.

Dietz, Elias. "The O Antiphons." *Cistercian Studies Quarterly* 58, no. 4 (2023): 375–88.

Donaldson, Terence L. "Supersessionism and Early Christian Self-Definition." *Journal of the Jesus Movement in Its Jewish Setting* 3 (2016): 1–32.

Edwards, Mark, Martin Goodman, and Simon Price. *Apologetics in the Roman Empire: Pagans, Jews and Christians.* Oxford University Press, 1999.

Eisenbaum, Pamela. *Paul Was Not a Christian: The Real Message of a Misunderstood Apostle.* Harper One, 2009.

Eusebius. *Eusebius' Life of Constantine*, edited by Averil Cameron and Stuart Hall. Clarendon Press, 1999.

Fein, Helen. 1987. "Dimensions of Antisemitism: Attitudes, Collective Accusations, and Actions." In *The Persisting Question: Sociological Perspectives and Social Contexts of Modern Antisemitism*, edited by H. Fein. DeGruyter, 1987.

Fisher, Edward J., and Leon Klenicki, eds., *Pope John Paul II: Spiritual Pilgrimage; Texts on Jews and Judaism*. Crossroad, 1995.

Fitzmyer, Joseph A. *The Biblical Commission's "Interpretation of the Bible in the Church": Text and Commentary*. Editrice Pontificio Istituto Biblico, 1995.

Flannery, Austin, ed., *Vatican Council II Constitutions, Decrees and Declarations*, Inclusive Language ed. Liturgical Press, 2014.

Fredriksen, Paula. *Jesus of Nazareth, King of the Jews. A Jewish Life and the Emergence of Christianity*. Vintage, 1999.

Fredriksen, Paula. "Christian Anti-Judaism: Polemics and Policies." In *The Cambridge History of Judaism IV*, edited by Steven T. Katz. Cambridge University Press, 2008.

Fredriksen, Paula. "Roman Christianity and the Post-Roman West: The Social Correlation of the *Contra Judaeos* Tradition." In *Jews, Christians, and the Roman Empire: The Poetics of Power in Late Antiquity*, edited by Natalie B. Dohrmann and Annette Yoshiko Reed. University of Pennsylvania Press, 2013.

Fredriksen, Paula. *Paul: The Pagans' Apostle*. Yale University Press, 2017.

Fredriksen, Paula. *When Christians Were Jews: The First Generation*. Yale University Press, 2018.

Fredriksen, Paula. "Paul, the Perfectly Righteous Pharisee." In *The Pharisees*, edited by Joseph Sievers and Amy-Jill Levine. Eerdmans, 2021.

Fredriksen, Paula, and Jesper Svartvik, eds. *Krister Stendahl among the Jews and Gentiles*. Paulist, 2018.
Fredriksen, Paula. "What Does It Mean to See Paul 'within Judaism?'" *Journal of Biblical Literature* 141, no. 2 (2022): 359–80.
Fredriksen, Paula. "Paul Within Judaism." In *Within Judaism? Interpretive Trajectories in Judaism, Christianity, and Islam from the First to the Twenty-First Century*, edited by Karin Hedner Zetterholm and Anders Runesson. Lexington Books/Fortress Academic, 2024.
Fredriksen, Paula. *Ancient Christianities: The First Five Hundred Years*. Princeton University Press, 2024.
French, David. "Why Are So Many Christians So Cruel?" *New York Times*, December 22, 2024. https://www.nytimes.com/2024/12/22/opinion/christmas-jesus-power-humility.html.
Freyne, Sean. *Jesus a Jewish Galilean: A New Reading of the Jesus Story*. London: T & T Clark, 2004.
Gager, John. *Attitudes Toward Judaism in Pagan and Christian Antiquity*. Oxford University Press, 1985.
Garber, Zev. *The Jewish Jesus: Revelation, Reflection and Reclamation*. Purdue University Press, 2011.
Graff, Gil. *Living Torah: Gateway to a Living Tradition*. Rowman and Littlefield, 2024.
Graham, William A. "Scripture." In *Encyclopedia of Religion*, vol. 12, 2nd ed., edited by Lindsay Jones. Macmillan Reference USA, 2005.
Graves, Michael. *The Inspiration and Interpretation of Scripture: What the Early Church Can Teach Us*. Eerdmans, 2014.
Green, Barbara "This Old Text: An Analogy for Biblical Interpretation." *Biblical Theology Bulletin* 36 (2006): 72–83.
Greenberg, Irving. *The Jewish Way: Living the Holidays*. Summit Books, 1988.

Greenberg, Irving. *Sage Advice: Pirkei Avot with Translation and Commentary*. Magid Books, 2016.

Greenberg, Irving. *The Triumph of Life: A Narrative Theology of Judaism*. Jewish Publication Society, 2024.

Gregerman, Adam. "Superiority without Supersessionism: Walter Kasper, The Gifts and Calling of God Are Irrevocable, and God's Covenant with the Jews." *Theological Studies* 79, no. 1 (2018): 36–59.

Gruen, Erich S. "Judaism in the Diaspora." In *Early Judaism: A Comprehensive Overview*, edited by John J. Collins and Daniel Harlow. Eerdmans, 2012.

Haber, Susan. "A Woman's Touch: Feminist Encounters with the Hemorrhaging Woman in Mark 5:24–24." *Journal for the Study of the New Testament* 26, no. 2 (2003): 171–92.

Haber, Susan. *They Shall Purify Themselves: Essays on Purity in Early Judaism*, edited by Adele Reinhartz. SBL Press, 2008.

Hagner, Donald. *The Jewish Reclamation of Jesus: An Analysis and Critique of Modern Jewish Study of Jesus*. Zondervan, 1984.

Haight, Roger. "Logos Christology Today." In *From Logos to Christ: Essays in Christology in Honour of Joanne Williams*. Wilfred Laurier University Press, 2010.

Harkins, Franklin T. "Nuancing Augustine's Hermeneutical Jew: Allegory and Actual Jews in the Bishop's Sermons." *Journal for the Study of Judaism in the Persian, Hellenistic, and Roman Period* 36, no. 1 (2005): 41–64.

Harkins, Paul W. *Saint John Chrysostom: Discourses against Judaizing Christians*. Catholic University of America Press, 1979.

Hasselhoff, George K. "Revising the Vulgate: Jerome and his Jewish Interlocutors." *Zeitschrift für Religions und Geistesgeschichte* 64, no. 3 (2012): 209–21.

Herbst, Matthew T. "Constantine the Great (r. 306–337 CE)." In *The Byzantine Empire: A Historical Perspective*, edited by James F. LePree and Ljudmila Dyukic. ABC-CLIO, 2019.

Heschel, Susannah. *The Aryan Jesus: Christian Theologians and the Bible in Nazi Germany*. Princeton University Press, 2008.

Heschel, Susannah. "Historiography of Antisemitism versus Anti-Judaism: A Response to Robert Morgan." *Journal for the Study of the New Testament* 33, no. 3 (2011): 258–61.

Heschel, Susannah, and Deborah Forger. "The Pharisees in Modern Scholarship." In *The Pharisees*, edited by Joseph Sievers and Amy-Jill Levine. Eerdmans, 2021.

Hesslein, Kayko Driedger. *Dual Citizenship: Two-Natures Christologies and the Jewish Jesus*. Bloomsbury Academic, 2015.

Hezser, Catherine. *The Social Structure of the Rabbinic Movement in Roman Palestine*. Mohr Siebeck, 1997.

Hezser, Catherine, ed. *The Oxford Handbook of Jewish Daily Life in Roman Palestine*. Oxford University Press, 2010.

Hezser, Catherine, ed. "Introduction." In *The Routledge Handbook of Jews and Judaism in Late Antiquity*. Routledge, 2024.

Hirshman, Marc. *A Rivalry of Genius: Jewish and Christian Biblical Interpretation in Late Antiquity,* translated by Batya Stein. State University of New York Press, 1996.

Hirshman, Marc. "Torah in Rabbinic Thought: The Theology of Learning." In *The Cambridge History of Judaism*, vol. 4, edited by Steven T. Katz. Cambridge University Press, 2006.

Homolka, Walter. *Jewish Jesus Research and Its Challenge to Christology Today*. Brill, 2016.

Hopkins, Gerard Manley. *Hopkins: Poetry and Prose*. Alfred A. Knopf, 1995.

Horner, Timothy J. *Listening to Trypho: Justin Martyr's Dialogue Reconsidered*. Peeters, 2001.
Hull, John. *What Prevents Christian Adults from Learning?* Trinity Press International, 1991.
Isaac, Jules. *The Teaching of Contempt*, translated by Helen Weaver. Holt, Rinehart, and Winston, 1964.
Isaac, Jules. *Jesus and Israel*, translated by Sally Gran. Holt, Rinehart, and Winston, 1971.
Jacobs, Andrew S. *Christ Circumcised: A Study in Early Christian History and Difference*. University of Pennsylvania Press, 2012.
Jacobs, Andrew S. "Christianizing the Roman Empire: Jews and the Law from Constantine to Justinian." In *The Cambridge Companion to Antisemitism*, edited by Steven T. Katz. Cambridge University Press, 2022.
Johnson, Elizabeth A. *Quest for the Living God: Mapping Frontiers in the Theology of God*. Continuum, 2007.
Johnson, Luke Timothy. *Contested Issues in Christian Origins and the New Testament*. Brill, 2013.
Joslyn-Siemiatkoski, Daniel. "Comparative Theology and the Status of Judaism: Hegemony and Reversals." In *The New Comparative Theology*, edited by Francis X. Clooney. T&T Clark, 2010.
Joslyn-Siemiatkoski, Daniel. *The More Torah, The More Life: A Christian Commentary on Mishnah Avot*. Peeters, 2018.
Karp, Jonathan. "Anti-Israelism," 2024. https://jewishreviewofbooks.com/american-jewry/15563/anti-israelism.
Kasper, Walter Cardinal. "The Commission on Religious Relations with the Jews: A Crucial Endeavour of the Catholic Church," 2002. https://www.bc.edu/content/dam/files/research_sites/cjl/texts/cjrelations/resources/articles/Kasper_6Nov02.htm.
Katz, Michael, and Gershon Schwartz. *Swimming in the Sea of Talmud*. Jewish Publication Society, 1998.

Katz, Steven T., ed. *The Cambridge History of Judaism*, IV. Cambridge University Press, 2006.
Katz, Steven T., ed. *The Cambridge Companion to Antisemitism*. Cambridge University Press, 2022.
Konradt, Matthias. "Matthew Within Judaism." In *Within Judaism: Interpretive Trajectories in Judaism, Christianity and Islam from the First to the Twenty-First Century*, edited by Karin Hedner Zetterholm and Anders Runesson. Mohr Siebeck, 2024.
Korner, Ralph J. *The Origin and Meaning of Ekklēsia in the Early Jesus Movement*. Brill, 2017.
Kraemer, David. "The Mishnah." In *The Cambridge History of Judaism*, IV, edited by Steven T. Katz. Cambridge University Press, 2006.
Kraemer, Ross S. *The Mediterranean Diaspora in Late Antiquity: What Christianity Cost Jews*. Oxford University Press, 2020.
Krewson, William L. *Jerome and the Jews: Innovative Supersessionism*. Wipf & Stock, 2017.
Kugel, James. *The Bible as It Was*. Harvard University Press, 1997.
Lanfranchi, Pierluigi. *Attitudes to the Sabbath in Three Apostolic Fathers: Didache, Ignatius and Barnabas*. Brill, 2008.
Leadbetter, Bill. "From Constantine to Theodosius." In *The Early Christian World*, 2nd ed., vol. 1, edited by Philip F. Esler. Routledge, 2017.
Letter to the Editor. *The Tablet*, July 3, 2021.
Levine, Amy-Jill. *The Misunderstood Jew: The Church and the Scandal of the Jewish Jesus*. HarperOne, 2006.
Levine, Amy-Jill. "Bearing False Witness: Common Errors Made about Early Judaism." In *The Jewish Annotated New Testament*, 2nd ed. Oxford University Press, 2017.

Lieu, Judith M. *Image and Reality: The Jews in the World of the Christians in the Second Century*. T&T Clark, 1996.
Lieu, Judith M. *Christian Identity in the Jewish and Graeco-Roman World*. Oxford University Press, 2004.
Lieu, Judith M. *Neither Jew nor Greek? Constructing Early Christianity*, 2nd ed. Bloomsbury T&T Clark, 2016.
Linder, Amnon. *The Jews in Roman Imperial Legislation*. Wayne State University Press, 1997.
Maccoby, Hyam, ed. and trans. *Judaism on Trial: Jewish-Christian Disputations in the Middle Ages*. Littman Library of Jewish Civilization, 1984.
Marshall, Mary M. *The Portrayal of the Pharisees in the Gospels and Acts*. Vandenhoeck and Ruprecht, 2015.
Martin, Matthew J. "Interpreting the *Theodotos* Inscription: Some Reflections on a First-Century Jerusalem Synagogue Inscription and E.P. Sanders' 'Common Judaism.'" *Ancient Near Eastern Studies* 39 (2002): 160–81.
Mason, Steve. "Why Josephus Matters," 2021. https://www.marginaliareviewofbooks.com/post/why-josephus-matters.
Mayer, Wendy. "Preaching Hatred? John Chrysostom, Neuroscience and the Jews." In *Revisioning John Chrysostom: New Approaches, New Perspectives*, edited by Wendy Mayer and Chris de Wet. Leiden 2019.
Mayers, Simon D. *From "the Pharisee" to "The Zionist Menace": Myth, Stereotype and Constructions of the Jews in English Catholic Discourse, 1896–1929*. Ph.D. Dissertation, University of Manchester (UK), 2012.
Marx, Dalia. *From Time to Time: Journeys in the Jewish Calendar*. Reform Jewish Publishing, 2023.
McGuckin, John A. *The Path of Christianity: The First Thousand Years*. IVP Academic, 2017.
Meier, John P. *A Marginal Jew: Rethinking the Historical Jesus 1: The Roots of the Problem and the Person*. Doubleday, 1991.

Meier, John P. *A Marginal Jew: Rethinking the Historical Jesus 2: Mentor, Message, and Miracles.* Yale University Press, 1994.

Meier, John P. *A Marginal Jew: Rethinking the Historical Jesus 3: Companions and Competitors.* Yale University Press, 2001.

Meier, John P. *A Marginal Jew Rethinking the Historical Jesus 4: Law and Love.* Yale University Press, 2009.

Meier, John P. *A Marginal Jew: Rethinking the Historical Jesus 5: Probing the Authenticity of the Parables.* Yale University Press, 2016.

Meyer, Barbara U. *Jesus the Jew in Christian Memory.* Cambridge University Press, 2020.

Meyers, Carol L. "Temple, Jews." In *The Anchor Bible Dictionary*, 6th ed., edited by David Noel Freedman. Yale University Press, 1992.

Mikva, Rachel S. *Dangerous Religious Ideas: The Deep Roots of Self-Critical Faith in Judaism, Christianity and Islam.* Beacon, 2020.

Mitchell, Stephen. *A History of the Later Roman Empire AD 284–641*, 2nd ed. John Wiley & Sons, 2014.

Moltmann, Jürgen. *The Crucified* God, translated by R. A. Wilson and J. Bowden. Fortress, 2015.

Moss, Yonatan. "From Syria All the Way to Rome: Ignatius of Antioch's Pauline Journey to Christianity." In *Journeys in the Roman East: Imagined and Real*, edited by Maren B. Niehoff. Mohr Siebeck, 2017.

Moyaert, Marianne. "The Gifts and Calling of God Are Irrevocable (Rom 11:29): A Theological Reflection." *Irish Theological Quarterly* 83, no. 1 (2017): 24–43.

Nanos, Mark D., and Magnus Zetterholm, eds. *Paul within Judaism: Restoring the First-Century Context to the Apostle.* Cascade, 2015.

Newman, Barbara. "The Passion of the Jews of Prague: The Pogrom of 1389 and the Lessons of a Medieval Parody." *Church History* 81 (2012): 1–26.

Newman, Hillel. "Jerome's Judaizers." *Journal of Early Christian Studies* 9, no. 4 (2001): 421–52.

Osborne, William. 2011. "A Linguistic Introduction to the Origins and Characteristics of Early Mishnaic Hebrew as It Relates to Biblical Hebrew." *Old Testament Essays*. 24, no. 1 (2011): 159–72.

Parvis, Sara, and Paul Foster, eds. *Justin Martyr and His Worlds*. Fortress Press, 2007.

Peppard, Michael. "Do We Share a Book? The Sunday Lectionary and Jewish-Christian Relations." *Studies in Christian-Jewish Relations* 1, no. 1 (2005): 89–102.

Peppard, Michael. *How Catholics Encounter the Bible*. Oxford University Press, 2024.

Petuchowski, Jacob. 1959. "The Bible of the Synagogue." *Commentary* 27 (1959): 142–50.

Piercy, Marge. "Meditation before Reading Torah." In *The Art of Blessing the Day*. Knopf, 2007.

Pontifical Biblical Commission. *The Interpretation of the Bible in the Church*. Libreria EditriceVaticana, 1993.

Pontifical Biblical Commission. *The Jewish People and Their Sacred Scripture in the Christian Bible*. Libreria Editrice Vaticana, 2002.

Rajak, Tessa. "Talking at Trypho: Christian Apologetics as Anti-Judaism in Justin's Dialogue with Trypho." In *The Roman Empire: Pagans, Jews and Christians*, edited by Mark Edwards, Martin Goodman, and Simon Price. Oxford University Press, 1999.

Reinhartz, Adele. *Befriending the Beloved Disciples: A Jewish Reading of the Gospel of John*. Continuum, 2005.

Reinhartz, Adele. *Cast Out of the Covenant: Jews and Anti-Judaism in the Gospel of John*. Lexington Books/Fortress Academic, 2018.

Robles, AD. *Social Justice Pharisees: Woke Church Tactics and How to Engage Them*. Morgan James Publishing, 2021.

Rokéah, David. *Justin Martyr and the Jews*. Brill, 2002.

Runesson, Anders. "Jewish and Christian Interaction from the First to the Fifth Centuries." In *The Early Christian World*, I, edited by Philip Esler. Routledge, 2000.

Runesson, Anders. *The Origins of the Synagogue: A Socio-Historical Study.* Almqvist and Wiksell, 2001.

Runesson, Anders. "The Origins of the Synagogue in Past and Present Research: Some Comments on Definitions, Theories, and Sources." *Studia Theologica* 57 (2003): 60–76.

Runesson, Anders. "Rethinking Early Jewish-Christian Relations: Matthean Community History as Pharisaic Intragroup Conflict." *Journal of Biblical Literature* 127, no. 1 (2008): 95–132.

Runesson, Anders. "Jewish and Christian Interactions from the First to the Fifth Centuries." In *The Early Christian World*, 2nd ed., vol. 1, edited by Philip F. Esler. Routledge, 2017.

Runesson, Anders. "Behind the Gospel of Matthew: Radical Pharisees in Post-War Galilee?" *Currents in Theology and Mission* 37 (2018): 460–71.

Runesson, Anders. *Judaism for Gentiles: Reading Paul Beyond the Paradigm of the Partings of the Ways.* Mohr Siebeck, 2022.

Runesson, Anders. "What Does It Mean to Read New Testament Texts 'within Judaism?'" *New Testament Studies* 69 (2023): 299–312.

Runesson, Anders, and Daniel M. Gurtner, eds. *Matthew within Judaism: Israel and the Nations in the First Gospel.* Society of Biblical Literature Press, 2020.

Runesson, Anders, Donald D. Binder, and Birger Olsson. *The Ancient Synagogue: A Source Book.* Brill, 2008.

Saint Ephrem the Syrian. *Songs for the Fast and Pasch.* Translated by Blake Hartung, J. Falconer, and J. E. Walter. Catholic University of America Press, 2022.

Saldarini, Anthony J. *Pharisees, Scribes and Sadducees in Palestinian Society: A Sociological Approach.* Michael Glazier, 1988.
Saldarini, Anthony J. "Delegitimation of Leaders in Matthew 23." *Catholic Biblical Quarterly* 54, no. 4 (1992): 659–80.
Saldarini, Anthony J. *Matthew's Christian-Jewish Community.* University of Chicago Press, 1994.
Samely, Alexander. *Forms of Rabbinic Literature and Thought.* Oxford University Press, 2007.
Sanders, E. P. *Paul and Palestinian Judaism.* SCM, 1977.
Sanders, E. P. *Jesus and Judaism.* Philadelphia: Fortress Press, 1985.
Sanders, E. P. *Judaism: Practice and Belief 63 BCE–66 CE.* London: SCM, 1992.
Sanders, E. P. "Covenantal Nomism Revisited," *Jewish Studies Quarterly* 16 (2009): 25–55.
Sandwell, Isabella. "Christian Self-Definition in the Fourth Century AD: John Chrysostom on Christianity, Imperial Rule and the City." In *Culture and Society in Later Roman Antioch,* edited by Isabella Sandwell and Janet Huskinson. Oxbow Books, 2004.
Sandwell, Isabella. *Religious Identity in Late Antiquity: Greeks, Jews, and Christians in Antioch.* Cambridge University Press, 2007.
Schäfer, Peter. *The Jewish Jesus: How Judaism and Christianity Shaped Each Other.* Princeton University Press, 2012.
Schoedel, William. *Ignatius of Antioch: A Commentary on the Letters of Ignatius of Antioch.* Edited by Helmut Koester. Fortress, 1985.
Schuller, Eileen. "Biblical Texts about Purity in Contemporary Christian Lectionaries." In *Purity, Holiness and Identity in Judaism and Christianity*, edited by Carl S.

Ehrlich, Anders Runesson, and Eileen Schuller. Mohr Siebeck, 2013.

Schwartz, Seth. *The Ancient Jews from Alexander to Muhammad*. Cambridge University Press, 2014.

Schwartz, Seth. "Jews, Judaism, and the Christianization of the Roman Empire." In *The Routledge Handbook of Jews and Judaism in Late Antiquity*, edited by Catherine Hezser. Routledge, 2024.

Shepardson, Christine. *Anti-Judaism and Christian Orthodoxy: Ephrem's Hymns in Fourth-Century Syria*. Catholic University of America Press, 2008.

Shepardson, Christine. *Controlling Contested Places: Late Antique Antioch and the Spatial Politics of Religious Controversy*. University of California Press, 2019.

Sheridan, Ruth. *Retelling Scripture: "The Jews" and the Scriptural Citations in John 1:19–12:15*. Brill, 2012.

Sievers, Joseph, and Amy-Jill Levine, eds. *The Pharisees*. Eerdmans, 2021.

Slusser, Michael, ed. *St. Justin Martyr: Dialogue with Trypho*. Translated by Thomas B. Falls. Catholic University of America Press, 2003.

Smith, Wilfred Cantwell. *What Is Scripture? A Comparative Approach*. Fortress, 1995.

"Statement by the French Bishops Commission for Relations with Jews." In *Stepping Stones for Further Jewish-Christian Relations: An Unabridged Collection of Christian Documents,* edited by Helga Croner. Paulist Stimulus Books, 1987.

Stendahl, Krister. "The Apostle Paul and the Introspective Conscience of the West." *Journal for the Scientific Study of Religion* 1, no. 2 (1962): 261–263.

Stendahl, Krister. "The Apostle Paul and the Introspective Conscience of the West." *Harvard Theological Review* 56, no. 3 (1963): 199–215.

Stendahl, Krister. *Paul among Jews and Gentiles and Other Essays*. Fortress, 1976.

Stendahl, Krister. "From God's Perspective We Are All Minorities." *Journal of Religious Pluralism*, 1993. https://www.jcrelations.net/article/from-gods-perspective-we-are-all-minorities.pdf.

Stendahl, Krister. "From God's Perspective We Are All Minorities." In *Defining New Christian/Jewish Dialogue*, edited by Irvin J. Borowsky. Crossroad, 2004.

Streeter, Joseph. "Conceptions of Tolerance in Antiquity and Late Antiquity." *Journal of the History of Ideas* 82, no. 3 (2021): 357–76.

Stroumsa, Guy G. "From Anti-Judaism to Antisemitism in Early Christianity?" In *Contra Iudaeos: Ancient and Medieval Polemics between Christians and Jews*, edited by Ora Limor and Guy G. Stroumsa. J. C. B. Mohr, 1996.

Stroumsa, Guy G. *The End of Sacrifice: Religious Transformations in Late Antiquity*. Translated by Susan Emanuel. University of Chicago Press, 2009.

Stroumsa, Guy G. *The Making of the Abrahamic Religions in Late Antiquity*. Oxford University Press, 2015.

Terrien, Samuel. *The Elusive Presence: Toward a New Biblical Theology*. Harper & Row, 1978.

Teter, Magda. *Christian Supremacy: Reckoning with the Roots of Antisemitism and Racism*. Princeton University Press, 2023.

Thatamanil, John. *Circling the Elephant: A Comparative Theology of Religious Diversity*. Fordham University Press, 2020.

Thiessen, Matthew. *Jesus and the Forces of Death: The Gospels' Portrayal of Ritual Impurity within First-Century Judaism*. Baker Academic, 2020.

Van Buren, Paul M. *A Theology of the Jewish-Christian Reality, Part 1: Discerning the Way*. Seabury Press, 1980.

Van Buren, Paul M. *A Theology of the Jewish-Christian Reality, Part 2: A Christian Theology of the People Israel.* Seabury, 1983.

Van Buren, Paul M. *A Theology of the Jewish-Christian Reality, Part 3: Christ in Context.* Harper & Row, 1988.

Van Maaren, John. "How Can the New Testament Writings Be Within Judaism? Distinguishing Ways of Asking and Answering the Question." *Zeitschrift für die Neutestamentliche Wissenschaft und die Kunde der älteren Kirche* 114, no. 2 (2023): 264–303.

Van Maaren, John. "Mark Within Judaism." In *Within Judaism: Interpretive Trajectories in Judaism, Christianity and Islam from the First to the Twenty-First Century.* Edited by Karin Hedner Zetterholm and Anders Runesson. Lexington Books/Fortress Academic, 2024.

Vermes, Geza. *Jesus the Jew: A Historian's Reading of the Gospels.* London: William Collins and Sons, 1973

Vermes, Geza. *The Religion of Jesus the Jew.* Minneapolis: Fortress, 1993.

Visotzky, Burton. *Reading the Book: Making the Bible a Timeless Text.* Doubleday, 1991.

Visotzky, Burton. "The Church Fathers on Jews and Judaism." In *The Routledge Handbook on Jews and Judaism in Late Antiquity,* edited by Catherine Hezser. Routledge, 2024.

Walter, J. Edward. *Ephrem the Syrian's Hymns on the Unleavened Bread.* Gorgias Press, 2012.

Walter, J. Edward, trans. *Teaching Songs on the Unleavened Bread.* Catholic University of America Press, 2022.

White, Caroline. 1990. *The Correspondence (394–419) between Jerome and Augustine of Hippo.* Edwin Mellen Press, 1990.

Williams, Megan Hale. 2008. "Lessons from Jerome's Jewish Teachers: Exegesis and Cultural Interaction in Late Antique Palestine." In *Jewish Biblical Interpretation* and *Cultural Exchange: Comparative Exegesis in Context*, edited by Natalia B. Dohrmann and David Stern. University of Pennsylvania Press, 2008.

Zetterholm, Karin Hedner. *Jewish Interpretation of the Bible: Ancient and Contemporary*. Fortress, 2012.

Zetterholm, Karin Hedner, Anders Runesson, Cecilia Wassen, and Magnus Zetterholm, eds. *Negotiating Identities: Conflict, Conversion, and Consolidation in Early Judaism and Christianity (200 BCE–600 CE)*. Lexington Books/Fortress Academic, 2022.

Zetterholm, Karin Hedner, and Anders Runesson, "Introduction: The 'Within Judaism' Perspective—An Emerging Paradigm Shift." In *Within Judaism? Interpretive Trajectories in Judaism, Christianity, and Islam from the First to the Twenty-First Century*, edited by Karin Hedner Zetterholm and Anders Runesson. Lexington Books/Fortress Academic, 2024.

# Index

Aelius Donatus, 88
*Against Apion* (Josephus), 38, 56
Alexander of Alexandria, 146
*Alternative für Deutschland* (AfD), 220
anachronisms, 17–18, 20, 21, 53, 210
antisemitism, 6, 16, 22, 149, 189
   Christian indifference toward, 186
   continuance into modern era, 5, 8, 34, 158
   Gospel of John as inspiring, 169, 177, 212–13, 227
   political and social guises of, 8–9
   social media as fueling, 9, 220
   in writers of the early church, 7, 74, 99, 115, 117
apocrypha, 162
Apollinaris of Laodicea, 88
*Apology against Jerome* (Rufinus), 91
Aquinas, Thomas, 120
Arianism, 84, 86–87, 107, 108–9, 146, 148, 160
*The Aryan Jesus* (Heschel), 6–7
Athanasius of Alexandria, 74, 107–9, 114

Augustine of Hippo, 89, 90–91
Auschwitz, 220
Australian Bishops Conference, 187–89

Bakker, Jim, 65–66
*Baltimore Catechism*, 119–20
Bar Kokhba Revolt, 82, 151–52, 153
Barabbas, 91–92, 171
Baranina, 90, 91–92
Ben Bag Bag, 137
Biden, Joe, 26
binaries, 17, 19–21, 29, 63, 109, 122
Brooks, David, 189–92
Buechner, Frederick, 205
Butcher, James, 26

Caiaphas, 169, 170–71
*Caiaphas the High Priest* (Reinhartz), 7
Caligula, Emperor, 152
*Cast Out of the Covenant* (Reinhartz), 173
Catholic lectionary, 200–204, 215
Catholic–Jewish Colloquium, 3, 124

Celsus, 72
Chagall, Marc, 160–61
Christian nationalism, 20, 130, 149, 160, 189, 220
*Christian Pharisees* (Butcher), 26
Chrysostom, John
 as bishop of Constantinople, 93–94, 116
 *Discourses Judaizing Christians*, 96–97, 98, 100
 Jews, condemning, 8, 88, 95–97, 107, 114, 115, 117, 143
 *Against the Jews*, 99
 Pseudo-Chrysostom, 101
Cicero, 70
Cirafesi, Wally V., 174–77
circumcision, 77, 129
 Gentiles, not required for, 67, 164, 211
 Judaism, associated with, 92, 151, 175
 Justin Martyr on spiritual circumcision, 79–80
 Paul as circumcised, 41, 42–43, 167
*Commentary on Matthew* (Jerome), 92–93
Commission on Religious Relations with the Jews, 126–27, 180–81
Constantine, Emperor, 84–86, 144–47
Council of Constantinople, 84, 87
Council of Nicaea, 211
 1,700th anniversary, 149
 Arius, denouncing, 160
 Constantine as convening, 146
 upholding teachings of, 84–87, 107, 147
covenantal nomism, 163
*Cunctos populos* edict, 87, 147
Cunningham, Philip, 29–30, 62–63

Damasus I, Pope, 88
Daniel, 104
Dead Sea Scrolls, 37, 57, 132, 161–62
Decius, Emperor, 144
Delitzsch, Franz, 61
*Dialogue with Trypho* (Justin Martyr), 134, 143, 157
 on the demise of Judaism, 81–82
 as the earliest refutation of Judaism, 83–84, 156
 prophets, on the Christian interpretation of, 124–25
 reconsideration of, 149–55
 Way of Christ, Justin advocating for, 78–79
diaspora. *See* Jewish diaspora
Didymus the Blind, 89
Diocletian, Emperor, 144, 145
Diodore of Tarsus, 94
*Disruptive Readings* (Cunningham), 63
Donaldson, Terence, 118
Donatist controversy, 145

early Christ followers, 13, 16, 65, 129
 circumcision debates, 43, 211
 Great Persecution of, 144
 identity, establishing, 66–67, 75

Jewish assemblies, co-existence with, 135, 143
Luke on the early communities, 42, 44
Wisdom literature, as referencing, 184
early church writers on Christ, 22, 127, 202
Chrysostom, 96, 97
Ignatius, 76–77
Jerome, 92–93
Jews, blaming for the death of Jesus, 107, 158
Justin Martyr, 80, 82, 84, 157
on the Passover of Jesus, 99–101
supersessionist beliefs, espousing, 126, 141
Torah, depicting Jesus in opposition to, 128
early Judaism, 161, 162, 176, 210–11, 217
Easter, 33, 201
Athanasius and Ephrem on, 107–8
date of Easter, establishing, 85–86
*Exsultet* as an Easter Vigil hymn, 120–22
in Gospel of John, 105
Edict of Milan, 144–45
Eisenbaum, Pamela, 167
Ephrem of Syria, 8, 74, 107, 109–15, 143
Essenes, 28, 37, 55, 57, 162
Eusebius, 85–86
Eustochium, 88–89, 116

Fein, Helen, 6

*Festal Letters* of Athanasius, 107–8
flawed metaphors, 17, 21, 98
Flynn, Michael, 20–21
Forger, Deborah, 61
Francis, Pope, 181, 195
Fredriksen, Paula, 168–69
French, David, 219, 220
"From God's Perspective We Are All Minorities" (Stendahl), 218

Galerius, Emperor, 144
Gamaliel, 44, 52
"The Gifts and Calling of God Are Irrevocable" (Commission on Religious Relations with the Jews), 180–82
*The Gifts and Calling of God Are Irrevocable* (Pontifical Biblical Commission), 127, 143
Great Revolt (66-70), 28, 36, 39, 56, 82, 152, 161
Greenberg, Irving, 165–66
Gregory Nazianzus, 88

Halsall, Paul, 99
Hamas–Israel war, 8
Hananel, Rabbi, 138
Hartley, L. P., 216
Hens-Piazza, Gina, 116
Herod the Great, 48, 152
Heschel, Abraham Joshua, 223
Heschel, Susannah, 6–7, 61
*Hexapla* (Origen), 89
Hillel the Elder, 61
historical criticism, 28, 116, 206–7, 209

historical reconstruction, 21–22, 35
holy envy, 221
Holy Thursday worship, 120
Hopkins, Gerard Manley, 182
Horner, Timothy J., 150–51

Ignatius of Antioch, 8, 74–78, 93, 100, 107, 115
Ingall, Carol K., 4–5
intolerance, 14, 83, 143, 145

Jacob of Sarug, 110
Jerome of Stridon, 74, 88–93, 115–17
Jesus Christ, 22, 40, 41, 56, 61, 205, 207, 218
  in the *Baltimore Catechism*, 119–20
  Barabbas as freed in place of Jesus, 91
  in Catholic education textbooks, 29–30
  coming of Christ, 82, 119, 124, 203
  Council of Nicaea as defining, 84, 85, 86, 146
  death of Jesus, 6, 48, 69, 85, 92, 104, 107, 226, 228, 229
  in *Dialogue with Trypho*, 124–25, 150, 154–55, 156–57
  *ekklēsia* as Christ assemblies, 18, 53, 133–34
  Judas and, 213–14
  Lamb of God, Jesus as, 99–100, 104, 108, 121
  Last Supper, Jesus at, 103, 120
  messiah, Jesus as, 31–32, 66, 79, 112, 113–14, 129, 173
  ministry of Jesus, 11, 202
  oppositional imagination, applying to narrative of, 63
  the Other, Jesus as, 178–80
  Paul as a follower of Christ, 16, 167, 211
  purity laws, reacting to, 214–17
  as raised from the dead, 66, 104–5
  in supersessionist thought, 119–21, 126, 194
  the Way of Christ, 7, 52, 78, 81, 101, 118, 123, 173, 177, 182, 229
  wisdom, Jesus as, 183–86
  *See also* early Christ followers; early church writers on Christ; Judaism and Jesus; Pharisees
*Jewish Antiquities* (Josephus), 37–38, 39
Jewish diaspora, 129, 131, 151, 175
Jewish diversity, 34, 60, 69, 74, 125, 131, 175–76, 195–96, 225
Jewish legalism, 29, 56, 96–97, 125–26, 161, 163–64, 181, 214, 215
*The Jewish People and Their Sacred Scriptures in the Christian Bible* (Pontifical Biblical Commission), 142–43, 228
*The Jewish Way: Living the Holidays* (Greenberg), 165–66

# Index

John, Gospel of, 15, 105, 201, 227
  Australian bishops, reflections on, 187–89
  death of Jesus, charging Jews with, 69, 229
  on Jesus and the Pharisees, 46–47, 48
  on Jesus washing the feet of disciples, 103–4
  on Jewish blame for crucifixion, 48, 106, 171–72, 188, 219
  on Jewish hostility toward Jesus, 106, 169–73, 176
  the Jews in John's Gospel, 186, 212–13
  passion narrative of, 106, 159, 188
  reading of within Judaism, 24, 169–78
  on salvation through Christ, 218
John Hyrcanus, 36
John the Baptist, 45
*John within Judaism* (Cirafesi), 174, 176
Johnson, Elizabeth, 207
Joseph of Arimathea, 172
Josephus, 29, 36–40, 51–52, 56, 162
Judah ha-Nasi, 135
Judah the Galilean, 39
Judaism and Jesus, 62, 189, 192
  Christ followers and the construction of Judaism, 69–74
  Christ-killers, Jews viewed as, 7, 86, 97, 111, 169–70, 187–88, 205, 212
  crucifixion, Jews blamed for, 5, 92, 96, 106–7, 149, 158–59, 160, 172, 188, 219, 228
  fulfillment of Judaism, Jesus viewed as, 23, 141, 194, 202
  Jewish Jesus, 10, 20, 21, 23–24, 117, 158, 159–66, 168, 178, 179, 180, 191, 210–11, 217
  Jewish rejection of Jesus, 7, 29
  John on Jewish hostility toward Jesus, 106, 169–73, 176
  living Torah of God, Jesus as, 24, 127, 159, 180–83, 221
  Passover imagery and Jesus, 99–100, 102–3, 107, 110, 114, 121
  synagogues, Jesus's visits to, 54, 129
Judas, 213–14
*Judean Wars* (Josephus), 37
Julian, Emperor, 85, 109, 147
justification, 163–64
Justin Martyr, 8, 115, 127
  circumcision, on the practice of, 79–80
  deeper understanding of Judaism, not seeking, 124–25
  in the early church, 143, 144
  in imaginary listening scenario, 149–51
  lasting influence on the church, 78–79, 84
  religious tolerance, as lacking in, 82–83, 117
  on the Sabbath, 80–81
  *See also Dialogue with Trypho*

Justinian I, Emperor, 147

Karp, Jonathan, 9
Kasper, Walter, 155
Keim, Karl Theodor, 61
Kingdom of God, 11, 59, 67, 103, 105, 106, 171, 229
Klenicki, Leon, 189
Konradt, Matthias, 191
Kraemer, Ross Shepard, 148
Krewson, William, 93
Kugel, James, 139

lectionary. *See* Catholic lectionary
Lee, Sara S., 2–3, 220
legalism. *See* Jewish legalism
Licinius, Emperor, 144–45
Lieu, Judith, 71
*Listening to Trypho* (Horner), 150
Luke, Gospel of, 55, 103, 131, 201, 216
   Antioch, on the first Christians in, 75
   Judas, grisly portrayal of, 213
   Paul, featuring in Acts of the Apostles, 42, 52
   Pentecost, on the Spirit received during, 105
   on the Pharisees, 40, 44, 45, 47–48
Luther, Martin, 163–64

Mark, Gospel of, 45, 183, 215
   on the Last Supper, 103
   on Pharisee hostility toward Jesus, 47–48
   as Year B of lectionary cycle, 201

Marshall, Mary, 44
martyrs, 75, 96, 116
Marx, Dalia, 154
Mary of Magdala, 53, 105
Mary of Nazareth, 168, 183, 201, 219
Mason, Steve, 36
Matthew, Gospel of, 55, 103, 182, 213
   Antioch as likely setting for, 75
   Beatitudes, 31, 190–91
   *ekklēsia*, use of term, 134
   as within Judaism, 191, 192
   in the lectionary cycle, 201, 203
   on missionary discipleship, 218
   negative portrait of Judaism, 15, 29
   on the Pharisees, 28, 40, 44–45, 48, 49–52, 56–58, 59–60, 211
Mayer, Wendy, 97–98
Mayers, Simon D., 9
Melito of Sardis, 100, 107
Meyer, Barbara, 178–79
*Mishnah* (rabbinic commentary), 140, 162, 182
   *Avot* tractate, 137, 155
   Oral Torah as embodied in, 135–38
   *Pirkei Avot* on transmission of the Torah, 181
   *Tishah B'Av*, on the disasters of, 154
Moltmann, Jürgen, 160–61
Moses, 58, 108, 118, 207, 216
   laws given through, 30, 36, 38–39, 185

Pharaoh, as challenging, 55
  in *Pirkei Avot* tractate, 181
Musk, Elon, 220

Nanos, Mark, 167
Nazism, 7, 160, 220, 226, 227
Nero, Emperor, 144
Nicene Creed, 84, 87, 108, 114, 146, 148
Nicodemus, 46, 52, 90
*Nostra Aetate* decree, 34
  church relationship to Judaism, rethinking, 178, 186–87
  death of Jesus, on interpreting in context, 5–6
  fiftieth anniversary reflections, 126–27, 180–81
  Jews, not blaming for crucifixion, 158–59, 228
  sixtieth anniversary, marking, 189, 224, 225–27, 230

*On Ephrem* (Jacob of Sarug), 110
*On the Unleavened Bread* (musical composition), 110–14
oppositional imagination, 11, 29, 62–64, 69, 127, 195
Origen of Alexandria, 89

*Pange Lingua* (hymn), 120, 121
Passover
  in early Church writings, 99–101, 101–7
  Easter, separating date from Passover, 85–86
  Ephrem on, 110, 113–14

paschal lamb, 99, 101–5, 108, 110, 114, 121, 136, 139
  in passion narrative, 171, 172
  as *Pesach*, 33, 101, 136–37
  seder meals during, 2, 5, 136–37, 165
  symbolism, appropriation of, 71, 74
patristic writers, 73, 75, 93–94, 140–41, 143
Paul, 65, 72, 105, 127, 186, 207, 228
  as a Christ follower, 16, 211
  as circumcised, 41, 42–43, 167
  as confounding, 42, 200
  convert, misguided classification as a, 18, 52
  *ekklēsia*, use of term, 133–34
  Fredriksen on the defamiliarized Paul, 169
  Gentiles, mission to, 13, 57, 168
  identification as a Pharisee, 35, 52, 59, 102, 162, 167, 179
  letters of, 40–42, 65, 75, 130, 133, 167, 202, 229
  Martin Luther, comparing to, 163–64
  Pharisees, declarations on, 40–44
*Paul and Palestinian Judaism* (Sanders), 163
*Paul Was Not a Christian* (Eisenbaum), 167
*Paul within Judaism* (Nanos/Zetterholm, ed.), 167
Paula, 88–89, 116
Pentecost, 33, 65, 105, 196
Peppard, Michael, 203

Pesach. *See* Passover
Pharisäer cocktail, 61
Pharisees, 22, 55, 62, 162, 211, 217, 228
  as antagonists of Jesus, 25, 29, 31–32, 34, 44, 59
  Caiaphas as a Pharisee, 169, 170–71
  Catholic religious education on, 29–30
  Christ followers as rivals of the Pharisees, 28, 57
  Christian self-understanding, Pharisees playing a role in, 16–17
  German Protestant theologians on, 61
  Josephus on the Pharisees, 36–40
  as legalistic, 22, 25, 27, 29, 61
  Matthew on, 28, 40, 44–45, 48, 49–52, 56–58, 59–60, 211
  in the oppositional imagination, 63–64
  pastoral settings, discussing in, 30–33, 196
  Paul as a Pharisee, 35, 41, 42, 52, 102, 162, 167, 179
  Paul on the Pharisees, 40–44
  *Pharisees: The Party Game*, 26–27
  Robles on Pharisees as the woke church, 25–26
  Runesson on Matthew's Pharisees, 58–59
  stereotypical view of, 9, 16–17, 28, 33, 61–62
Philo of Alexandria, 54–55
Piercy, Marge, 209
Pius XII, Pope, 195
Pontifical Biblical Commission, 127, 142–43, 177
Pontius Pilate, 48, 91, 106, 171–72, 188, 229
"Preaching Hatred?" (Mayer), 97–98
*Pro Flacco* (Cicero), 70
*Prologue to Isaiah* (Jerome), 92
Pseudepigrapha, 162
*PTL Club* (televangelist show), 65–66
purity and impurity, 56, 98–99, 135, 168, 197, 214–17

QAnon, 19
"Questions 'Which Touch on the Heart of Our Faith'" (Boys), 1

rabbinic tradition, 21, 49, 71, 161, 210
  early church writers, comparing rabbis to, 140–43
  emerging rabbinic movement, 90, 129
  *Mishnah* as rabbinic commentary, 135–38, 140, 154, 155, 162, 181–82
  reinventing Judaism, rabbinic role in, 128, 134–35
  *Talmud* as rabbinic commentary, 23, 131, 138–39, 182
Rahner, Karl, 207
Rajak, Tessa, 81
Rashi, 138
ReAwaken America movement, 20–21
Reformation, 163
Reid, Barbara, 116
Reinhartz, Adele, 7, 173–74, 177
*Religious Education* (journal), 3

# Index

replacement theology, 23
Robles, AD, 25–26
*Rosh Hashanah*, 95, 165
Rufinus of Aquileia, 91–92
Runesson, Anders, 58, 60

Sabbath, 5, 50, 54, 57, 79, 112
  *Avot* as studied on Shabbat, 137
  Ignatius on Christian keeping of, 76, 77–78
  Jesus, observance of, 48, 179
  Jesus as healing on, 47, 170
  Justin Martyr as characterizing, 80, 81
  live-streaming services during coronavirus pandemic, 138
  *melakhot* as work forbidden on, 136
  Pharisees, Jesus eating Sabbath meal with, 45–46
Sacouman, Lesley, 220
sacrifice, 50, 80, 92, 153
  cultic sacrifice, 128, 133, 144
  Ephrem on sacrifice, 111–13
  Jesus, sacrificial death of, 99–100
  paschal sacrifices, 101–5, 108, 110, 139
  purity and sacrificial offerings, 214, 216
Sadducees, 28, 37–38, 42, 57
Sanders, Ed Parish, 163, 164, 167
Schwartz, Shuly Rubin, 4–5
Second Temple Judaism, 28, 52, 71, 105, 133, 142, 166
  destruction of Second Temple, 36, 56, 152–53, 154
  diversity as marking, 34, 176

early Judaism as final phase of, 161
Essenes as a dissenting faction in, 37
Passover celebrations during, 102
Sefaria (website), 194–95
self-critical faith, 13–14
Septuagint (LXX), 54, 66, 89–91, 133
*Shavuot*, celebration of, 33, 102, 105
Shepardson, Christine, 97
Shimon bar Kosiba, 151–52
*Shoah* (Holocaust), 34, 160, 226, 227
Singer, Michael, 2, 3–4
Smith, Wilfred Cantwell, 208
social justice, 26
*Social Justice Pharisees* (Robles), 25–26
Stendahl, Krister, 163–64, 167, 217–19, 221
Stone, Roger, 20–21
Stroumsa, Guy, 115
*Sukkot*, festival of, 95, 102, 131
supersessionism, 93, 118–22, 126, 194
synagogues, 134, 149, 154
  coronavirus pandemic, adapting to, 137–38
  describing and defining, 53–55
  Jesus's visits to, 54, 129
  John Chrysostom, negative view of, 97, 98
  Pharisees seeking seats of honor in, 46, 49
  synagogue Bible, contents of, 140
  Torah studied in, 54, 57, 131, 132, 133

*The Tablet* (periodical), 26
Tacitus, 70–71
*Talmud* (rabbinic commentary), 23, 131, 138–39, 182
*Tanakh* (Jewish Bible), 55, 115, 133, 209
*targum* translations, 140
Teter, Magda, 118
Theodosius I, Emperor, 87, 147
Theodosius II, Emperor, 147
tolerance, 82–83, 145
Torah, 43, 80, 128, 129, 185, 192, 226
   Ben Bag Bag on elucidating Torah, 137
   Christian understanding of, 220–21
   debates on, 57, 58, 211
   Essenes, adherence to, 37
   interpretation of the Torah, 55–56
   Jesus as embodying Torah, 178–79
   Jesus as the living Torah of God, 24, 127, 159, 180–83, 191, 221
   Jesus as Torah-faithful, 105, 126
   Living Library of Torah website, 194–95
   Luther on living up to demands of, 163
   *midrashim* as commenting on, 139–40
   *Mishnah* and, 136, 155
   Oral Torah, 55, 135, 138, 181–82
   Pharisees as interpreting, 30, 36, 40, 47, 48, 49, 52
   rabbis as studying, 134–35
   *Shavuot* as celebrating giving of the Torah, 33, 102
   supersession of the Torah by Christ, 118, 123, 126
   synagogues, Torah studied in, 54, 57, 131, 132, 133
   *Tanakh*, as part of, 209
*Tosefta* (rabbinic texts), 138
Trump, Donald—Trump administration, 9, 17, 149, 219
"Truth and Peace" (Australian Bishops Conference), 187–88

Valerius Flavius, Lucius, 70
Van Buren, Paul, 125–26
Vatican II, 120, 201. *See also Nostra Aetate* decree

Weill, Raymond, 132
Wellhausen, Julius, 61
*What Is Scripture* (Smith), 208
*White Crucifixion* (painting), 160
works righteousness, 163, 164
"Wreck of the Deutschland" (poem), 182

*Yellow Crucifixion* (painting), 160–61
*Yerushalmi* Talmud, 131, 138
Yom Kippur observance, 95, 165

Zakok, 39
zero-sum problems, 20–21
Zetterholm, Magnus, 167
Zionism, 8–9